Comptroller of the Currency
Administrator of National Banks

I0423770

Truth in Lending Act

Comptroller's Handbook

December 2010

CCE

Truth in Lending Act   Table of Contents

This booklet provides background information and optional expanded examination procedures for the Truth in Lending Act (TILA) and Regulation Z, which implements the TILA.

Examiners will select from the procedures those that are necessary after completing a compliance core assessment. For guidance in completing a core assessment, refer to the "Community Bank Supervision," "Large Bank Supervision," and "Internal and External Audits" booklets in the Comptroller's Handbook and the "Compliance Management System" booklet in the Comptroller's Handbook for Consumer Compliance. Complaint information received by the Office of the Ombudsman, Customer Assistance Group, may also be useful in completing the assessment.

Background and Summary

The TILA, 15 USC 1601 et seq., was enacted on May 29, 1968, as title I of the Consumer Credit Protection Act (Public Law 90-321). The TILA, implemented by Regulation Z (12 CFR 226), became effective July 1, 1969.

The TILA was first amended in 1970 to prohibit unsolicited credit cards. Additional major amendments to the TILA and Regulation Z were made by the Fair Credit Billing Act of 1974, the Consumer Leasing Act of 1976, the Truth in Lending Simplification and Reform Act of 1980, the Fair Credit and Charge Card Disclosure Act of 1988, the Home Equity Loan Consumer Protection Act of 1988, the Home Ownership and Equity Protection Act of 1994 (HOEPA), the TILA Amendments of 1995, and the Economic Growth and Regulatory Paperwork Reduction Act of 1996 (EGRPRA).

Regulation Z also was amended to implement section 1204 of the Competitive Equality Banking Act of 1987, and in 1988, to include adjustable rate mortgage (ARM) loan disclosure requirements. All consumer leasing provisions were deleted from Regulation Z in 1981 and transferred to Regulation M (12 CFR 213).

The HOEPA imposed new disclosure requirements and substantive limitations on certain closed-end mortgage loans bearing rates or fees above a certain percentage or amount. The law also included new disclosure requirements to assist consumers in comparing the costs and other material considerations of a reverse mortgage transaction and authorized the Board of Governors of the Federal Reserve System (Board) to prohibit specific acts and practices in connection with mortgage transactions. Regulation Z was amended in 2001 to implement these legislative changes to TILA.

The TILA Amendments of 1995 dealt primarily with tolerances for real estate secured credit. Regulation Z was amended on September 14, 1996 to incorporate changes to the TILA that limit lenders' liability for disclosure errors in loans secured by real estate consummated after September 30, 1995. The EGRPRA amendments were made to simplify and improve disclosures related to credit transactions.

The Electronic Signatures in the Global and National Commerce Act (the E-Sign Act), 15 USC 7001 et seq., was enacted in 2000 and did not require implementing regulations. On November 9, 2007, the amendments to Regulation Z and the official staff commentary were issued to simplify the regulation and provide guidance on the electronic delivery of disclosures consistent with the E-Sign Act.

In July 2008, Regulation Z was amended to protect consumers in the mortgage market from unfair, abusive, or deceptive lending and servicing practices. Specifically, the change applied protections to a newly defined category of "higher-priced mortgages" that includes virtually all closed-end subprime loans secured by a consumer's principal dwelling. The revisions also applied new protections to mortgage loans secured by dwellings, regardless of loan price, and required the delivery of early disclosures for more types of transactions. The revisions banned several advertising practices deemed deceptive or misleading. The Mortgage Disclosure Improvement Act of 2008 (MDIA) broadened and added to the requirements of the Board's July 2008 final rule by requiring early truth-in-lending disclosures for more types of transactions and by adding a waiting period between the time when disclosures are given and the transaction is consummated.

In December 2008, the Board adopted two final rules pertaining to open-end (not home-secured) credit. The first rule involved Regulation Z revisions and made comprehensive changes applicable to several disclosures required for applications and solicitations, new accounts, periodic statements, changes in terms notifications, and advertisements. The second rule was published under the Federal Trade Commission (FTC) Act and issued jointly with the Office of Thrift Supervision and the National Credit Union Administration. It sought to protect consumers from unfair acts or practices involving consumer credit card accounts. Before these rules took effect, however, the Credit Card Accountability, Responsibility, and Disclosure Act of 2009 (Credit CARD Act) amended TILA and established new requirements for open-end consumer credit plans. Several provisions of the Credit CARD Act are similar to provisions in the Board's December 2008 TILA revisions and the joint FTC Act rule, but other portions of the Credit CARD Act address practices or mandate disclosures that were not addressed in these rules.

The Credit CARD Act provisions are effective in three stages. The provisions in the first stage (effective August 20, 2009) involve rules regarding mailing of periodic statements and advance notice of rate increases and other significant changes in account terms. The provisions in the second stage (effective February 22, 2010) involve rules regarding interest rate increases and other changes in terms, over-the-limit and other fees, evaluation of consumers' repayment ability, payments and billing, and student cards. Finally, the provisions in the third stage (effective August 22, 2010) address the reasonableness and proportionality of penalty fees and charges and re-evaluation of rate increases. Changes to Regulation Z that were not made pursuant to the Credit CARD Act became effective July 1, 2010.

In 2009, Regulation Z was amended following the passage of the Higher Education Opportunity Act adding disclosure and timing requirements that apply to lenders making private education loans.

Format of Regulation Z

The disclosure rules creditors must follow differ depending on whether or not the creditor is offering open-end credit, such as credit cards or home-equity lines of credit, or closed-end credit, such as car loans or mortgages.

Subpart A [sections 226.1 through 226.4] provides general information that applies to open-end and closed-end credit transactions. It sets forth definitions and stipulates which transactions are covered and which are exempt from the regulation. It also contains the rules for determining which fees are finance charges.

Subpart B [sections 226.5 through 226.16] contains disclosure rules for home-equity lines of credit, credit and charge card accounts, and other open-end credit. It also covers rules for resolving billing errors, calculating the annual percentage rate (APR), credit balances, and advertising open-end credit. Special rules apply to credit card transactions only, such as certain prohibitions on the issuance of credit cards and restrictions on the right to offset a cardholder's indebtedness. Additional special rules apply to home-equity lines of credit, such as certain prohibitions against closing accounts or changing account terms.

Subpart C [sections 226.17 through 226.24] includes provisions for closed-end credit. Residential mortgage transactions, demand loans, and installment credit contracts, including direct loans by banks and purchased dealer paper, are included in the closed-end credit category. It also contains disclosure rules for regular and variable rate loans, refinancings and assumptions, credit balances, calculating the APR, and advertising closed-end credit.

Subpart D [sections 226.25 through 226.30] applies to both open-end and closed-end credit and sets forth a creditor's duty to retain evidence of compliance with the regulation. It also clarifies the relationship between the regulation and state law, and requires creditors to set a cap for variable rate transactions secured by a consumer's dwelling.

Subpart E [sections 226.31 through 226.39] contains special requirements for mortgages that fit the criteria in 226.32(a) ("high-cost mortgages"), 226.33(a) ("reverse mortgages"), and 226.35(a) ("higher-priced mortgage loans"), as well as loans secured by a consumer's principal dwelling. It also includes new notification requirements to borrowers when their mortgage loan is acquired by, or otherwise sold, transferred, or assigned to a third party in section 226.39.

Subpart F [sections 226.46 through 226.48] includes disclosure and timing requirements that apply to creditors making private education loans. It limits certain practices by creditors, including "co-branding" products with educational institutions in the marketing of private student loans. The rule requires creditors to obtain self-certification forms signed by consumers before consummating loans. The rule also requires creditors with preferred lender arrangements with educational institutions to provide certain information to those institutions.

Subpart G [sections 226.51 through 226.59] relates to credit card accounts under open-end (not home-secured) consumer credit plans (except for section 226.57(c), which applies to all open-end credit plans). This subpart contains rules on the evaluation of a consumer's ability to pay, limits on fees during the first year after an account opening, limits and prohibitions on penalty fees, rules on allocation of payments in excess of the minimum payment, and limits on the imposition of finance charges. The subpart limits increases in the APR, fees, and charges, and prohibits the assessment of fees for over-the-limit transactions unless the consumer opts in to the payment of over-the-limit transactions. It also includes rules for reporting and marketing open-end credit to college students and requirements for posting on the Internet credit card account agreements under open-end (not home-secured) consumer credit plans. In addition, this subpart includes requirements to reevaluate rate increases.

The appendixes to the regulation set forth model forms and clauses that creditors may use when providing open-end and closed-end disclosures. The appendixes contain detailed rules for calculating the APR for open-end credit (appendix F) and closed-end credit (appendixes D and J). The last two appendixes (appendixes K and L) provide total annual loan-cost rate computations and assumed loan periods for reverse mortgage transactions.

Official staff interpretations of the regulation are published in a commentary that is normally updated annually in March. Good faith compliance with the commentary protects creditors from civil liability under the act. In addition, the commentary includes mandates, which are not necessarily explicit in Regulation Z, on disclosures or other actions required of creditors. In order to comply with Regulation Z, it is critical to reference and rely on the commentary.

Electronic Disclosures

Disclosures may be provided to the consumer in electronic form, subject to compliance with the consumer consent and other applicable provisions of the Electronic Signatures in Global and National Commerce Act (E-Sign Act) (15

USC 7001 et seq.). The E-Sign Act does not mandate that institutions or consumers use or accept electronic records or signatures. It permits institutions to satisfy any statutory or regulatory requirements by providing the information electronically after obtaining the consumer's affirmative consent. Before consent can be given, consumers must be provided with the following information:

- Any right or option to have the information provided in paper or nonelectronic form.

- The right to withdraw the consent to receive information electronically and the consequences, including fees, of doing so.

- The scope of the consent (for example, whether the consent applies only to a particular transaction or to identified categories of records that may be provided during the course of the parties' relationship).

- The procedures to withdraw consent and to update information needed to contact the consumer electronically.

- The methods by which a consumer may obtain, upon request, a paper copy of an electronic record after consent has been given to receive the information electronically and whether any fee will be charged.

The consumer must consent electronically or confirm consent electronically in a manner that "reasonably demonstrates that the consumer can access information in the electronic form that will be used to provide the information that is the subject of the consent." After the consent, if an institution changes the hardware or software requirements such that a consumer may be prevented from accessing and retaining information electronically, the institution must notify the consumer of the new requirements and must allow the consumer to withdraw consent without charge.

Note: The following narrative does not discuss all the sections of Regulation Z but rather highlights only certain sections of the regulation and the Truth in Lending Act.

Subpart A—General

Purpose of the TILA and Regulation Z

The TILA is intended to ensure that credit terms are disclosed in a meaningful way so consumers can compare credit terms more readily and knowledgeably. Before its enactment, consumers were faced with a bewildering array of credit terms and rates. It was difficult to compare loans because they were seldom presented in the same format. Now, all creditors must use the same credit terminology and expressions of rates. In addition to providing a uniform system for disclosures, the act:

- Protects consumers against inaccurate and unfair credit billing and credit card practices.

- Provides consumers with rescission rights.

- Provides for rate caps on certain dwelling-secured variable rate loans.

- Imposes limits on home equity lines of credit and certain closed-end home mortgages.

- Delineates and prohibits unfair or deceptive mortgage lending practices.

The TILA and Regulation Z do not, however, tell banks how much interest they may charge or whether they must grant loans to consumers.

Summary of Coverage [Sections 226.1 and 226.2]

Lenders must carefully consider several factors when deciding if loans require Truth in Lending disclosures or are subject to other Regulation Z requirements. A chart in the appendix of this booklet, "Coverage Considerations under Regulation Z," helps lenders make such decisions.

Regulation Z and its commentary address in more detail the factors included in the chart. For example, section 226.1(c) of the regulation specifies what kinds of institutions and borrowers are covered, and relevant definitions appear in section 226.2.

Exempt Transactions [Section 226.3]

The following transactions are exempt from Regulation Z:

- Credit extended primarily for a business, commercial, or agricultural purpose.

- Credit extended to other than a natural person (including credit to government agencies or instrumentalities).

- Credit in excess of $25,000 not secured by real property or personal property used or expected to be used as the consumer's principal dwelling.

- Public utility credit.

- Credit extended by a broker-dealer registered with the Securities and Exchange Commission (SEC) or the Commodity Futures Trading Commission (CFTC), involving securities or commodities accounts.

- Home fuel budget plans.

- Certain student loan programs.

However, when a credit card is involved, generally exempt credit (e.g., business purpose credit) is subject to the requirements that govern the issuance of credit cards and liability for their unauthorized use. Credit cards must not be issued on an unsolicited basis and, if a credit card is lost or stolen, the cardholder must not be held liable for more than $50 for the unauthorized use of the card (Regulation Z, footnote 4).

When determining if credit is for consumer purposes, the creditor must evaluate all of the following:

- Any statement obtained from the consumer describing the purpose of the proceeds:

- For example, a statement that the proceeds will be used for a vacation trip would indicate a consumer purpose.
- If the loan has a mixed-purpose (e.g., proceeds will be used to buy a car that will be used for personal and business purposes), the lender must look to the primary purpose of the loan to decide if disclosure is necessary. A statement of purpose from the consumer will help the lender make that decision.
- A checked box indicating that the loan is for a business purpose, absent any documentation showing the intended use of the proceeds, could be insufficient evidence that the loan did not have a consumer purpose.

- The consumer's primary occupation and how it relates to the use of the proceeds. The higher the correlation between the consumer's occupation and the property purchased from the loan proceeds, the greater the likelihood that the loan has a business purpose. For example, proceeds used to purchase dental supplies for a dentist would indicate a business purpose.

- Personal management of the assets purchased from proceeds. The less the borrower is personally involved in managing the investment or enterprise purchased by the loan proceeds, the less likely the loan will have a business purpose. For example, money borrowed to purchase stock in an automobile company by an individual who does not work for that company would indicate a personal investment and a consumer purpose.

- Size of the transaction. The larger the size of the transaction, the more likely the loan will have a business purpose. For example, if the loan is for a $5 million real estate transaction, that might indicate a business purpose.

- Relative amount of income derived from the property acquired by the loan proceeds. The less the income derived from the acquired property relative to the borrower's total income, the more likely the loan will have a consumer purpose. For example, if the borrower has an annual salary of $100,000 and receives about $500 in annual dividends from the acquired property, that would indicate a consumer purpose.

All five factors must be evaluated before the lender can conclude that disclosures are not necessary. Normally, no one factor by itself is sufficient to determine the applicability of Regulation Z. In any event, the bank may routinely furnish disclosures to the borrower. Disclosure under such circumstances does not determine that the transaction is covered under the Regulation Z but can assure protection to the bank and compliance with the law.

Determination of Finance Charge and APR

Finance Charge (Open-End and Closed-End Credit) [Section 226.4]

The finance charge is a measure of the cost of consumer credit represented in dollars and cents. Along with APR disclosures, the disclosure of the finance charge is central to the uniform credit cost disclosure envisioned by the TILA.

Finance charges include any charges or fees payable directly or indirectly by the consumer and imposed directly or indirectly by the financial institution either as an incident to or as a condition of an extension of consumer credit. The finance charge on a loan always includes any interest charges and often, other charges. Regulation Z includes examples, applicable both to open-end and closed-end credit transactions, of what must, must not, or need not be included in the disclosed finance charge [section 226.4(b)].

The finance charge does not include any charge of a type payable in a comparable cash transaction. Examples of charges payable in a comparable cash transaction may include taxes, title, license fees, or registration fees paid in connection with an automobile purchase.

Accuracy Tolerances (Closed-End Credit) [Sections 226.18(d) and 226.23(h)]

Regulation Z provides finance charge tolerances for legal accuracy that should not be confused with those provided in the TILA for reimbursement under regulatory agency orders. As with disclosed APRs, if a disclosed finance charge were legally accurate, it would not be subject to reimbursement.

Under the TILA and Regulation Z, finance charge disclosures for open-end credit must be accurate as there is no tolerance for finance charge errors. However, both the TILA and Regulation Z permit various finance charge accuracy tolerances for closed-end credit.

Tolerances for the finance charge in a closed-end transaction, other than a mortgage loan, are generally $5 if the amount financed is less than or equal to $1,000 and $10 if the amount financed exceeds $1,000. The finance charge in a closed-end mortgage transaction consummated on or after September 30, 1995 is considered accurate:

- If the disclosed finance charge does not vary from the actual finance charge by more than $100, or

- If the disclosed finance charge is greater than the actual finance charge.

Tolerances for the finance charge in rescindable mortgage transactions are different. After the three-business-day rescission period is over, the finance charge in the closed-end credit transaction is considered accurate if:

- Except as otherwise provided, the disclosed finance charge does not vary from the actual finance charge by more than one-half of 1 percent of the credit extended or $100, whichever is greater.

- The disclosed finance charge does not vary from the actual finance charge by more than 1 percent of the credit extended or $100, whichever is greater, for the initial and subsequent refinancings of residential mortgage transactions when the new loan is made by a different financial institution. (This does not apply to HOEPA mortgage loans subject to section 226.32, transactions in which there are new advances and new consolidations.)

Special rules apply to the finance charge tolerances if the (closed-end credit) rescindable mortgage transaction is involved in foreclosure action.

- The disclosed finance charge is considered accurate if it does not vary from the actual finance charge by more than $35.

- Overstatements are not considered violations.

- The consumer can rescind if a mortgage broker fee that should have been included in the finance charge was not included.

Note: Normally, the finance charge tolerance for a rescindable transaction is either 0.5 percent of the credit transaction or, for certain refinancings, 1 percent of the credit transaction. However, in the event of a foreclosure, the consumer may exercise the right of rescission if the disclosed finance charge is understated by more than $35.

Calculating Finance Charge (Closed-End Credit)

One of the more complex tasks under Regulation Z is determining if a charge associated with an extension of credit must be included in, or excluded from, the disclosed finance charge. The finance charge initially includes any charge that is, or will be, connected with a specific loan. Charges imposed by third parties are finance charges if the bank requires use of the third party. Charges imposed by settlement or closing agents are finance charges if the bank requires the specific service that gave rise to the charge and the charge is not otherwise excluded.

See the "Finance Charge" chart in the appendix of this booklet for a brief summary of the rules that must be considered when determining what is a finance charge.

Prepaid Finance Charges [Section 226.18(b)(3)]

A prepaid finance charge is any finance charge paid separately to the bank or to a third party, in cash or by check before or at closing, settlement, or consummation of a transaction, or withheld from the proceeds of the credit at any time. Prepaid finance charges effectively reduce the amount of funds available for the consumer's use.

Examples of finance charges frequently prepaid by consumers are borrower's points, loan origination fees, real estate construction inspection fees, odd days' interest (interest attributable to part of the first payment period when that period is longer than a regular payment period), mortgage guarantee insurance fees paid to the Federal Housing Administration, private mortgage insurance (PMI) paid to such companies as the Mortgage Guaranty Insurance Company (MGIC), and, in non-real-estate transactions, credit report fees.

Precomputed Finance Charges

A precomputed finance charge includes, for example, interest added to the note amount that is computed by the add-on, discount, or simple interest methods. If reflected in the face amount of the debt instrument as part of the consumer's obligation, finance charges that are not viewed as prepaid finance charges are treated as precomputed finance charges that are earned over the life of the loan.

APR Definition and Disclosure [Sections 226.18(a) and 226.22 (Closed-End Credit)]

Credit costs may vary depending on the interest rate, the amount of the loan and other charges, the timing and amounts of advances, and the repayment schedule. The APR, which must be disclosed in nearly all consumer credit transactions, is designed to take into account all relevant factors and to provide a uniform measure for comparing the cost of various credit transactions.

The APR is a measure of the cost of credit, expressed as a nominal yearly rate. It relates the amount and timing of value received by the consumer to the amount and timing of payments made. The disclosure of the APR is central to the uniform credit cost disclosure envisioned by the TILA.

The value of a closed-end credit APR must be disclosed as a single rate only, if the loan has a single interest rate, a variable interest rate, a discounted variable interest rate, or graduated payments based on separate interest rates (step rates), and it must appear with the segregated disclosures. Segregated disclosures are grouped together and do not contain any information not directly related to the disclosures required under section 226.18.

Because an APR measures the total cost of credit, including such costs as transaction charges or premiums for credit guarantee insurance, it is not an "interest" rate, as that term is generally used. APR calculations do not rely on definitions of interest in state law and often include charges, such as a commitment fee paid by the consumer, that are not viewed by some state usury statutes as interest. Conversely, an APR might not include a charge, such as a credit report fee in a real property transaction, which some state laws might view as interest for usury purposes. Furthermore, measuring the timing of value received and of payments made is essential if APR calculations are to be accurate, and in accordance with the Regulation Z parameters.

The APR is often considered to be the finance charge expressed as a percentage. However, two loans could require the same finance charge and still have different APRs because of differing values of the amount financed or of payment schedules. For example, two loans could each have a finance charge of $978.52, but the APR on loan one is 12 percent and the APR on loan two is 13.26 percent. The APRs differ because the amount financed in loan one is $5,000 and the borrower makes 36 equal monthly payments of $166.07 each, and the amount financed in loan two is $4,500 and the borrower makes 35 equal monthly payments of $152.18 each and a final payment of $152.22. The APRs on these loans are not the same because an APR reflects not only the finance charge but also the amount and timing of value received by the consumer in relation to the amount and timing of payments made.

The APR is a function of:

- The amount financed, which is not necessarily equivalent to the loan amount. For example, if the consumer must pay at closing a separate 1 percent loan origination fee (prepaid finance charge) on a $100,000 residential mortgage loan, the loan amount is $100,000, but the amount financed would be $100,000 less the $1,000 loan fee, or $99,000.

- The finance charge, which is not necessarily equivalent to the total interest amount. (Interest is not defined by Regulation Z; rather, it is defined by state or other federal law). For example, if the consumer must pay a $25 credit report fee for an auto loan, the fee must be included in the finance charge. The finance charge in that case is the sum of the interest on the loan (i.e., interest generated by the application of a percentage rate against the loan amount) plus the $25 credit report fee. If the consumer must pay a $25 credit report fee for a loan secured by real property, the credit report fee must be excluded from the finance charge. Assuming there are no additional fees or charges assessed in the connection with the mortgage loan, the finance charge would be only the interest on the loan. Refer to the section on finance charge for clarification.

- The payment schedule, which does not necessarily include only principal and interest (P + I) payments. For example, if the consumer borrows $2,500 for a vacation trip at 14 percent simple interest per annum and repays that amount with 25 equal monthly payments beginning one month from consummation of the transaction, the monthly P + I payment will be $115.87, if all months are considered equal, and the amount financed would be $2,500. If the consumer's payments are increased by $2 a month to pay a non-financed (for illustrative purpose, there is no interest component) $50 loan fee over the life of the loan, the amount financed would remain at $2,500 but the payment schedule would be increased to $117.87 a month, the finance charge would increase by $50, and there would be a corresponding increase in the APR. This would be the case whether or not state law defines the $50 loan fee as interest.

  If the loan above has 55 days to the first payment and the consumer prepays interest at consummation ($24.31 to cover the first 25 days), the amount financed would be $2,500 minus $24.31, or $2,475.69. Although the amount financed has been reduced to reflect the consumer's reduced use of available funds at consummation, the time interval during which the consumer has use of the $2,475.69, 55 days to the first payment, has not changed. Because the first payment period exceeds the limits of the regulation's minor irregularities provisions (see section 226.17(c)(4)), it may not be treated as regular. In calculating the APR, the first payment period must include the additional 25 days (i.e., the first payment period may not be treated as one month).

Banks may, if permitted by state or other law, precompute interest by applying a rate against a loan balance using a simple interest, add-on, discount or some other method, and may earn interest using a simple interest accrual system, the "rule of 78's" (if permitted by law) or some other method. Even if the bank's internal interest earnings and accrual methods involve a simple interest rate based on a 360-day year that is applied over 365 actual days (that fact is important only for determining the accuracy of the payment schedule), it is not relevant in calculating an APR, because an APR is not an interest rate (as that term is commonly used under state or other law).

Because the APR normally need not rely on the internal accrual systems of a bank, it can be computed after the loan terms have been agreed upon (as long as it is disclosed before consummation of the transaction).

Special Requirements for Calculating the Finance Charge and APR

The finance charge and APR, more than any other disclosures, enable consumers to understand the cost of credit and to comparison shop for credit. Therefore, proper calculation of the finance charge and APR are of primary importance. Additionally, section 226.17(a)(2) requires that the terms "finance charge" and "annual percentage rate" be disclosed more conspicuously than any other required disclosure. A creditor's failure to disclose those values accurately can result in significant monetary damages to the creditor, either from a class action lawsuit or from a regulatory agency's order to reimburse consumers for violations of law.

Footnote 45d to section 226.22 of regulation Z provides that if an APR or finance charge is disclosed incorrectly, the error is not, in itself, a violation of the regulation if:

- The error resulted from a corresponding error in a calculation tool used in good faith by the bank.

- Upon discovery of the error, the bank promptly discontinues use of that calculation tool for disclosure purposes.

- The bank notifies the Federal Reserve Board in writing of the error in the calculation tool.

When a bank claims it used a calculation tool in good faith, it assumes a reasonable degree of responsibility for ensuring that the tool in question provides the accuracy the regulation requires. For example, the bank might verify the results obtained using the tool by comparing those results to the figures obtained by using another calculation tool. The bank might also verify that the tool, if it is designed to operate under the actuarial method, produces figures similar to those provided by the examples in appendix J to the regulation. The calculation tool should be checked for accuracy before it is first used and periodically thereafter.

Subpart B—Open-End Credit

Time of Disclosures (Open-End Credit) [Section 226.5(b)]

For credit card accounts under open-end (not home-secured) consumer credit plans, creditors must adopt reasonable procedures designed to ensure that periodic statements are mailed or delivered at least 21 days prior to the payment due dates disclosed on the periodic statements and that required minimum payments are not treated as late for any purpose if they are received within 21 days after mailing or delivery of the statements. For all open-end consumer credit accounts, creditors must adopt reasonable procedures designed to ensure that periodic statements are mailed or delivered at least 21 days prior to the dates on which a grace period (if any) expires and that finance charges are not imposed as a result of the loss of a grace period if payments are received within 21 days after mailing or delivery of statements. For purposes of this requirement, a "grace period" is defined as a period within which any credit extended may be repaid without incurring a finance charge due to a periodic interest rate.

Finance Charge (Open-End Credit) [Section 226.6(a)]

Each finance charge imposed must be individually itemized. The aggregate total amount of the finance charge need not be disclosed.

Determining the Balance and Computing the Finance Charge

The examiner must know how to compute the balance to which the periodic rate is applied. Common methods used are the previous balance method, the daily balance method, and the average daily balance method:

- Previous balance method. The balance on which the periodic finance charge is computed is based on the balance outstanding at the start of the billing cycle. The periodic rate is multiplied by this balance to compute the finance charge.

- Daily balance method. A daily periodic rate is applied to either the balance on each day in the cycle or the sum of the balances on each of the days in the cycle. If a daily periodic rate is multiplied by the balance on each day in the billing cycle, the finance charge is the sum of the products. If the daily periodic rate is multiplied by the sum of all the daily balances, the result is the finance charge.

- Average daily balance method. The average daily balance is the sum of the daily balances (either including or excluding current transactions) divided by the number of days in the billing cycle. A periodic rate is then multiplied by the average daily balance to determine the finance charge. If the periodic rate is a daily one, the product of the rate multiplied by the average balance is multiplied by the number of days in the cycle.

In addition to those common methods, banks have other ways of calculating the balance to which the periodic rate is applied. By reading the bank's explanation, the examiner should be able to calculate the balance to which the periodic rate was applied. In some cases, the examiner may need to obtain additional information from the bank to verify the explanation disclosed. Any inability to understand the disclosed explanation should be discussed with management, who should be reminded of Regulation Z's requirement that disclosures be clear and conspicuous.

If a balance is determined without first deducting all credits and payments made during the billing cycle, that fact and the amount of the credits and payments must be disclosed.

If the bank uses the daily balance method and applies a single daily periodic rate, disclosure of the balance to which the rate was applied may be stated as any of the following:

- A balance for each day in the billing cycle. The daily periodic rate is multiplied by the balance on each day and the sum is the finance charge.

- A balance for each day in the billing cycle on which the balance in the account changes. The finance charge is figured by the same method as discussed previously, but the statement shows the balance only for those days on which the balance changed.

- The sum of the daily balances during the billing cycle. The balance on which the finance charge is computed is the sum of all the daily balances in the billing cycle. The daily periodic rate is multiplied by that balance to determine the finance charge.

- The average daily balance during the billing cycle. If this is stated, the bank may, at its option, explain that the average daily balance is or can be multiplied by the number of days in the billing cycle and the periodic rate applied to the product to determine the amount of interest.

If the bank uses the daily balance method, but applies two or more daily periodic rates, the sum of the daily balances may not be used. Acceptable ways of disclosing the balances include:

- A balance for each day in the billing cycle.

- A balance for each day in the billing cycle on which the balance in the account changes.

- Two or more average daily balances. If the average daily balances are stated, the bank may, at its option, explain that interest is or may be determined by multiplying each of the average daily balances by the number of days in the billing cycle; or if the daily rate varied during the cycle, by multiplying each of the results by the applicable daily periodic rate, and then adding these products together.

In explaining the method used to find the balance on which the finance charge is computed, the bank need not reveal how it allocates payments or credits. That information may be disclosed as additional information, but all required information must be clear and conspicuous.

Finance Charge Resulting From Two or More Periodic Rates

Some banks use more than one periodic rate in computing the finance charge. For example, one rate may apply to balances up to a certain amount and another rate to balances more than that amount. If two or more periodic rates apply, the bank must disclose all rates and conditions. The range of balances to which each rate applies also must be disclosed. It is not necessary, however, to break the finance charge into separate components based on the different rates.

Subsequent Disclosures (Open-End Credit) [Section 226.9]

Creditors are required to provide consumers with 45 days' advance written notice of rate increases and other significant changes to the terms of their credit card account agreements. The list of "significant changes" includes most fees and other terms that consumers should be aware of before they use their accounts. Examples of such fees and terms include:

- Penalty fees.

- Transaction fees.

- Fees imposed for the issuance or availability of the open-end plan.

- Grace period.

- Balance computation method.

Changes that do not require advance notice include:

- Reductions of finance charges.

- Terminations of account privileges resulting from agreements involving court proceedings.

- Increases in the APR upon expiration of a specified period of time previously disclosed in writing.

- Increases in the variable APRs that change according to an index not under the control of card issuers.

- Rate increases due to the completion of, or failure of a consumer to comply with, the terms of a workout or temporary hardship arrangement, if those terms are disclosed prior to commencement of the arrangement.

A creditor may suspend account privileges, terminate an account, or lower the credit limit without notice. However, a creditor that lowers the credit limit may not impose an over-the-limit fee or penalty rate as a result of the consumer exceeding the new credit limit without a 45-day advance notice that the credit limit has been reduced.

For significant changes in terms (with the exception of rate changes, increases in minimum payments, certain changes in the balance computation method, and when changes result from a consumer's failure to make a required minimum periodic payment within 60 days after the due date), creditors must also provide consumers the right to reject the changes. If a consumer does reject the change prior to the effective date, the creditor may not apply the change to the account [section 226.9(h)(2)(i)].

In addition, when a consumer rejects a change or increase, the creditor must not:

- Impose a fee or charge or treat the account as in default solely as a result of the rejection, or

- Require repayment of the balance on the account using a method that is less beneficial to the consumer than one of the following methods:

  (1) Repayment period prior to the rejection.
  (2) Amortization period of not less than five years from the date of rejection.
  (3) Minimum periodic payment that includes a percentage of the balance that is not more than twice the percentage included prior to the date of rejection.

Annual Percentage Rate (Open-End Credit)

Accuracy Tolerance [Section 226.14]

The disclosed APR on an open-end credit account is accurate if it is within one-eighth of 1 percentage point of the APR calculated under Regulation Z.

Determination of APR

The regulation states two basic methods for determining the APR in open-end credit transactions. The first involves multiplying each periodic rate by the number of periods in a year. This method is used for disclosing:

- Corresponding APR in the initial disclosures.

- Corresponding APR on periodic statements.

- APR in application or solicitation disclosures for credit card accounts.

- APR in early disclosures for home-equity plans.

- APR in advertising.

- APR in oral disclosures.

The corresponding APR is prospective. In other words, it does not involve any particular finance charge or periodic balance. The second method is the quotient method, used in computing the APR for periodic statements. The quotient method reflects the annualized equivalent of the rate that was actually applied during a cycle. This rate, also known as the historical rate, will differ from the corresponding APR if the creditor applies minimum, fixed, or transaction charges to the account during the cycle.

If the finance charge is determined by applying one or more periodic rates to a balance, and does not include any of the charges just mentioned, the bank may compute the historical rate using the quotient method. Using that method, the bank divides the total finance charge for the cycle by the sum of the balances to which the periodic rates were applied and multiplies the quotient (expressed as a percentage) by the number of cycles in a year.

Alternatively, the bank may use the quotient method for computing the corresponding APR by multiplying each periodic rate by the number of periods in one year. If the finance charge includes a minimum, fixed, or transaction charge, then the bank must use the appropriate variation of the quotient method (see section 226.14(c) for more details). When transaction charges are imposed, the bank should refer to appendix F of Regulation Z for computational examples.

The regulation also contains a computation rule for small finance charges. If the finance charge includes a minimum, fixed, or transaction charge, and the total finance charge for the cycle does not exceed 50 cents, the bank may multiply each applicable periodic rate by the number of periods in a year to compute the corresponding APR.

Optional calculation methods also are provided for accounts involving daily periodic rates [section 226.14(d)].

Brief Outline for Open-End Credit APR Calculations
on Periodic Statements

Note: Assume monthly billing cycles for each of the calculations below.

I. APR when finance charge is determined solely by applying one or more periodic rates.

    A. Monthly periodic rates:

        1. Monthly rate x 12 = APR

    or

        2. (Total finance charge / applicable balance[1]) x 12 = APR
    This calculation also can be used when different rates apply to different balances.

    B. Daily periodic rates [section 226.14(d)]:

    Daily rate x 365 = APR

    or

---

[1] For the following formulas, the APR cannot be determined if the applicable balance is zero. The amount of applicable balance is determined by the balance calculation method and may include the average daily balance, adjusted balance, or previous balance method.

(Total finance charge / average daily balance) x 12 = APR

or

(Total finance charge / sum of balances) x 365 = APR

II. APR when finance charge includes a minimum, fixed, or other charge that is not calculated using a periodic rate (and does not include charges related to a specific transaction, like cash advance fees).

A. Monthly periodic rates [section 226.14(c)(2)]:

1. (Total finance charge / amount of applicable balance) x 12 = APR[2]

B. Daily periodic rates [section 226.14(c)]:

1. (Total finance charge / amount of applicable balance) x 365 = APR

2. The following may be used if at least a portion of the finance charge is determined by the application of a daily periodic rate. If not, use the formula above.

a. (Total finance charge / average daily balance) x 12 = APR

or

3. (Total finance charge / sum of balances) x 365 = APR

C. Monthly and daily periodic rates:

If the finance charge imposed during the billing cycle does not exceed $0.50 for a monthly or longer billing cycle (or pro rata part of $0.50 for a billing cycle shorter than monthly), the APR may be calculated by multiplying the monthly rate by 12 or the daily rate by 365.

---

[2] Loan fees, points, or similar finance charges that relate to the opening of the account must not be included in the calculation of the APR.

III. If the total finance charge includes a charge related to a specific transaction (such as a cash advance fee), even if the total finance charge also includes any other minimum, fixed, or other charge not calculated using a periodic rate, then the monthly and daily APRs are calculated as follows: (total finance charge divided by the greater of the transaction amounts that created the transaction fees or the sum of the balances and other amounts on which a finance charge was imposed during the billing cycle[3]) times number of billing cycles in a year (12) equals APR.[4]

Minimum Payments [Section 226.7(b)(12)]

For credit card accounts under open-end credit plans, card issuers generally must disclose on periodic statements the estimate of the amount of time and the total cost (principal and interest) involved in paying balances in full when making only the minimum payments, the estimate of the monthly payment amounts required to pay off the balances in 36 months, and the total cost (principal and interest) of repaying the balances in 36 months. Card issuers also must disclose minimum payment warnings and estimates of the total interest that consumers would save if they repaid their balance in 36 months, instead of making minimum payments.

Timely Settlement of Estates [Section 226.11(c)]

Issuers are required to establish procedures to ensure that an administrator of an estate can resolve the outstanding credit card balance of a deceased account holder in a timely manner. If an administrator requests the amount of the balance:

- The issuer is prohibited from imposing additional fees on the account.

- The issuer is required to disclose the amount of the balance to the administrator in a timely manner (safe harbor of 30 days).

---

[3] The sum of the balances may include the average daily balance, adjusted balance, or previous balance method. Where a portion of the finance charge is determined by application of one or more daily periodic rates, the sum of the balances also means the average of daily balance.

[4] Cannot be less than the highest periodic rate applied, expressed as an APR.

- If the balance is paid in full within 30 days after disclosure of the balance, the issuer must waive or rebate any trailing or residual interest charges that accrued on the balance following the disclosure.

Subpart G—Special Rules Applicable to Credit Card Accounts and Open-End Credit Offered to College Students

Evaluation of the Consumer's Ability to Pay [Section 226.51]

Regulation Z requires a credit card issuer to consider a consumer's ability to pay before opening a new credit card account or increasing the credit limit for an existing credit card account. Additionally, the rule provides specific requirements before opening a new credit card account or increasing the credit limit on an existing account when the consumer is younger than 21.

When evaluating a consumer's ability to pay, the credit card issuer must perform a review of a consumer's income or assets and current obligations. A creditor is permitted, however, to rely on information provided by the consumer. The rule does not require an issuer to verify a consumer's statements. A card issuer may also consider information obtained through any empirically derived, demonstrably and statistically sound model that reasonably estimates a consumer's income or assets.

The rule also requires that the credit card issuer consider at least one of the following:

- Ratio of debt obligations to income.

- Ratio of debt obligations to assets.

- Income of the consumer will have after paying debt obligations (i.e., residual income).

The rule also states that it is unreasonable for an issuer to fail to review any information about a consumer's income, assets, or current obligations, or to issue a credit card to a consumer who does not have any income or assets.

Because a credit card issuer typically requires a consumer to make a minimum monthly payment equal to a percentage of the total balance (plus, in some cases, accrued interest and fees), the creditor is required to consider the consumer's ability to make the required minimum payments. The card issuer must also establish and maintain reasonable written policies and procedures to consider a consumer's income or assets and current obligations. Because the minimum payment is unknown at account opening, the rule requires that a creditor use a reasonable method to estimate a consumer's minimum payment.

The regulation provides a safe harbor for the issuer to estimate the required minimum periodic payment if the card issuer:

1. Assumes utilization, from the first day of the billing cycle, of the full credit line that the issuer is considering offering to the consumer and

2. Uses a minimum payment formula employed by the issuer for the product the issuer is considering offering to the consumer or, in the case of an existing account, the minimum payment formula that currently applies to that account, provided that

    a. If the minimum payment formula includes interest charges, the card issuer estimates those charges using an interest rate that the issuer is considering offering to the consumer for purchases or, in the case of an existing account, the interest rate that currently applies to purchases, and

    b. If the applicable minimum payment formula includes mandatory fees, the card issuer must assume that such fees have been charged to the account.

Specific Requirements for Underage Consumers [Section 226.51(b)(1)]

Regulation Z prohibits the issuance of a credit card to a consumer younger than 21 unless the consumer has submitted a written application and the creditor has:

- Information indicating that the underage consumer has an independent means of repaying any debts incurred in connection with the account, or

- The signature of a cosigner who has attained the age of 21, who has the means to repay debts incurred by the underage consumer in connection with the account and who assumes joint liability for such debts.

If the account is opened based on a cosigner's ability to pay, the issuer must also obtain written consent from the cosigner before increasing the credit limit.

Limitations of Fees [Section 226.52]

Limitations during first year after account opening

During the first year after accounts are opened, issuers are prohibited from requiring consumers to pay fees (other than fees for late payments, returned payments, and exceeding their credit limit) that in the aggregate exceed 25 percent of the initial credit limit.

Limitations on penalty fees

TILA requires that penalty fees imposed by card issuers be reasonable and proportional to the violation of the account terms. Among other things, the regulation prohibits credit card issuers from charging a penalty fee of more than $25 for paying late or otherwise violating the account's terms for the first violation (or $35 for an additional violation of the same type during the next six billing cycles), unless the issuer determines that a higher fee represents a reasonable proportion of the costs it incurs as a result of that type of violation and reevaluates that determination at least once every twelve months.

Credit card issuers are banned from charging penalty fees that exceed the dollar amount associated with the consumer's violation of the terms or other requirements of the account. For example, card issuers are no longer permitted to charge a $39 fee when a consumer is late making a $20 minimum payment. Instead, in this example, the fee cannot exceed $20. The regulation also bans penalty fees where there is no dollar amount associated with the violation, such as "inactivity" fees based on the consumer's failure to use the account to make new purchases. It also prohibits issuers from charging multiple penalty fees based on a single late payment or other violation of the account terms.

Payment Allocation [Section 226.53]

When different rates apply to different balances on a credit card account, an issuer is required to allocate payments in excess of the minimum payment to first pay the balance with the highest APR, and any remaining portion to the other balances in descending order based on the applicable APR. For a deferred interest program, however, the issuer must allocate excess payments first to the deferred interest balance during the last two billing cycles of the deferred interest period. In addition, during a deferred interest period, the issuer is permitted (but not required) to allocate excess payments in the manner requested by the consumer.

Double-Cycle Billing and Partial Grace Period [Section 226.54]

Issuers are generally prohibited from imposing finance charges on balances for days in previous billing cycles as a result of the loss of a grace period. In addition, when a consumer pays some, but not all, of a balance prior to the expiration of a grace period, an issuer is prohibited from imposing finance charges on the portion of the balance that has been repaid.

General Prohibition on Applying Increased Rates to Existing Balances [Section 226.55]

There are some general exceptions to the prohibition against applying increased rates to existing balances:

- A temporary rate lasting at least six months expires and the issuer has complied with applicable disclosure requirements.

- The rate is increased due to the operation of an index available to the general public and not under the card issuer's control (i.e., the rate is a variable rate).

- The minimum payment has not been received within 60 days after the due date.

- The consumer successfully completes or fails to comply with the terms of a workout arrangement.

- The APR on an existing balance has been reduced pursuant to the Servicemembers Civil Relief Act (SCRA). The creditor is permitted to increase the rate once the SCRA ceases to apply, but only to the rate that applied prior to the reduction.

Regulation Z's limitations on the application of increased rates to existing balances continue to apply when the account is closed, acquired by another institution through a merger or the sale of a credit card portfolio, or when the balance is transferred to another credit account issued by the same creditor (or its affiliate or subsidiary).

For new transactions, a creditor is generally prevented from increasing the APR during the first year after an account is opened. After the first year, the creditor is permitted to increase the APR that applies to new transactions so long as the creditor complies with the regulation's 45-day advance notice requirement (section 226.9).

Fees for Transactions That Exceed the Credit Limit [Section 226.56]

Consumer consent requirement. Regulation Z requires an issuer to obtain a consumer's express consent (or opt-in) before the issuer may impose any fees on a consumer's credit card account for making an extension of credit that exceeds the account's credit limit. Prior to providing such consent, a consumer must be notified by the issuer of any fees that may be assessed for an over-the-limit transaction. If the consumer consents, the issuer is also required to provide a notice of the consumer's right to revoke that consent on the front page of any periodic statement that reflects the imposition of an over-the-limit fee.

Prior to obtaining a consumer's consent to the payment of over-the-limit transactions, the issuer must provide the consumer with a notice disclosing, among other things, the dollar amount of any charges that will be assessed for an over-the-limit transaction, as well as any increased rate that may apply if the consumer exceeds the credit limit. Issuers are prevented from assessing any over-the-limit fee or charge on an account unless the consumer consents to the payment of transactions that exceed the credit limit.

Prohibited practices. Even if the consumer has affirmatively consented to the issuer's payment of over-the-limit transactions, Regulation Z prohibits certain issuer practices involving the assessment of over-the-limit fees or charges. An issuer can only charge one over-the-limit fee or charge per billing cycle. In addition, an issuer cannot impose an over-the-limit fee on the account for the same transaction in more than three billing cycles. Furthermore, fees may not be imposed for the second or third billing cycle unless the consumer has failed to reduce the account balance below the credit limit by the payment due date in that cycle.

Regulation Z also prevents unfair or deceptive acts or practices in connection with the manipulation of credit limits in order to increase over-the-limit fees or other penalty charges. Specifically, issuers are prohibited from engaging in three practices:

- Assessing an over-the-limit fee because the creditor failed to promptly replenish the amount of credit available to the consumer following the crediting of the consumer's payment.

- Conditioning the amount of available credit on the consumer's consent to the payment of over-the-limit transactions (e.g., opting in to an over-the-limit service to obtain a higher credit limit).

- Imposing any fee if the credit limit is exceeded solely because of the issuer's assessment of accrued interest charges or fees on the consumer's account.

Special Rules for Marketing to Students [Section 226.57]

Regulation Z establishes several requirements related to the marketing of credit cards and other open-end consumer credit plans to students enrolled at institutions of higher education. The regulation limits a creditor's ability to offer a college student any tangible item to induce the student to apply for or participate in an open-end consumer credit plan offered by the creditor.

Specifically, Regulation Z prohibits these types of offers:

- On the campus of an institution of higher education.

- Near the campus of an institution of higher education.

- At an event sponsored by or related to an institution of higher education.

A tangible item means physical items, such as gift cards, T-shirts, or magazine subscriptions, but does not include non-physical items such as discounts, reward points, or promotional credit terms. With respect to offers "near" the campus, the commentary to the regulation defines a location within 1,000 feet of the border of a campus as "near the campus."

Regulation Z also requires card issuers to submit annual reports to the Board containing the terms and conditions of business, marketing, or promotional agreements with institutions of higher education, or with alumni organizations or foundations affiliated with institutions of higher education.

Online Disclosure of Credit Card Agreements [Section 226.58]

The regulation requires that issuers post credit card agreements on their Web sites and submit those agreements to the Board for posting on a Web site maintained by the Board. There are three exceptions for when issuers are not required to provide statements to the Board:

- The issuer has fewer than 10,000 open credit card accounts.

- The agreement is not offered to the public and the agreement is used only for one or more private label credit card plans, each of which has fewer than 10,000 open accounts.

- The agreement is offered solely as part of a product test offered only to a limited group of consumers for a limited time, and is used for fewer than 10,000 open accounts.

Reevaluation of Rate Increases [Section 226.59]

For any rate increase imposed on or after January 1, 2009 that requires 45 days advance notice, the regulation requires card issuers to review the account no less frequently than once every six months and, if appropriate based on that review, reduce the annual percentage rate. The requirement to reevaluate rate increases applies both to increases in annual percentage rates based on consumer-specific factors, such as changes in the consumer's creditworthiness, and to increases in annual percentage rates imposed based on factors that are not specific to the consumer, such as changes in market conditions or the issuer's cost of funds. If based on its review a card issuer is required to reduce the rate applicable to an account, the final regulation requires that the rate be reduced within 45 days after completion of the evaluation.

This review must consider either the same factors on which the increase was originally based or the factors the card issuer currently considers in determining the annual percentage rate applicable to similar new credit card accounts. However, the first two reviews of rate increases between January 1, 2009 and February 21, 2010 must use the factors the card issuer currently considers in determining the annual percentage rate applicable to similar new credit card accounts.

Open-End Advertising [Section 226.16]

If an advertisement for credit states specific credit terms, it must state only those terms that actually are or will be arranged or offered by the creditor. Additionally, advertisements may not refer to an APR as "fixed" unless the advertisement also specifies a time period that the rate will be fixed and that the rate will not increase during that period. If a time period is not specified, the advertisement may refer to a rate as fixed only if the rate will not increase while the plan is open.

If an advertisement sets forth certain terms required to be disclosed, further disclosures are triggered. If any charges are set forth in an advertisement, either affirmatively or negatively, the advertisement must also clearly and conspicuously state the following:

- Any minimum, fixed, transaction, activity or similar charge that could be imposed.

- Any periodic rate that may be applied and expressed as an APR as determined under section 226.14(b). If the plan provides for a variable periodic rate, that fact must be disclosed and

- Any membership or participation fee that could be imposed.

In addition, if any charges or payment terms are set forth, affirmatively or negatively, in an advertisement for a home-equity plan, the advertisement also must clearly and conspicuously set forth the following:

- Any loan fee that is a percentage of the credit limit under the plan and an estimate of any other fees imposed for opening the plan, stated as a single dollar amount or a reasonable range.

- Any periodic rate used to compute the finance charge, expressed as an APR as determined under section 226.14(b)

- The maximum APR that may be imposed in a variable-rate plan.

Regulation Z also contains provisions regarding advertising of promotional rates, payments, and tax implications for home-equity plans, promotional rates for open-end (not home-secured) plans, and deferred interest or similar offers relating to open-end (not home-secured) plans. Required disclosures in advertisements are subject to the general "clear and conspicuous" standard for open-end credit. Commentary provisions clarify how the clear and conspicuous standard applies to advertisements of home-equity plans with promotional rates or payments, and to Internet, television, and oral advertisements of home-equity plans. The regulation allows alternative disclosures for television and radio advertisements for home-equity plans. The regulation also requires that advertisements adequately disclose not only promotional plan terms but also the rates or payments that apply over the term of the plan.

Regulation Z also contains provisions implementing the Bankruptcy Abuse Prevention and Consumer Protection Act of 2005, which requires disclosure of the tax implications of certain home-equity plans.

Subpart C—Closed-End Credit

What follows is not a complete discussion of the TILA's requirements for closed-end credit. The information provided here merely clarifies confusing terms and requirements. Refer to sections 226.17 through 226.24 and related commentary for a more thorough understanding of the act.

Finance Charge (Closed-End Credit) [Section 226.17(a)]

The aggregate total amount of the finance charge must be disclosed. Each finance charge imposed need not be individually itemized and must not be itemized with the segregated disclosures.

Annual Percentage Rate (Closed-End Credit) [Section 226.22]

Accuracy Tolerances

The disclosed APR on a closed-end transaction is accurate for:

- Regular transactions (which include any single advance transaction with equal payments and equal payment periods, or an irregular first payment period or a first or last irregular payment), if it is within one-eighth of 1 percentage point of the APR calculated under Regulation Z (section 226.22(a)(2)).

- Irregular transactions (which include multiple advance transactions and other transactions not considered regular), if it is within one-quarter of 1 percentage point of the APR calculated under Regulation Z (section 226.22(a)(3)).

- Mortgage transactions, if it is within one-eighth of 1 percentage point for regular transactions or one-quarter of 1 percentage point for irregular transactions or in a transaction secured by real property or a dwelling:

i. The rate results from the disclosed finance charge and the disclosed finance charge is considered accurate under section 226.18(d)(1) or, for purposes of rescission, the disclosed finance charge is considered accurate under 226.23(g) or (h) (section 226.22(a)(4)), or

ii. The disclosed finance charge is calculated incorrectly but is considered accurate under section 226.18(d)(1) or section 226.23(g) or (h) and either:

   a. The finance charge is understated and the disclosed APR is also understated but is closer to the actual APR than the APR that would be considered accurate under section 226.22(a)(4), or

   b. The disclosed finance charge is overstated and the disclosed APR is also overstated but is closer to the actual APR than the APR that would be considered accurate under section 226.22(a)(4).

For example, in an irregular transaction subject to a tolerance of one-quarter of 1 percentage point, if the actual APR is 9.00 percent and a $75 omission from the finance charge corresponds to a rate of 8.50 percent that is considered accurate under section 226.22(a)(4), a disclosed APR of 8.65 percent is considered accurate under section 226.22(a)(5). However, a disclosed APR below 8.50 percent or above 9.25 percent would not be considered accurate.

Refer to the Accuracy Tolerance Charts in this booklet.

Note: There is an additional tolerance for mortgage loans when the disclosed finance charge is calculated incorrectly but is considered accurate under section 226.18(d)(1) or section 226.23(g) or (h) (section 226.22(a)(5)).

Construction Loans [Section 226.17(c)(6) and Appendix D]

Construction and certain other multiple advance loans pose special problems in computing the finance charge and APR. In many instances, the amount and dates of advances are not predictable with certainty because they depend on the progress of the work. Regulation Z provides that the APR and finance charge for such loans may be estimated for disclosure.

At its option, the bank may rely on the representations of other parties to acquire necessary information (for example, it might look to the consumer for the dates of advances). In addition, if either the amounts or dates of advances are unknown (even if some of them are known), the bank may, at its option, use appendix D to the regulation to make calculations and disclosures. The finance charge and payment schedule obtained through appendix D may be used with volume one of the Federal Reserve Board's APR tables or with any other appropriate computation tool to determine the APR. If the bank elects not to use appendix D, or if appendix D cannot be applied to a loan (e.g., appendix D does not apply to a combined construction-permanent loan if the payments for the permanent loan begin during the construction period), the bank must make its estimates under section 226.17(c)(2) and calculate the APR using multiple advance formulas.

On loans involving a series of advances under an agreement to extend credit up to a certain amount, a bank may treat all of the advances as a single transaction or disclose each advance as a separate transaction. If advances are disclosed separately, disclosures must be provided before each advance occurs, with the disclosures for the first advance provided before consummation.

In a transaction that finances the construction of a dwelling that may or will be permanently financed by the same bank, the construction and permanent financing phases may be disclosed in any of three ways:

- As a single transaction, with one disclosure combining both phases.

- As two separate transactions, with one disclosure for each phase. If the consumer is obligated for both construction and permanent phases at the outset, both sets of disclosures must be given to the consumer initially, before consummation of each transaction occurs.

- As more than two transactions, with one disclosure for each advance and one for the permanent financing phase.

If two or more disclosures are furnished, buyer's points or similar amounts imposed on the consumer may be allocated among the transactions in any manner the bank chooses, as long as the charges are not applied more than once.

If the creditor requires interest reserves for construction loans, special appendix D rules apply that can make the disclosure calculations quite complicated. The amount of interest reserves included in the commitment amount must not be treated as a prepaid finance charge.

If the lender uses appendix D for construction-only loans with required interest reserves, the lender must estimate construction interest using the interest reserve formula in appendix D. The lender's own interest reserve values must be completely disregarded for disclosure purposes.

If the lender uses appendix D for combination construction-permanent loans, the calculations can be much more complex. Appendix D is used to estimate the construction interest, which is then measured against the lender's contractual interest reserves.

If the interest reserve portion of the lender's contractual commitment amount exceeds the amount of construction interest estimated under appendix D, the excess value is considered part of the amount financed if the lender has contracted to disburse those amounts whether or not they ultimately are needed to pay for accrued construction interest. If the lender will not disburse the excess amount when it is not needed to pay for accrued construction interest, the excess amount must be ignored for disclosure purposes.

Calculating the Annual Percentage Rate [Section 226.22]

The APR must be determined using either of the following methods:

- The actuarial method, which is defined by Regulation Z and explained in appendix J to the regulation, or

- The U.S. Rule, which is permitted by Regulation Z and briefly explained in appendix J to the regulation. The U.S. Rule is an accrual method that surfaced in an early nineteenth century United States Supreme Court case, Story v. Livingston (38 U.S. 359).

Whichever method the bank uses, the rate calculated will be accurate if the institution is able to "amortize" the amount financed while it generates the finance charge under the accrual method selected. Banks also may rely on minor irregularities and accuracy tolerances in the regulation, both of which permit somewhat imprecise, but still legal, APRs to be disclosed.

360-Day and 365-Day Years [Section 226.17(c)(3)]

Confusion often arises over the use of the 360-day or 365-day year in computing interest, particularly when the finance charge is computed by applying a daily rate to an unpaid balance. The method to apply should be explained clearly in the legal obligation. Many single payment loans or loans payable on demand are in this category. There are also loans in this category that call for periodic installment payments.

Regulation Z does not require one method of interest computation over another (although state law may). It permits banks to disregard the fact that months have different numbers of days when calculating and making disclosures. This means banks may base their disclosures on calculation tools that assume all months have an equal number of days, even if their practice is to take account of the variations in months to collect interest.

For example, a bank may calculate disclosures using a financial calculator based on a 360-day year with 30-day months, when, in fact, it collects interest by applying a factor of 1/365 of the annual interest rate to actual days.

Disclosure violations may occur, however, when a bank applies a daily interest factor based on a 360-day year to the actual number of days between payments. In those situations, the bank must disclose the higher values of the finance charge, the APR, and the payment schedule resulting from this practice.

For example, a 12 percent simple interest rate divided by 360 days results in a daily rate of 0.033333 percent. If no charges are imposed except interest, and the amount financed is the same as the loan amount, applying the daily rate on a daily basis for a 365-day year on a $10,000 one-year, single-payment, unsecured loan results in an APR of 12.17 percent (0.033333% x 365 = 12.17%), and a finance charge of $1,216.67. There would be a violation if the APR were disclosed as 12 percent or if the finance charge were disclosed as $1,200 (12% x $10,000).

However, if there is no other charge except interest, the application of a 360-day-year daily rate over 365 days on a regular loan would not result in an APR in excess of the one-eighth of 1 percentage point APR tolerance unless the nominal interest rate is greater than 9 percent. For irregular loans, with one-quarter of 1 percentage point APR tolerance, the nominal interest rate would have to be greater than 18 percent to exceed the tolerance.

Variable Rate Information [Section 226.18(f)]

If the terms of the legal obligation allow the bank, after consummation of the transaction, to increase the APR, the bank must furnish the consumer with certain information on variable rates. Graduated payment mortgages and step-rate transactions without a variable rate feature are not considered variable rate transactions. In addition, variable rate disclosures are not applicable to rate increases resulting from delinquency, default, assumption, acceleration, or transfer of the collateral.

Some of the more important transaction-specific variable rate disclosure requirements under section 226.18 follow:

- Disclosures for variable rate loans must be given for the full term of the transaction and must be based on the terms in effect at the time of consummation.

- If the variable rate transaction includes either a seller buy down that is reflected in a contract or a consumer buy down, the disclosed APR should be a composite rate based on the lower rate for the buy down period and the rate that is the basis for the variable rate feature for the remainder of the term.

- If the initial rate is not determined by the index or formula used to make later interest rate adjustments, as in a discounted variable rate transaction, he disclosed APR must reflect a composite rate based on the initial rate for as long as it is applied and, for the remainder of the term, the rate that would have been applied using the index or formula at the time of consummation (i.e., the fully indexed rate).

- If a loan contains a rate or payment cap that would prevent the initial rate or payment, at the time of the adjustment, from changing to the fully indexed rate, the effect of that rate or payment cap must be reflected in the disclosures.

- The index at consummation need not be used if the contract allows the lender to delay implementation of changes in an index value (e.g., the contract indicates that future rate changes are based on the index value in effect for some specified period, such as 45 days before the change date). Instead, the bank may use any rate from the date of consummation back to the beginning of the specified period (e.g., during the previous 45-day period).

- If the initial interest rate is set according to the index or formula used for later adjustments, but is set at a value as of a date before consummation, disclosures should be based on the initial interest rate, even though the index may have changed by the consummation date.

For variable-rate loans that are not secured by the consumer's principal dwelling or that are secured by the consumer's principal dwelling but have a term of one year or less, creditors must disclose the circumstances under which the rate may increase, any limits on the increase, the effect of an increase, and an example of the payment terms that would result from an increase [section 226.18(f)(1)].

For variable-rate consumer loans secured by the consumer's principal dwelling and having a maturity of more than one year, creditors must state that the loan has a variable-rate feature and that disclosures were previously provided [section 226.18(f)(2)]. Extensive disclosures about the loan program are provided when consumers apply for such a loan [section 226.19(b)], and throughout the loan term when the rate or payment amount is changed [section 226.20(c)].

Payment Schedule [Section 226.18(g)]

The disclosed payment schedule must reflect all components of the finance charge. It includes all payments scheduled to repay loan principal, interest on the loan, and any other finance charge payable by the consumer after consummation of the transaction.

However, any finance charge paid separately before or at consummation (e.g., odd days' interest) is not part of the payment schedule. It is a prepaid finance charge that must reduce the value of the amount financed.

At the creditor's option, the payment schedule may include amounts beyond the amount financed and finance charge (e.g., certain insurance premiums or real estate escrow amounts such as taxes added to payments). However, when calculating the APR, the creditor must disregard such amounts.

If the obligation is a renewable balloon payment instrument that unconditionally obligates the bank to renew the short-term loan at the consumer's option or to renew the loan subject to conditions within the consumer's control, the payment schedule must be disclosed using the longer term of the renewal period or periods. The long-term loan must be disclosed with a variable rate feature.

If there are no renewal conditions or if the bank guarantees to renew the obligation in a refinancing, the payment schedule must be disclosed using the shorter balloon payment term. The short-term loan must be disclosed as a fixed rate loan, unless it contains a variable rate feature during the initial loan term.

Amount Financed [Section 226.18(b)]

Definition

The "amount financed" is the net amount of credit extended for the consumer's use. It should not be assumed that the amount financed under the regulation is equivalent to the note amount, proceeds, or principal amount of the loan. The amount financed normally equals the total of payments less the finance charge.

To calculate the amount financed, all amounts and charges connected with the transaction, either paid separately or included in the note amount, must first be identified. Any prepaid, precomputed, or other finance charge must then be determined.

The amount financed must not include any finance charges. If finance charges have been included in the obligation (either prepaid or precomputed), they must be subtracted from the face amount of the obligation when determining the amount financed. The resulting value must be reduced further by an amount equal to any prepaid finance charge paid separately. The final resulting value is the amount financed.

When calculating the amount financed, finance charges (if in the note amount or paid separately) should not be subtracted more than once from the total amount of an obligation. Charges not in the note amount and not included in the finance charge (e.g., an appraisal fee paid separately in cash on a real estate loan) are not required to be disclosed under Regulation Z and must not be included in the amount financed.

In a multiple advance construction loan, proceeds placed in a temporary escrow account and awaiting disbursement in draws to the developer are not considered part of the amount financed until actually disbursed. Thus, if the entire commitment amount is disbursed into the lender's escrow account, the lender must not base disclosures on the assumption that all funds were disbursed immediately, even if the lender pays interest on the escrowed funds.

Required Deposit [Section 226.18(r)]

A "required deposit," with certain exceptions, is one that the bank requires the consumer to maintain as a condition of the specific credit transaction. It can include a compensating balance or a deposit balance that secures the loan. The effect of a required deposit is not reflected in the APR. Also, a required deposit is not a finance charge because it is eventually released to the consumer. A deposit that earns at least 5 percent per year need not be considered a required deposit.

Calculating the Amount Financed

A consumer signs a note secured by real property in the amount of $5,435. The note amount includes $5,000 in proceeds disbursed to the consumer, $400 in precomputed interest, $25 paid to a credit reporting agency for a credit report, and a $10 service charge. Additionally, the consumer pays a $50 loan fee separately in cash at consummation. The consumer has no other debt with the bank. The amount financed is $4,975.

The amount financed may be calculated by first subtracting all finance charges included in the note amount ($5,435 − $400 − $10 = $5,025). The $25 credit report fee is not a finance charge because the loan is secured by real property. The $5,025 is further reduced by the amount of prepaid finance charges paid separately, for an amount financed of $5,025 − $50 = $4,975. The answer is the same if finance charges included in the obligation are considered prepaid or precomputed finance charges.

The bank may treat the $10 service charge as an addition to the loan amount and not as a prepaid finance charge. If it does, the loan principal would be $5,000. The $5,000 loan principal does not include either the $400 or the $10 precomputed finance charge in the note. The loan principal is increased by other amounts that are financed which are not part of the finance charge (the $25 credit report fee) and reduced by any prepaid finance charges (the $50 loan fee, not the $10 service charge) to arrive at the amount financed: $5,000 + $25 − $50 = $4,975.

Other Calculations

The bank may treat the $10 service charge as a prepaid finance charge. If it does, the loan principal would be $5,010. The $5,010 loan principal does not include the $400 precomputed finance charge. The loan principal is increased by other amounts that are financed which are not part of the finance charge (the $25 credit report fee) and reduced by any prepaid finance charges (the $50 loan fee and the $10 service charge withheld from loan proceeds) to arrive at the same amount financed: $5,010 + $25 − $50 − $10 = $4,975.

Closed-End Credit APR and Finance Charge Tolerance Charts

The appendix of this booklet contains five charts that show how accuracy tolerances apply to finance charges and APRs for disclosure and reimbursement purposes. These charts are:

- "Closed-End Credit: Finance Charge Accuracy Tolerances."

- "Closed-End Credit: Accuracy and Reimbursement Tolerances for Understated Finance Charges."

- "Closed-End Credit: Accuracy Tolerances for Overstated Finance Charges."

- "Closed-End Credit: Accuracy Tolerances for Overstated APRs."

- "Closed-End Credit: Accuracy and Reimbursement Tolerances for Understated APRs."

Refinancings [Section 226.20]

When an obligation is satisfied and replaced by a new obligation to the original bank (or a holder or servicer of the original obligation) and is undertaken by the same consumer, it must be treated as a refinancing for which a complete set of new disclosures must be furnished. A refinancing may involve the consolidation of several existing obligations, disbursement of new money to the consumer, or the rescheduling of payments under an existing obligation. In any form, the new obligation must completely replace the earlier one to be considered a refinancing under the regulation. The finance charge on the new disclosure must include any unearned portion of the old finance charge that is not credited to the existing obligation [section 226.20(a)].

The following transactions are not considered refinancings even if the existing obligation is satisfied and replaced by a new obligation undertaken by the same consumer:

- Renewal of an obligation with a single payment of principal and interest or with periodic interest payments and a final payment of principal with no change in the original terms.

- APR reduction with a corresponding change in the payment schedule.

- Agreement involving a court proceeding.

- Changes in credit terms arising from the consumer's default or delinquency.

- Renewal of optional insurance purchased by the consumer and added to an existing transaction if required disclosures were provided for the initial purchase of the insurance.

However, even if the old obligation is not canceled and a new one created, a new transaction subject to new disclosures results if the bank:

- Increases the rate based on a variable rate feature that was not previously disclosed, or

- Adds a variable rate feature to the obligation.

If, at the time a loan is renewed, the rate is increased, the increase is not considered a variable rate feature. It is the cost of renewal, similar to a flat fee, as long as the new rate remains fixed during the remaining life of the loan. If the original debt is not canceled in connection with such a renewal, the regulation does not require new disclosures. Also, changing the index of a variable rate transaction to a comparable index is not considered adding a variable rate feature to the obligation.

Closed-End Advertising [Section 226.24]

The regulation requires that advertisements for mortgage loans provide, in a clear and conspicuous manner, accurate and balanced information about rates, monthly payments, and other loan features. The advertising rules ban several deceptive or misleading advertising practices, including representations that a rate or payment is "fixed" when in fact it can change.

If an advertisement for credit states specific credit terms, it must state only those terms that actually are or will be arranged or offered by the creditor.

Disclosures required by this section must be made "clearly and conspicuously." In general, to meet this standard, credit terms need not be printed in a certain type size or appear in any particular place in the advertisement. For an advertisement for credit secured by a dwelling, a clear and conspicuous disclosure means that the required information is disclosed with equal prominence and in close proximity to the advertised rates or payments triggering the required disclosures.

If an advertisement states a rate of finance charge, it must state the rate as an "annual percentage rate," using that term. If the APR may be increased after consummation, the advertisement must state that fact.

If an advertisement is for credit not secured by a dwelling, the advertisement must not state any other rate, except that a simple annual rate or periodic rate that is applied to an unpaid balance may be stated in conjunction with, but not more conspicuously than, the APR.

If an advertisement is for credit secured by a dwelling, the advertisement must not state any other rate, except that a simple annual rate that is applied to an unpaid balance may be stated in conjunction with, but not more conspicuously than, the APR. That is, an advertisement for credit secured by a dwelling may not state a periodic rate, other than a simple annual rate, that is applied to an unpaid balance.

The following phrases—so-called triggering terms—require additional disclosures:

- Amount or percentage of any down payment.

- Number of payments or period of repayment.

- Amount of any payment.

- Amount of any finance charge.

An advertisement stating a triggering term must also state the following terms as applicable:

- Amount or percentage of any down payment.

- Terms of repayment, which reflect the repayment obligations over the full term of the loan, including any balloon payment.

- "Annual percentage rate," using that term, and, if the rate may be increased after consummation, that fact.

For an advertisement secured by a dwelling, other than a television or radio advertisement, that states a simple annual rate of interest and more than one simple annual rate of interest that applies over the term of the advertised loan, the advertisement must state in a clear and conspicuous manner:

- Each simple rate of interest that will apply. In variable-rate transactions, a rate determined by adding an index and margin must be disclosed based on a reasonably current index and margin.

- Period of time during which each simple annual rate of interest will apply.

- APR for the loan.

The regulation prohibits in advertisements for closed-end mortgage loans the following seven deceptive or misleading acts or practices:

- Stating that rates or payments for loans are "fixed" when those rates or payments can vary without adequately disclosing that the interest rate or payment amounts are "fixed" only for a limited period of time, rather than for the full term of the loan.

- Making comparisons between actual or hypothetical credit payments or rates and any payments or rates available for the advertised product that are not available for the full term of the loan, with certain exceptions for advertisements for variable rate products.

- Characterizing the products offered as "government loan programs," "government-supported loans," or otherwise endorsed or sponsored by a federal or state government entity when the advertised products are not government-supported or government-sponsored loans.

- Displaying the name of the consumer's current mortgage lender, unless the advertisement also prominently discloses that the advertisement is from a mortgage lender not affiliated with the consumer's current lender.

- Making claims of debt elimination if the product advertised would merely replace one debt obligation with another.

- Creating a false impression that the mortgage broker or lender is a "counselor" for the consumer.

- In foreign-language advertisements, providing certain information, such as a low introductory "teaser" rate, in a foreign language, while providing required disclosures only in English.

Subpart D—Miscellaneous

Civil Liability [TILA Sections 130 and 131]

If a creditor fails to comply with any requirements of the TILA, other than with the advertising provisions of chapter 3, it may be held liable to the consumer for:

- Actual damage.

- Cost of any legal action together with reasonable attorney's fees in a successful action.

If it violates certain requirements of the TILA, the creditor also may be held liable for either of the following:

- In an individual action, twice the amount of the finance charge involved, but not less than $100 or more than $1,000. Exception: In an individual action relating to a closed-end credit transaction secured by real property or a dwelling, twice the amount of the finance charge involved, but not less than $200 or more than $2,000.

- In a class action, such amount as the court may allow. The total amount of recovery, however, cannot be more than $500,000 or 1 percent of the creditor's net worth, whichever is less.

Civil actions that may be brought against a creditor also may be maintained against any assignee of the creditor if the violation is apparent on the face of the disclosure statement or other documents assigned, except where the assignment was involuntary.

A creditor that fails to comply with TILA's requirements for loans that meet the criteria in section 226.32(a) ("high-cost mortgage loans") or section 226.35(a) ("higher-priced mortgage loans") may be held liable to the consumer for all finance charges and fees paid to the creditor. For high-cost mortgage loans (under section 226.32(a)), any subsequent assignee is subject to all claims and defenses that the consumer could assert against the creditor, unless the assignee demonstrates that it could not reasonably have determined that the loan was subject to section 226.32.

Criminal Liability [TILA Section 112]

Anyone who willingly and knowingly fails to comply with any requirement of the TILA will be fined not more than $5,000 or imprisoned for not more than one year, or both.

Administrative Actions [TILA Section 108]

The TILA authorizes federal regulatory agencies to require banks to make monetary and other adjustments to the consumers' accounts when the true finance charge or APR exceeds the disclosed finance charge or APR by more than a specified accuracy tolerance. That authorization extends to unintentional errors, including isolated violations (e.g., an error that occurred only once or errors, often without a common cause, that occurred infrequently and randomly).

Under certain circumstances, the TILA requires federal regulatory agencies to order banks to reimburse consumers when understatement of the APR or finance charge involves:

- Patterns or practices of violations (e.g., errors that occurred, often with a common cause, consistently or frequently, reflecting a pattern with a specific type or types of consumer credit).

- Gross negligence.

- Willful noncompliance intended to mislead the person to whom the credit was extended.

Any proceeding that may be brought by a regulatory agency against a creditor may be maintained against any assignee of the creditor if the violation is apparent on the face of the disclosure statement or other documents assigned, except where the assignment was involuntary [section 131].

Relationship to State Law [TILA Section 111]

State laws that impose responsibilities on banks offering consumer credit, or that require such institutions or consumers to follow certain procedures, or that grant rights to consumers or banks in consumer credit contracts:

- May be preempted by the TILA.

- May not be preempted by the TILA, or

- May be substituted for the TILA and Regulation Z requirements. The TILA does not preclude preemption of state law by other federal statues, such as the National Bank Act.

State law provisions are preempted to the extent that they contradict the requirements in the following chapters of the TILA and the implementing sections of Regulation Z:

- Chapter 1, "General Provisions," which contains definitions and acceptable methods for determining finance charges and APRs.

- Chapter 2, "Credit Transactions," which contains disclosure requirements, rescission rights, and certain credit card provisions.

- Chapter 3, "Credit Advertising," which contains consumer credit advertising rules and APR oral disclosure requirements.

For example, a state law would be preempted if it required a bank to use the term "nominal annual interest rate" in lieu of "annual percentage rate."

Conversely, state law provisions are not preempted under the TILA if they call for, without contradicting chapters 1, 2, or 3 of the TILA or the implementing sections of Regulation Z, either of the following:

- Disclosure of information not otherwise required. A state law that requires disclosure of the minimum periodic payment for open-end credit, for example, would not be preempted by the TILA.

- Disclosures more detailed than those required. A state law that requires itemization of the amount financed, for example, would not be preempted, unless it contradicts the TILA by requiring the itemization to appear with the disclosure of the amount financed in the segregated closed-end credit disclosures.

The relationship between state law and chapter 4 of the TILA ("Credit Billing") involves two parts. The first part is concerned with sections 161 (correction of billing errors) and 162 (regulation of credit reports) of the act; the second part addresses the remaining sections of chapter 4.

State law provisions are preempted if they differ from the rights, responsibilities, or procedures in sections 161 or 162. An exception is made, however, for state law that allows a consumer to inquire about an account and requires the bank to respond to such inquiry beyond the time limits provided by the TILA. Such a state law would not be preempted for the extra time period.

State law provisions are preempted if they result in violations of sections 163 through 171 of chapter 4. For example, a state law that allows the card issuer to offset the consumer's credit-card indebtedness against funds held by the card issuer would be preempted, because it would violate 12 CFR 226.12(d). Conversely, a state law that requires periodic statements to be sent more than 14 days before the end of a free-ride period would not be preempted, because no violation of the TILA is involved.

A bank, state, or other interested party may ask the Federal Reserve Board to determine if state law contradicts chapters 1 through 3 of the TILA or Regulation Z. They also may ask if the state law is different from, or would result in violations of, chapter 4 of the TILA and the implementing provisions of Regulation Z. If the Board determines that a disclosure required by state law (other than a requirement relating to the finance charge, APR, or the disclosures required under section 226.32) is substantially the same in meaning as a disclosure required under the act or Regulation Z, generally creditors in that state may make the state disclosure in lieu of the federal disclosure.

Subpart E—Special Rules for Certain Home Mortgage Transactions

General Rules [Section 226.31]

The requirements and limits of this subpart are in addition to and not in lieu of those in other subparts of Regulation Z. The disclosures for high-cost and reverse mortgage transactions must be made clearly and conspicuously in writing, in a form that the consumer may keep.

Closed-End Home Mortgages Subject to Section 32 (HOEPA Loans)

This section's requirements apply to a consumer credit transaction secured by the consumer's principal dwelling, in which either:

- The APR at consummation exceeds by more than 8 percentage points for first-lien mortgage loans, or by more than 10 percentage points for subordinate-lien mortgage loans, the yield on Treasury securities having comparable periods of maturity to the loan's maturity (as of the 15th day of the month immediately preceding the month in which the application for the extension of credit is received by the creditor), or

- The total points and fees (see definition below) payable by the consumer at or before loan closing exceeds the greater of 8 percent of the total loan amount or $592 for 2011. (This dollar amount is adjusted annually based on changes in the Consumer Price Index. See staff commentary to section 32(a)(1)(ii) for a historical list of dollar amount adjustments.) [section 226.32(a)(1)].

Exemptions

The following transactions are exempted from compliance with section 226.32:

- Residential mortgage transactions (generally purchase money mortgages).

- Reverse mortgage transactions subject to section 226.33.

- Open-end credit plans subject to Subpart B of Regulation Z.

Points and Fees

Points and fees include the following:

- All items required to be disclosed under section 226.4(a) and (b), except interest or the time-price differential.

- All compensation paid to mortgage brokers.

- All items listed in section 226.4(c)(7), other than amounts held for future taxes, unless all of the following conditions are met:

  - Charge is reasonable.

  - Creditor receives no direct or indirect compensation in connection with the charge.

  - Charge is not paid to an affiliate of the creditor.

- Premiums or other charges, paid at or before closing if paid in cash or financed, for optional credit life, accident, health, or loss-of-income insurance, and other debt-protection or debt cancellation products written in connection with the credit transaction (section 226.32(b)(1)).

Prohibited Acts or Practices in Connection With Credit Subject to Section 226.32 (HOEPA Loans)

Among other requirements, a creditor extending mortgage credit subject to section 226.32 (HOEPA loans) must not make such loans based on the value of the consumer's collateral without regard to the consumer's repayment ability at loan consummation, including mortgage-related obligations. Mortgage-related obligations are expected property taxes, premiums for mortgage-related insurance required by the creditor, and similar expenses. A creditor, in determining a consumer's repayment ability, must also verify the income or assets, including expected income and assets that it relies on by using tax returns, payroll receipts, financial institution records, or other third party documents that provide reasonably reliable evidence of the consumer's income or assets. A creditor also must verity the consumer's current obligations.

A presumption of compliance is available for some transactions, but only if the creditor:

- Verifies the consumer's repayment ability as required.

- Determines the consumer's repayment ability using the largest payment of principal and interest scheduled in the first seven years following consummation and taking into account current obligations and mortgage-related obligations.

- Assesses the consumer's repayment ability taking into account either the ratio of total debts to income or the income the consumer will have after paying debt obligations.

For HOEPA loans, the regulation prohibits the imposition of prepayment penalties under certain circumstances, and in no case may a penalty be imposed after two years following consummation.

The regulation prohibits prepayment penalties at any time for a HOEPA loan if:

- Other applicable law (e.g., state law) prohibits such penalty.

- Penalty will apply after the first two years following consummation.

- Penalty applies where the source of the prepayment funds is a refinancing by the same mortgage lender or an affiliate.

- Consumer's mortgage payment can change during the first four years of the loan term (applicable only to loans originated on or after October 1, 2009), or

- Consumer's total monthly debt payments (at consummation), including amounts owed under the mortgage, exceed 50 percent of the consumer's monthly gross income.

- The regulation prohibits creditors from structuring home-secured loans as open-end plans to evade these requirements.

Reverse Mortgages [Section 226.33]

A reverse mortgage is a non-recourse transaction secured by the consumer's principal dwelling which ties repayment (other than upon default) to the homeowner's death or permanent move from, or transfer of the title of, the home.

Higher-Priced Mortgage Loans [Section 226.35]

A mortgage loan subject to section 226.35 ("higher-priced" mortgage loan) is a consumer credit transaction secured by the consumer's principal dwelling with an APR that exceeds the average prime offer rate for a comparable transaction as of the date the interest rate is set by:

- 1.5 or more percentage points for loans secured by a first lien on a dwelling, or

- 3.5 or more percentage points for loans secured by a subordinate lien on a dwelling.

Average prime offer rate means an APR that is derived from average interest rates, points, and other loan pricing terms currently offered to consumers by a representative sample of creditors for mortgage transactions that have low-risk pricing characteristics. The Federal Reserve Board publishes average prime offer rates for a broad range of types of transactions in a table updated at least weekly, as well as the methodology it uses to derive these rates. These rates are available on the Web site of the Federal Financial Institutions Examination Council (www.ffiec.gov).

A higher-priced mortgage loan does not include:

- A transaction to finance the initial construction of a dwelling.

- A temporary "bridge" loan with a term of 12 months or less.

- A reverse mortgage subject to section 226.33.

- A home equity line of credit subject to section 226.5(b).

- Among other requirements, a creditor extending a higher-priced mortgage loan must not make such loans based on the value of the consumer's collateral without regard for the consumer's repayment ability as of consummation, including mortgage-relat ed obligations. Mortgage-related obligations are expected property taxes, premiums for mortgage-related insurance required by the creditor, and similar expenses. A creditor must also verify amounts of income or assets, including expected income and assets, that it relies on to determine repayment ability using tax returns, payroll receipts, financial institution records, or other third party documents that provide reasonably reliable evidence of the consumer's income or assets. A creditor also must verity the consumer's current obligations.

A presumption of compliance is available for some transactions, but only if the creditor:

- Verifies the consumer's repayment ability as required.

- Determines the consumer's repayment ability using the largest payment of principal and interest scheduled in the first seven years following consummation and taking into account current obligations and mortgage-related obligations.

- Assesses the consumer's repayment ability taking into account either the ratio of total debts to income or the income the consumer will have after paying debt obligations.

The regulation prohibits prepayment penalties at any time for higher-priced mortgage loans if:

- Other applicable law (e.g., state law) prohibits such penalty.

- Penalty applies after the two-year period following consummation.

- Source of prepayment funds is a refinancing by the same mortgage lender or an affiliate.

- Consumer's mortgage payment can change during the first four years of the loan term.

- Consumer's total monthly debt payments (at consummation), including amounts owed under the mortgage, exceed 50 percent of the consumer's monthly gross income.

The regulation prohibits creditors from structuring home-secured loans as open-end plans to evade these requirements.

With few exceptions, a creditor may not grant a higher-priced mortgage loan secured by a first lien on a principal dwelling unless an escrow account is established before consummation for payment of property taxes and premiums for mortgage-related insurance required by the creditor. The exceptions involve loans secured by shares in a cooperative or condominium units where the condominium association has an obligation to maintain a master insurance policy. A creditor may allow a consumer to cancel the escrow account one year after consummation if a consumer's written cancellation request is received no earlier than 365 days after consummation.

Prohibited Acts or Practices in Connection with Credit Secured by a Consumer's Principal Dwelling [Section 226.36]

Coercion of Appraiser

Creditors and mortgage brokers are prohibited from coercing a real estate appraiser to misstate a home's value. Examples of actions that violate that prohibition include telling an appraiser what minimum value is necessary to approve the loan or failing to compensate when values do not meet minimum requirements. Actions that do not violate this section include, for example, asking an appraiser to consider additional information for the basis of valuation or requesting the appraiser to correct factual inaccuracies in the appraisal.

Loan Servicing Practices

Companies that service mortgage loans are prohibited from engaging in certain practices, such as pyramiding late fees. In addition, servicers are required to credit consumers' loan payments as of the date of receipt and provide a payoff statement within a reasonable time of request.

Specifically, for a consumer credit transaction secured by a consumer's principal dwelling, a loan servicer cannot:

- Fail, with limited exception, to credit a payment to the consumer's loan account as of the date of receipt.

- Impose on the consumer any late fee or delinquency charge in connection with a timely payment made in full, when the only delinquency is attributable to late fees or delinquency charges assessed on an earlier payment.

- Fail to provide, within a reasonable time after receiving a request from the consumer or person acting on behalf of the consumer, an accurate statement of the total outstanding balance that would be required to satisfy the consumer's obligations in full as of a specific date.

Notification of Sale or Transfer of Mortgage Loans [Section 226.39]

No later than 30 calendar days after the date of transfer[5] of a mortgage loan to a "covered person,"[6] the covered person shall notify the consumer in writing, clearly and conspicuously, in a form that the consumer may keep, of such transfer and include:

- Identification of the loan that was sold, assigned, or otherwise transferred.

- Name, address, and telephone number of the covered person.

- Date of transfer.

- Name, address, and telephone number of an agent or party authorized to receive notice of the right to rescind and resolve issues concerning the consumer's payments on the loan.

- Location where the transfer of ownership of the debt to the covered person is or may be recorded (note, however, that if the transfer of ownership has not been recorded in public records at the time the disclosure is provided, the covered person complies with this paragraph by stating this fact).

- At the option of the covered person, any other information regarding the transaction.

---

[5] The date of transfer to the covered person may, at the covered person's option, be either the date of acquisition recognized in the books and records of the acquiring party, or the date of transfer recognized in the books and records of the transferring party.

[6] A "covered person" means any person, as defined in 12 CFR 226.2(a)(22), that becomes the owner of an existing mortgage loan by acquiring legal title to the debt obligation, whether through a purchase, assignment, or other transfer, and who acquires more than one mortgage loan in any 12-month period. For purposes of this section, a servicer of a mortgage loan shall not be treated as the owner of the obligation if the servicer holds title to the loan or it is assigned to the servicer solely for the administrative convenience of the servicer in servicing the obligation. See section 226.39(a)(1).

This notice of sale or transfer must be provided for any consumer credit transaction that is secured by the principal dwelling of a consumer. Thus, it applies to both closed-end mortgage loans and open-end home equity lines of credit (HELOC). The notification is required even if the loan servicer remains the same.

Regulation Z also establishes special rules regarding the delivery of the notice when there is more than one covered person:

In a joint acquisition of a loan, the covered persons must provide a single disclosure that lists the contact information for all covered persons. However, if one of the covered person is authorized to receive a notice of rescission and to resolve issues concerning the consumer's payments, the disclosure may state contact information only for that covered person. In addition, if the multiple covered persons each acquire a partial interest in the loan pursuant to separate and unrelated agreements, they may provide either a single notice or separate notices. Finally, if a covered person acquires a loan and subsequently transfers it to another covered person, a single notice may be provided on behalf of both of them, as long as the notice satisfies the timing and content requirements with respect to each of them.

In addition, there are three exceptions to the requirement to provide the notice of sale or transfer:

1. A covered person sells, assigns, or otherwise transfers its entire interest in the loan on or before the 30th calendar day following the date of transfer.

2. A party temporarily becomes a covered person because of a repurchase agreement that obligates the transferor to repurchase the loan, unless the transferor does not repurchase the loan and the acquiring party recognizes the transaction as an acquisition on its books and records.

3. A party acquires only a partial interest in the loan and the transaction does not result in a change in the party authorized to receive the consumer's rescission notice and to resolve issues concerning the consumer's payment on the loan.

Subpart F—Special Rules for Private Education Loans

Special Disclosure Requirements for Private Education Loans [Section 226.46]

The disclosures required under Subpart F apply only to private education loans. Except where specifically provided otherwise, the requirements and limitations of Subpart F are in addition to the requirements of the other subparts of Regulation Z.

A private education loan means an extension of credit that:

- Is not made, insured, or guaranteed under title IV of the Higher Education Act of 1965.

- Is extended to a consumer expressly, in whole or part, for postsecondary educational expenses, regardless of whether the loan is provided by the educational institution that the student attends.

- Does not include open-end credit or any loan that is secured by real property or a dwelling.

A private education loan does not include an extension of credit in which the covered educational institution is the creditor if:

- The term of the extension of credit is 90 days or less.

- An interest rate will not be applied to the credit balance and the term of the extension of credit is one year or less, even if the credit is payable in more than four installments.

Content of Disclosures [Section 226.47]

Disclosure Requirements

This section establishes the content that a creditor must include in disclosures to the consumer at the following three different stages in the private education loan origination process:

- Application or Solicitation Disclosures: With any application or solicitation.

- Approval Disclosures: With any notice of approval of the private education loan.

- Final Disclosures: After the consumer accepts the loan; note section 226.48(d) requires that the disclosures must be provided at least three business days prior to disbursement of the loan funds.

Rights of the Consumer

The creditor must disclose that, if approved for the loan, the consumer has the right to accept the loan on the terms approved for up to 30 calendar days. The disclosure must inform the consumer that the rate and terms of the loan will not change during this period, except for changes to the rate based on adjustments to the index used for the loan and other changes permitted by law. The creditor must disclose that a consumer also has the right to cancel the loan, without penalty, until midnight of the third business day following the date on which the consumer receives the final disclosures.

Limitations on Private Educational Loans [Section 226.48]

This section contains rules and limitations on private education loans, including:

- A prohibition on co-branding in the marketing of private education loans.

- Rules governing arrangements in which educational institutions endorse a particular creditor's private education loans.

- Rules governing the 30 calendar-day acceptance period and three business-day cancellation period and prohibition on disbursement of loan proceeds until the cancellation period has expired.

- The requirement that the creditor obtain a self-certification form from the consumer before consummation.

- The requirement that creditors in preferred lender arrangements provide certain information to covered educational institutions.

Co-Branding Prohibited

Regulation Z prohibits creditors from using the name, emblem, mascot, or logo of a covered institution (or other words, pictures, or symbols readily identified with a covered institution) in the marketing of private education loans in a way that implies endorsement by the educational institution. Marketing that refers to an educational institution does not imply endorsement if the marketing includes a clear and conspicuous disclosure that is equally prominent and closely proximate to the reference to the institution that the educational institution does not endorse the creditor's loans, and that the creditor is not affiliated with the educational institution. There is also an exception in cases where the educational institution actually does endorse the creditor's loans, but the marketing must make a clear and conspicuous disclosure that is equally prominent and closely proximate to the reference to the institution that the creditor, and not the educational institution, is making the loan.

Specific Defenses [TILA Sections 108 and 130]

Defense Against Civil, Criminal, and Administrative Actions

A bank in violation of TILA may avoid liability by doing all of the following:

- Discovering the error before an action is brought against the bank, or before the consumer notifies the bank, in writing, of the error.

- Notifying the consumer of the error within 60 days of discovery.

- Making the necessary adjustments to the consumer's account, also within 60 days of discovery. (The consumer will pay no more than the lesser of the finance charge actually disclosed or the dollar equivalent of the APR actually disclosed.)

The above three actions also may allow the bank to avoid a regulatory order to reimburse the customer.

An error is "discovered" if it is:

- Discussed in a final, written report of examination.

- Identified through the bank's own procedures.

- An inaccurately disclosed APR or finance charge included in a regulatory agency notification to the bank.

When a disclosure error occurs, the bank is not required to redisclose after a loan has been consummated or an account has been opened. If the bank corrects a disclosure error by merely re-disclosing required information accurately, without adjusting the consumer's account, the bank may still be subject to civil liability and an order to reimburse from its regulator.

The circumstances under which a bank may avoid liability under the TILA do not apply to violations of the Fair Credit Billing Act (chapter 4 of the TILA).

Additional Defenses Against Civil Actions

The bank may avoid liability in a civil action if it shows by a preponderance of evidence that the violation was not intentional and resulted from a bona fide error that occurred despite the maintenance of procedures to avoid the error.

Examples of a bona fide error include clerical, calculation, computer malfunction, programming, or printing errors. It does not include an error of legal judgment.

A violation that occurred unintentionally could be difficult to prove if the bank is unable to produce explicit evidence that it has an internal controls program designed to ensure compliance. A bank can strengthen its defense if it has demonstrated a commitment to compliance and it has adopted policies and procedures to detect errors before disclosures are furnished to consumers.

Statute of Limitations [TILA Sections 108 and 130]

Civil actions may be brought within one year after the violation occurred. For private education loans, civil actions may be brought within one year from the date on which the first regular payment of principal and interest is due. After that time, and if allowed by state law, the consumer may still assert the violation as a defense if a bank were to bring an action to collect the consumer's debt.

Neither criminal actions nor regulatory administrative enforcement actions are subject to the TILA one-year statute of limitations. However, enforcement actions under the interagency policy guide for erroneously disclosed APRs and finance charges are subject to TILA time limitations. Those limitations range from the date of the bank's last regulatory examination, to as far back as 1969, depending on when loans were made, when violations were identified, whether or not the violations were repeat violations, and other factors.

There is no time limit on willful violations intended to mislead the consumer.

A summary of the primary time limitations follows:

- For open-end credit, reimbursement applies to violations not older than two years.

- For closed-end credit, the OCC directs reimbursement for loans with violations occurring since the immediately preceding examination of any type.

Rescission Rights (Open-End and Closed-End Credit) [Sections 226.15 and 226.23]

The TILA provides that for certain transactions secured by the consumer's principal dwelling, a consumer has three business days after becoming obligated on the debt to rescind the transaction. The right of rescission allows consumers time to reexamine their credit agreements and cost disclosures and to reconsider if they want to place their homes at risk as security for the credit. Transactions exempt from the right of rescission include residential mortgage transactions [defined in section 226.2(a)(24)] and refinancings or consolidations with the original creditor where no "new money" is advanced.

If a transaction is rescindable, consumers must be given a notice explaining that the creditor has a security interest in the consumer's home, that the consumer may rescind, how the consumer may rescind, the effects of rescission, and the date the rescission period expires.

To rescind a transaction, a consumer must notify the creditor in writing by midnight of the third business day after the latest of three events: (1) consummation of the transaction, (2) delivery of material TILA disclosures, or (3) receipt[7] of the required notice of the right to rescind. For purposes of rescission, business day means every calendar day except Sundays and the legal public holidays (section 226.2(a)(6)). The term "material disclosures" is defined in section 226.23(a)(3) to mean the required disclosures of the APR, the finance charge, the amount financed, the total of payments, the payment schedule, and certain disclosures and limitations contained in Regulation Z relating to HOEPA and higher-priced mortgage loans.

The creditor may not disburse any monies (except into an escrow account) and may not provide services or materials until the three-day rescission period has elapsed and the creditor is reasonably satisfied that the consumer has not rescinded. If the consumer rescinds the transaction, the creditor must refund all amounts paid by the consumer (even amounts disbursed to third parties) and terminate its security interest in the consumer's home.

A consumer may waive the three-day rescission period and receive immediate access to loan proceeds if the consumer has a "bona fide personal financial emergency." The consumer must give the creditor a signed and dated waiver statement that describes the emergency, specifically waives the right, and bears the signatures of all consumers entitled to rescind the transaction. The consumer provides the explanation for the bona fide

---

[7] 12 CFR 226.15(b) and 226.23(b)(1) were amended to address the electronic delivery of the notice of the right to rescind. If a paper notice of the right to rescind is used, a creditor must deliver two copies of the notice to each consumer entitled to rescind. However, under the final rule on electronic delivery of disclosures, if the notice is in electronic form, in accordance with the consumer consent and other applicable provisions of the E-Sign Act, only one copy to each customer is required.

personal financial emergency, but the creditor decides the sufficiency of the emergency.

If the required rescission notice or material TILA disclosures are not delivered or if they are inaccurate, the consumer's right to rescind may be extended from three days to as much as three years. On certain loans in foreclosure and in conjunction with recent case law, the consumer's right to rescind can be extended for a period of greater than three years when a consumer files bankruptcy, and the consumer used that as a defense to a foreclosure action.

Interagency Administrative Enforcement Policy

On September 8, 1998, the federal financial regulatory agencies issued a revised "Joint Statement of Policy on the Administrative Enforcement of the TILA—Restitution." (See the appendix of this booklet for this document and related guidance in question-and-answer form.) The policy summarizes and explains how the agencies interpret the reimbursement provisions of section 108(e) of the TILA. It also describes corrective actions the financial regulatory agencies believe appropriate.

The regulatory agencies anticipate that most banks will comply voluntarily with the reimbursement provisions of the TILA. However, if a bank does not act voluntarily to correct violations, the agencies generally are required by law to use their cease and desist authority to order correction of a clear and consistent pattern or practice of violations, gross negligence, or a willful violation that was intended to mislead the person to whom the credit was extended.

Enforcement Policy Applicability to Indirect Paper

Even if a third party rather than the bank makes an improper disclosure on a loan for which the bank is the creditor (i.e., if the bank is the entity to which the obligation is initially payable), the bank is cited for the violation and may be required to reimburse affected consumers under the enforcement policy.

If the third party is the creditor, a bank's acceptance of the third party's disclosures containing reimbursable violations normally reflects only a need for improved internal controls. However, if affected consumers have not been reimbursed, the OCC will report such third-party violations (consistent with the requirements of the Right to Financial Privacy Act of 1978) to the national headquarters of the regulatory agency supervising the creditor.

Adjustable Rate Mortgages

OCC's ARM Regulation

The OCC's ARM regulation (12 CFR 34) is intended to encourage national bank participation in the residential mortgage market. It provides a flexible framework within which banks may design ARMs that best meet their needs and those of their borrowers. National banks may make long-term mortgage loans with interest rates that can be adjusted to reflect changes in their cost of funds. At the same time, the regulation protects consumers by requiring national banks, for certain consumer ARMs, to link interest rates to an independent index or a combination of indices.

The OCC's ARM regulation permits national banks to design their own ARM loan programs, subject to certain rules. Banks may offer more than one ARM loan program as long as the various programs are offered to all borrowers in a manner that does not discriminate on any prohibited basis. Banks may impose limitations that are more restrictive than those provided in the regulation. Also, banks may continue to offer fixed rate mortgages.

While providing the flexibility desired by national banks, the OCC's ARM regulation helps protect the interests of borrowers. Subsequent notifications aid ARM borrowers in monitoring the pay down of their loans and determining if changes in installment payment amounts or rates of amortization best serve their needs. Because the regulation protects consumers primarily by ensuring proper disclosure rather than restricting ARM terms, the OCC views failure to provide timely and substantively complete disclosures as a serious violation of the regulation.

History and Requirements

National bank ARM loans may be subject to the OCC's ARM regulation, to special provisions on variable rate loans in the Regulation Z, or to both. The

OCC's ARM regulation was issued originally in March 1981, as 12 CFR 29, and amended significantly on March 7, 1983.

To achieve greater uniformity among the ARM regulations of several financial regulatory agencies, the OCC's regulation was rewritten completely, effective March 11, 1988, with optional compliance until October 1, 1988. The revised regulation was incorporated into 12 CFR 34, which is the OCC's regulation governing real estate lending activity of national banks, as Subpart B. The original Part 29 continued to be available until October 1, 1988.

The revised OCC ARM regulation modified the definition of an ARM, reduced the circumstances under which independent indexes are required, and deferred all ARM disclosure requirements to Regulation Z, as amended December 29, 1987. Subpart B was again modified and simplified effective April 19, 1996, and April 24, 2008.

The OCC's ARM regulation covers any extension of credit made by a national bank with an interest rate subject to adjustment and for the purpose of purchasing or refinancing the purchase of a one- to four-family dwelling and secured by that dwelling. OCC ARMs may either be open-end or closed-end credit.

Under the OCC ARM regulation, ARMs that are subject both to 12 CFR 34 and 12 CFR 226.19(b) must be tied to an independent index or combination of indices. Regulation Z requires ARMs subject to 12 CFR 226.19(b) to have early and comprehensive initial shopping disclosures, as well as notifications of interest rate changes. Disclosure requirements reflect the belief that the marketplace operates efficiently only if both buyers and sellers are well informed about the transaction. Consumers must be equipped to evaluate a variety of complex mortgage instruments, including ARMs. Initial shopping disclosures serve the dual purpose of educating consumers about the nature of ARMs and equipping them to shop for the appropriate one.

Loans subject to the ARM requirements of Regulation Z are closed-end consumer credit transactions secured by the consumer's principal dwelling with a maturity greater than one year and an APR that may increase. Regulation Z ARMs include purchase-money mortgage loans, as well as closed-end credit extended for other reasons (e.g., for home improvement).

See the "Summary of Coverage Rules for ARMs" in the appendix of this booklet for a comparison of ARM coverage requirements between the OCC's ARM regulation and the closed-end ARM requirements of Regulation Z.

The Board's changes to Regulation Z, effective on December 18, 1987, required creditors to provide comprehensive information about the variable rate features of closed-end ARMs. National bank and other creditor compliance with the Regulation Z ARM amendments became mandatory on October 1, 1988.

With the regulatory changes that became mandatory October 1, 1988, the only national bank federal disclosure requirements that remained for open-end ARMs were the regular open-end credit disclosures required by Regulation Z. However, in November 1988, the Home Equity Loan Consumer Protection Act became law. That statute required the FRB to amend Regulation Z to include special disclosure requirements for any open-end consumer credit plan secured by the consumer's dwelling. Additional comprehensive disclosure requirements were also included for variable rate plans.

Credit subject to the variable rate disclosure provisions of the Home Equity Loan Consumer Protection Act are open-end consumer credit transactions with variable rates of interest that are secured by the consumer's dwelling. Such disclosure requirements would apply both to open-end credit consumer ARMs, as defined by the OCC, as well as to any other consumer home equity line of credit (HELOC) secured by the consumer's dwelling. Also, the statute applies to both variable and fixed rate HELOCs.

Objective: Determine the bank's compliance with the TILA and Regulation Z, including whether there are reimbursable violations and compliance with the FFIEC Policy Guide on Reimbursement.

Use the TILA Worksheets to determine compliance. Refer to the Summary of the TILA Worksheets for guidance on which worksheets to use. When verifying APR accuracy, use the OCC's APRWIN program located in the applications section of your computer software.

Summary of the TILA Worksheets

Loan Type	Worksheets
Closed-End Consumer (Not Secured by Real Estate)	Worksheet #3—Closed-End Credit Forms Review
	Worksheet #5—Closed-End Credit File Review
Closed-End Consumer (Secured by Real Estate)	Worksheet #3—Closed-End Credit Forms Review
	Worksheet #5—Closed-End Credit File Review
	Worksheet #7—Right of Rescission Credit File Review
	Worksheet #13—Special Rules for Certain Home Mortgage Transactions Credit File Review
	Worksheet #15—High-Cost Mortgages
Closed-End Residential Mortgage	Worksheet #3—Closed-End Credit Forms Review
	Worksheet #5—Closed-End Credit File Review
	Worksheet #7—Right of Rescission Credit File Review
	Worksheet #13—Special Rules for Certain Home Mortgage Transactions Credit File Review
	Worksheet #15—High-Cost Mortgages
Adjustable Rate Mortgage	Worksheet #3—Closed-End Credit Forms Review
	Worksheet #5—Closed-End Credit File Review
	Worksheet #4—Closed-End Credit ARM Forms Review
	Worksheet #6—Closed-End Credit ARM File Review
	Worksheet #7—Right of Rescission Credit File Review
	Worksheet #13—Special Rules for Certain Home Mortgage Transactions Credit File Review
	Worksheet #15—High-Cost Mortgages
Home Equity Loan	Worksheet #3—Closed-End Credit Forms Review
	Worksheet #5—Closed-End Credit File Review
	Worksheet #7—Right of Rescission Credit File Review
	Worksheet #13—Special Rules for Certain Home Mortgage Transactions Credit File Review
	Worksheet #15—High-Cost Mortgages
Open-End Home-Secured	Worksheet #7—Right of Rescission Credit File Review
	Worksheet #9—Open-End Home-Secured Credit Forms Review
	Worksheet #11—Open-End Credit File Review
	Worksheet #12—HELOC Credit File Review
	Worksheet #14—Periodic Billing Statements Review
Open-End Not Home-Secured	Worksheet #8—Open-End Not Home-Secured Credit Forms Review
	Worksheet #10—Credit and Charge Card Forms Review
	Worksheet #11—Open-End Credit File Review
	Worksheet #14—Periodic Billing Statements Review
	Worksheet #16—Special Credit Card Rules Review
Advertising—Closed-End Credit	Worksheet #1—Closed-End Credit Advertising
Advertising—Open-End/HELOC	Worksheet #2—Open-End/HELOC Advertising
Reimbursements-All Loan Types	Worksheet #17—Reimbursement Review

Worksheet #1—
Closed-End Credit Advertising

Use this worksheet when reviewing closed-end credit advertisements. To complete, review advertising files, including electronic advertisements, from the last twelve months and place a check in each applicable box. This worksheet can be used for reviewing audit work papers, evaluating bank policies, performing expanded procedures, and training as appropriate. Only complete those sections of the worksheet that specifically relate to the issue being reviewed, evaluated, or tested, and retain those completed sections in the work papers.

When reviewing audit or evaluating bank policies, a "No" answer indicates a possible exception/deficiency and should be explained in the work papers. When performing expanded procedures, a "No" answer indicates a violation and should be explained in the work papers. If a line item is not applicable within the area you are reviewing, indicate "NA."

Underline the applicable use: Audit   Bank Policies   Expanded Procedures

#1—Closed-End Credit Advertising Worksheet										
Identify Advertisement:										
Advertisement Type:										
Date or Period Run:	Yes	No	Yes	No	Yes	No	Yes	No	Yes	No
1. Are all required disclosures made clearly and conspicuously? [226.24(b)] Note: The disclosures required by 226.24 may be provided to the consumer in electronic form without regard to the consumer consent or other provisions of the E-Sign Act in the circumstances set forth in those sections. [226.17(a)(1)]										
2. If credit terms are specific, are terms stated that actually are or will be arranged or offered by the creditor? [226.24(a)]										
3. If the advertisement states a rate of finance charge, is it stated as an "annual percentage rate?" [226.24(c)]										
4. Is the APR stated more conspicuously than the simple interest rate (if stated)? [226.24(c)]										
5. If the APR is stated and may be increased after consummation, does the advertisement state that fact? [226.24(c)]										
6. If triggering terms were used [226.24(d)(1)], did the advertisement include, as applicable: a. Amount or percentage of the down payment? [226.24(d)(2)(i)]										

#1—Closed-End Credit Advertising Worksheet										
Identify Advertisement:										
Advertisement Type:										
Date or Period Run:	Yes	No	Yes	No	Yes	No	Yes	No	Yes	No
b. Repayment terms over the full term of the loan, including any balloon payment? [226.24(d)(2)(ii)]										
c. APR? [226.24(d)(2)(iii)]										
d. The fact that the APR may be increased after consummation, if applicable? [226.24(d)(2)(iii)]										
7. If an advertisement for credit secured by a dwelling states a simple annual rate of interest and more than one simple annual rate of interest will apply over the term of the advertised loan, does the advertisement disclose in a clear and conspicuous manner:										
a. Each simple annual rate of interest that will apply; for variable-rate transactions, are the rates disclosed based on a reasonably current index and margin?										
b. Time period during which each simple annual rate of interest will apply?										
c. APR for the loan; if the APR is variable, does the APR comply with the accuracy standards in 226.17(c) and 226.22? [226.24(f)(2)]										
8. If an advertisement for credit secured by a dwelling states the amount of any payment, does the advertisement disclose in a clear and conspicuous manner:										
a. Amount of each payment that will apply over the term of the loan, including any balloon payment; in variable-rate transactions, are the payments disclosed based on										

#1—Closed-End Credit Advertising Worksheet										
Identify Advertisement:										
Advertisement Type:										
Date or Period Run:	Yes	No	Yes	No	Yes	No	Yes	No	Yes	No
a reasonably current index and margin?										
b. Period of time during which each payment will apply?										
c. For first lien loans, the fact that the payments do not include amounts for taxes and insurance premiums, if applicable, and that the actual payment obligation will be greater? [226.24(f)(3)]										
Note: Steps 7 and 8 do not apply to an envelope in which an application or solicitation is mailed, or to a banner advertisement or pop-up advertisement linked to an application or solicitation provided electronically. [226.24(f)(4)]										
9. If an advertisement distributed in paper form or through the internet is for a loan secured by the consumer's principal dwelling, and the advertisement states that the advertised extension of credit may exceed the fair market value of the dwelling, does the advertisement clearly and conspicuously state that:										
a. The interest on the portion of the credit extension that is greater than the fair market value of the dwelling is not tax deductible for Federal income tax purposes? [226.24(h)(1)]										
b. The consumer should consult a tax adviser for further information regarding the deductibility of interest and charges? [226.24(h)(2)]										
10. Are advertisements for credit secured by a dwelling void of misleading statements, including:										

#1—Closed-End Credit Advertising Worksheet										
Identify Advertisement:										
Advertisement Type:										
Date or Period Run:	Yes	No	Yes	No	Yes	No	Yes	No	Yes	No
a. Misleading advertising of "fixed" rates and payments?										
b. Misleading comparisons in advertisements?										
c. Misrepresentations about government endorsements?										
d. Misleading use of the current lender's name?										
e. Misleading claims of debt elimination?										
f. Misleading use of the term "counselor?"										
g. Misleading foreign-language advertisements? [226.24(i)]										

Worksheet #2—
Open-End/Home Equity Line of Credit Advertising

Use this worksheet when reviewing open-end and HELOC advertisements. To complete, review advertising files, including electronic advertisements, from the last twelve months and place a check in each applicable box. This worksheet can be used for reviewing audit work papers, evaluating bank policies, performing expanded procedures, and training as appropriate. Only complete those sections of the worksheet that specifically relate to the issue being reviewed, evaluated or tested, and retain those completed sections in the work papers.

When reviewing audit or evaluating bank policies, a "No" answer indicates a possible exception/deficiency and should be explained in the work papers. When performing expanded procedures, a "No" answer indicates a violation and should be explained in the work papers. If a line item is not applicable within the area you are reviewing, indicate "NA."

Underline the applicable use: Audit   Bank Policies   Expanded Procedures

#2—Open-End/Home Equity Line of Credit Advertising Worksheet										
Identify Advertisement:										
Advertisement Type:										
Date of Period Run:										
	Yes	No	Yes	No	Yes	No	Yes	No	Yes	No
1. If terms are specific, are terms stated that actually are or will be arranged or offered by the creditor? [226.16(a)]										
2. If triggering terms were used on any open-end plan advertisement [226.6(b)] did the advertisement also clearly and conspicuously include: a. Any minimum, fixed, transaction, activity or similar fee that could be imposed? [226.16(b)(1)(i)] b. Any periodic rates stated as an APR? [226.16(b)(1)(ii)] c. The fact that the plan provides for a variable periodic rate, if applicable? [226.16(b)(1)(ii)] d. Any membership or participation fee that could be imposed? [226.16(b)(1)(iii)] Note: The disclosures required by 226.5a, 226.5b, and 226.16 may be provided to the										

#2—Open-End/Home Equity Line of Credit Advertising Worksheet										
Identify Advertisement:										
Advertisement Type:										
Date of Period Run:	Yes	No	Yes	No	Yes	No	Yes	No	Yes	No
consumer in electronic form without regard to the consumer consent or other provisions of the E-Sign Act in the circumstances set forth in those sections. [226.5(a)(iii)]										
3. If an advertisement refers to an APR as fixed (or similar term), does the advertisement also specify a time period for which the rate will be fixed and not increase, or if no such time period is provided, specify that the rate will not increase while the plan is open? [226.16(f)]										
4. For open-end (not home-secured) plans, for any APR that is an introductory rate, is the term "introductory" or "intro" in immediate proximity to each listing of the introductory rate? [226.16(g)(3)]										
5. For open-end (not home-secured) plans, are the required disclosures for promotional rates made in a clear and conspicuous manner, and where applicable, in a prominent location closely proximate to the first listing of the promotional rate? [226.16(g)(4)]										
6. For open-end (not home-secured) plans, if the APR is stated in a written or electronic advertisement does the advertisement include, in a clear and conspicuous manner, when the promotional rate will end and what APR will apply after the end of the promotional period? [226.16(g)(4)(i) and (ii)] If the APR is variable, did the APR comply with the accuracy standards in 226.5a(c)(2), 226.5a(d)(3), 226.5a(e)(4), or 226.16(b)(1)(ii)? [226.16(g)(4)(ii)] If such rate cannot be determined at the time disclosures are given because the rate depends at least in part on a later										

#2—Open-End/Home Equity Line of Credit Advertising Worksheet										
Identify Advertisement:										
Advertisement Type:										
Date of Period Run:	Yes	No	Yes	No	Yes	No	Yes	No	Yes	No
determination of the consumer's creditworthiness, does the advertisement disclose, in a clear and conspicuous manner, the specific rates or the range of rates that might apply? [226.16(g)(4)(ii)]										
7. If a deferred interest offer is advertised for an open-end credit plan not subject to 226.5b is the deferred interest period stated in a clear and conspicuous manner in the advertisement? [226.16(h)(3)] If the phrase "no interest" or similar term regarding the possible avoidance of interest obligations under the deferred interest program is stated, is the term "if paid in full" stated in a clear and conspicuous manner preceding the disclosure of the deferred interest period in the advertisement? [226.16(h)(3)] If the deferred interest offer is included in a written or electronic advertisement, are the deferred interest period and, if applicable, the term "if paid in full" stated in immediate proximity to each statement of "no interest," "no payments," "deferred interest," "same as cash," or similar term regarding interest or payments during the deferred interest period? [226.16(h)(3)]										
8. If any deferred interest offer is advertised for an open-end credit plan not subject to 226.5b are the language requirements of 226.16(h)(4)(i) and (h)(4)(ii) stated in the advertisement and are they similar to Sample G–24 in Appendix G? If the deferred interest offer is included in a written or electronic advertisement, is this information stated in a prominent location closely proximate to the first										

#2—Open-End/Home Equity Line of Credit Advertising Worksheet										
Identify Advertisement:										
Advertisement Type:										
Date of Period Run:	Yes	No	Yes	No	Yes	No	Yes	No	Yes	No
statement of "no interest," "no payments," "deferred interest," "same as cash," or similar term regarding interest or payments during the deferred interest period? [226.16(h)(4)] Note: Steps 5, 6, and 8 do not apply to an envelope or other enclosure in which an application or solicitation is mailed, or to a banner advertisement or pop-up advertisement linked to an application or solicitation provided electronically. [226.16(h)(5)]										
9. Does the creditor offer a college student any tangible item to induce such student to apply for, or open, an open-end consumer credit plan if such offer is made on or near the campus of an institution of higher education, or at an event sponsored by or related to an institution of higher education? [226.57(c)]										
Additional Requirements for Home Equity Lines of Credit [226.5b]										
10. If triggering terms were used [226.6(b)], or the payment terms were set forth for a HELOC did the advertisement also include, clearly and conspicuously: a. Any loan fee that is a percentage of the credit limit? [226.16(d)(1)(i)] b. An estimate of any other fees for opening the plan stated as a single dollar amount or reasonable range? [226.16(d)(1)(i)] c. Any periodic rate stated as an APR? [226.16(d)(1)(ii)] d. The highest APR that may be imposed for a variable-rate plan? [226.16(d)(1)(iii)]										

#2—Open-End/Home Equity Line of Credit Advertising Worksheet										
Identify Advertisement:										
Advertisement Type:										
Date of Period Run:										
	Yes	No	Yes	No	Yes	No	Yes	No	Yes	No
11. For HELOCs, if a discounted or premium rate plan, does the ad state how long the initial APR will be in effect and provide a reasonably current, fully indexed APR with equal prominence? [226.16(d)(2)]										
12. For HELOCs, if a minimum periodic payment is disclosed, does the advertisement disclose, if applicable, and with equal prominence and in close proximity to the minimum periodic payment statement, the fact that a balloon payment will result and the amount and timing of the balloon payment if the consumer makes only minimum payments for the maximum permissible period? [226.16(d)(3)]										
13. For HELOCs, if there is a reference to tax deductibility, does the reference refrain from misleading language? [226.16(d)(4)]										
14. If an advertisement distributed in paper form or through the internet is for a home-equity plan secured by the consumer's principal dwelling, and the advertisement states that the advertised extension of credit may exceed the fair market value of the dwelling, does the advertisement clearly and conspicuously state that:										
a. The interest on the portion of the credit extension that is greater than the fair market value of the dwelling is not tax deductible for Federal income tax purposes? [226.16(d)(4)(i)]										
b. The consumer should consult a tax adviser for further information regarding the deductibility of										

#2—Open-End/Home Equity Line of Credit Advertising Worksheet										
Identify Advertisement:										
Advertisement Type:										
Date of Period Run:	Yes	No	Yes	No	Yes	No	Yes	No	Yes	No
interest and charges? [226.16(d)(4)(ii)]										
15. Does the advertisement refrain from misleading terms, such as referring to the HELOC as "free money"? [226.16(d)(5)]										
16. For HELOCs, are the required disclosures for promotional APRs and payments made and are they clear and conspicuous and with equal prominence and close proximity to each listing of the promotional rate or payment? [226.16(d)(6)(ii)]										
17. For HELOCs, do the promotional disclosures include, in a clear and conspicuous manner, the period of time during which the promotional rate or promotional payment will apply? [226.16(d)(6)(ii)(A)]										
18. For HELOCs, do the promotional rate disclosures include, in a clear and conspicuous manner, any APR that will apply under the plan? And, if such rate is variable, is the APR disclosed in accordance with the accuracy standards in 226.5b or 226.16(b)(1)(ii), as applicable? [226.16(d)(6)(ii)(B)]										

#2—Open-End/Home Equity Line of Credit Advertising Worksheet										
Identify Advertisement:										
Advertisement Type:										
Date of Period Run:										
	Yes	No	Yes	No	Yes	No	Yes	No	Yes	No
19. For HELOCs, are the amounts and time period of any promotional payments that will apply under the plan disclosed in a clear and conspicuous manner? In variable-rate transactions, are the payments that will be determined based on application of an index and margin disclosed based on a reasonably current index and margin? [226.16(d)(6)(ii)(C)] Note: Steps 16, 17, 18, and 19 do not apply to an envelope or other enclosure in which an application or solicitation is mailed, or to a banner advertisement or pop-up advertisement linked to an application or solicitation provided electronically. [226.16(d)(6)(iii)]										
20. For television and radio advertisements stating any of the terms requiring additional disclosures under 226.16(b)(1) or (d)(1), did the advertisement either state the information required by 226.16(b)(1)(ii) or (d)(1)(ii), as applicable? Did the advertisement list a toll-free telephone number, or any telephone number that allows a consumer to reverse the phone charges when calling for information, along with a reference that such number may be used by consumers to obtain the additional cost information?[226.16(e)]										

Worksheet #3—
Closed-End Credit Forms Review

Use this worksheet when reviewing closed-end credit forms other than those secured by the customer's principal dwelling for a term of more than one year. To complete, review the forms, including those furnished to dealers, and place a check in each applicable box. Determine the accuracy of the disclosures by comparing them to the contract and other bank documents. Forms that include or involve current transactions, such as change-in-terms notices, periodic billing statements, rescission notices, and billing error communications, are verified for accuracy when the file review worksheets are completed. This worksheet can be used for reviewing audit work papers, evaluating bank policies, performing expanded procedures, and training as appropriate. Only complete those sections of the worksheet that specifically relate to the issue being reviewed, evaluated or tested, and retain those completed sections in the work papers.

When reviewing audit or evaluating bank policies, a "No" answer indicates a possible exception/deficiency and should be explained in the work papers. When performing expanded procedures, a "No" answer indicates a violation and should be explained in the work papers. If a line item is not applicable within the area you are reviewing, indicate "NA."

Underline the applicable use: Audit   Bank Policies   Expanded Procedures

#3—Closed-End Credit Forms Review Worksheet										
Product Type:	Yes	No	Yes	No	Yes	No	Yes	No	Yes	No
1. Are disclosures and electronic disclosures clear, conspicuous, grouped, segregated, and in writing in a form the consumer can keep? [226.17(a)(1)] Note: Closed-end disclosures may be provided to the consumer in electronic form, subject to compliance with the consumer consent and other applicable provisions of the E-Sign Act. [226.17(a)(1)]										
2. Except for private education loans, are terms "finance charge" and "APR" together with the corresponding amount or percentage rate more conspicuous than other terms, except for the creditor's identity? [226.17(a)(2)]										
3. For private education loans, are the terms "finance charge" (when required to be disclosed under 226.18(d)) and "interest rate" more conspicuous than any other disclosure except for the creditor's identity under 226.18(a)? [226.46(c)]										
4. Is the creditor identified (may be apart from other disclosures)? [226.18(a)]										

#3—Closed-End Credit Forms Review Worksheet										
Product Type:	Yes	No	Yes	No	Yes	No	Yes	No	Yes	No
5. Is there a brief description of the Amount Financed? [226.18(b)]										
6. Is there a separate itemization of the Amount Financed or a statement that the consumer may request and receive a written itemization? [226.18(c)]										
7. Is there a brief description of the finance charge? [226.18(d)]										
8. Is there a brief description of the APR? [226.18(e)]										
9. Do the disclosures for variable rate loans that are not secured by the customer's principal dwelling or, if secured by the consumer's principal dwelling, that have a term of one year or less include: a. Circumstances that permit rate increases? [226.18(f)(1)(i)] b. Limits on the increase: Periodic? [226.18(f)(1)(ii)] Lifetime? [226.18(f)(1)(ii)] c. Effects of increase? [226.18(f)(1)(iii)] d. Hypothetical example of new payment terms? [226.18(f)(1)(iv)]										
10. Is the payment schedule included? [226.18(g)]										
11. Is there a description of the "Total of Payments," unless it's a single payment loan? [226.18(h)]										
12. Is a demand feature disclosed, if applicable? [226.18(i)]										
13. Is the total sales price included and described (if a credit sale)? [226.18(j)]										
14. Does the disclosure include whether or not a penalty/rebate is imposed for prepayment? [226.18(k)]										
15. Is a late payment charge (dollar amount or percent) disclosed, if applicable? [226.18(l)]										
16. Is there a security interest disclosure, if applicable? [226.18(m)]										
17. If credit life insurance and debt cancellation premiums have been excluded from the										

#3—Closed-End Credit Forms Review Worksheet										
Product Type:	Yes	No	Yes	No	Yes	No	Yes	No	Yes	No
finance charge, has the bank:										
a. Disclosed that insurance coverage is not required?										
b. Disclosed the premium for initial term?										
c. Obtained the customer's signature or initials as an affirmative request for the insurance? [226.18(n) and 226.4(d)]										
18. If the property insurance premium has been excluded from finance charge, has the bank:										
a. Disclosed that the consumer may choose the insurance company?										
b. Disclosed the cost of the insurance for the initial term if obtained from or through the bank? [226.18(n) and 226.4(d)]										
19. Are the disclosures required under 226.4(e) to exclude certain fees required by law, such as a filing fee or certain insurance premiums from the finance charge provided? [226.18(o)]										
20. Is there a statement referring to the contract document for specified information? [226.18(p)]										
21. Is there an appropriate assumption disclosure for residential mortgage transactions? [226.18(q)]										
22. If a deposit is required as a condition of the transaction, has the bank disclosed that the APR does not reflect its effect? [226.18(r)]										
23. Is the maximum interest rate disclosed (variable rate)? [226.30(b)]										
24. Has the creditor retained evidence of compliance with regulation Z for two years after the date disclosures were required to be made or action was required to be taken? [226.25(a)]										

Worksheet #4—
Closed-End Credit—Adjustable Rate Mortgage Forms Review

Use this worksheet when reviewing variable rate loans or ARMs with a maturity greater than one year secured by the principal dwelling of the borrower. To complete, review the forms, including any electronic forms, and place a check in each applicable box. Determine the accuracy of the disclosures by comparing them to the contract and other bank documents. Forms that include or involve current transactions, such as change-in-terms notices, periodic billing statements, rescission notices, and billing error communications, are verified for accuracy when the file review worksheets are completed. This worksheet can be used for reviewing audit work papers, evaluating bank policies, performing expanded procedures, and training as appropriate. Only complete those sections of the worksheet that specifically relate to the issue being reviewed, evaluated or tested, and retain those completed sections in the work papers.

When reviewing audit or evaluating bank policies, a "No" answer indicates a possible exception/deficiency and should be explained in the work papers. When performing expanded procedures, a "No" answer indicates a violation and should be explained in the work papers. If a line item is not applicable within the area you are reviewing, indicate "NA."

Underline the applicable use:　　　　Audit　　　　　　Bank Policies　　　　Expanded Procedures

#4—Closed-End Credit Adjustable Rate Mortgage Forms Review Worksheet										
Product Type:	Yes	No	Yes	No	Yes	No	Yes	No	Yes	No
1. Is the fact that the note contains a variable rate feature disclosed? [226.18(f)(2)(i)]										
2. Is there a statement that variable rate disclosures were provided earlier? [226.18(f)(2)(ii)] Note: Closed-end disclosures may be provided to the consumer in electronic form, subject to compliance with the consumer consent and other applicable provisions of the E-Sign Act. [226.17(a)(1)]										
Disclosure at Time of Application (one for each program in which the consumer expresses an interest) [226.19(b)(2)]										
3. Are disclosures provided either at time of application or before consumer pays any nonrefundable fee or, if the application is received from a mortgage broker or over the telephone, mailed within three business days following receipt of the application? [226.19(b) and footnote 45b] Note: The disclosures required by 226.19(b) may be provided to the consumer in electronic form without regard to the consumer consent or other provisions of the										

#4—Closed-End Credit Adjustable Rate Mortgage Forms Review Worksheet										
Product Type:										
	Yes	No	Yes	No	Yes	No	Yes	No	Yes	No
E-Sign Act in the circumstances set forth in those sections. [226.17(a)(1)]										
4. Do variable rate program disclosures provide:										
a. The booklet entitled "Consumer Handbook on ARMs," or a suitable substitute? [226.19(b)(1)]										
b. A statement that interest rate, payment or the term can change? [226.19(b)(2)(i)]										
c. The index/formula with source of information disclosed? [226.19(b)(2)(ii)]										
d. An explanation of the interest rate/payment determination and margin? [226.19(b)(2)(iii)]										
e. A statement that consumer should ask for the current margin and interest rate? [226.19(b)(2)(iv)]										
f. The fact that interest rate is discounted, if applicable, and a statement that the consumer should ask about the amount of discount? [226.19(b)(2)(v)]										
g. The frequency of interest rate and payment changes? [226.19(b)(2)(vi)]										
h. The rules relating to changes? [226.19(b)(2)(vii)]										
i. An historical example or the maximum interest rate and payment? [226.19(b)(2)(viii)]										
j. An explanation of how the loan payment can be calculated based on example? [226.19(b)(2)(ix)]										
k. The fact that the loan program contains a demand feature? [226.19(b)(2)(x)]										

#4—Closed-End Credit Adjustable Rate Mortgage Forms Review Worksheet									
Product Type:	Yes	No	Yes	No	Yes	No	Yes	No	Yes No
l. Information on, and timing of, adjustment notices? [226.19(b)(2)(xi)]									
m. A statement that disclosures for other variable rate loan programs are available? [226.19(b)(2)(xii)]									
5. Has the creditor retained evidence of compliance with regulation Z for two years after the date disclosures were required to be made or action was required to be taken? [226.25(a)]									

Worksheet #5—
Closed-End Credit File Review

Use this worksheet when reviewing closed-end credit loans. The worksheet contains all the standard closed-end credit disclosure requirements and should be used with the other closed-end worksheets. Determine the accuracy of the disclosures by comparing them to the contract and other bank documents. To complete, review loan files and place a check in each applicable box.

This worksheet can be used for reviewing audit work papers, evaluating bank policies, performing expanded procedures, and training as appropriate. Only complete those sections of the worksheet that specifically relate to the issue being reviewed, evaluated or tested, and retain those completed sections in the work papers.

When reviewing audit or evaluating bank policies, a "No" answer indicates a possible exception/deficiency and should be explained in the work papers. When performing expanded procedures, a "No" answer indicates a violation and should be explained in the work papers. If a line item is not applicable within the area you are reviewing, indicate "NA."

Underline the applicable use: Audit   Bank Policies   Expanded Procedures

#5—Closed-End Credit File Review Worksheet										
Product Type: Name of Borrower: Account Number:	Yes	No	Yes	No	Yes	No	Yes	No	Yes	No
1. Except for private education loans, are disclosures furnished before consummation? [226.17(b)] Note: Closed-end disclosures may be provided to the consumer in electronic form, subject to compliance with the consumer consent and other applicable provisions of the E-Sign Act. [226.17(a)(1), 226.39(b)(1)]										
2. Is the amount financed disclosed and accurate? [226.18(b)]										
3. Is there a separate itemization of the amount financed (RESPA–GFE, if applicable, may be substituted)? [226.18(c)]										
4. Is the finance charge disclosed and accurate? [226.4, 226.18(d) and footnote 41]										
5. Is the APR disclosed and accurate? [226.18(e) footnote 42 and 226.22(a)]										
6. Are the following required disclosures on variable rate loans (other than those secured by the consumer's principal dwelling with a term of more than one year) provided?										

#5—Closed-End Credit File Review Worksheet										
Product Type:										
Name of Borrower:										
Account Number:	Yes	No	Yes	No	Yes	No	Yes	No	Yes	No

a. Circumstances that permit rate increase? [226.18(f)(1)(i)]
 	
   b. Limits on the increase:
     Periodic? [226.18(f)(1)(ii)]
     Lifetime? [226.18(f)(1)(ii)]
 	
   c. Effects of increase? [226.18(f)(1)(iii)]
 	
   d. Hypothetical example of new payment terms? [226.18(f)(1)(iv)]										

7. Are the following required disclosures provided if the annual percentage rate may increase after consummation on variable rate loan transaction secured by the consumer's principal dwelling with a term greater than one year: a. The fact that the transaction contains a variable-rate feature? b. A statement that variable-rate disclosures have been provided earlier? [226.18(f)(2)]										
8. Is the payment schedule (amount, timing, and number of payments) provided and accurate? [226.18(g)]										
9. Is the total of payments provided and accurate? [226.18(h)]										
If the obligation has a demand feature, is that fact disclosed and if the disclosures are based on an assumption of one year as provided in section 226.17(c)(5), is that fact disclosed? [226.18(i)]										
10. If a credit sale, is the total sale price accurate? [226.18(j)]										
11. Is the security interest described accurately, if applicable? [226.18(m)]										
12. Is the credit life insurance premium or debt cancellation fee for the initial term accurately disclosed, if applicable? [226.18(n) and 226.4(d)]										

#5—Closed-End Credit File Review Worksheet										
Product Type: **Name of Borrower:** **Account Number:**										
	Yes	No	Yes	No	Yes	No	Yes	No	Yes	No
13. Is the cost of insurance for the initial term accurately disclosed if from or through the creditor? [226.18(n) and 226.4(d)]										
14. Are deposits required for credit transactions disclosed accurately? [226.18(r)]										
15. Are residential mortgage transaction closing fees that are excluded from the disclosed finance charge bona fide and reasonable? [226.4(c)(7)]										
16. Is the maximum interest rate in the contract (variable rate mortgage) disclosed? [226.30(a)]										
17. For mortgage transactions subject to RESPA secured by the consumer's dwelling, does the creditor provide a good faith estimate of the disclosures required by 226.18 within three business days after receiving the consumer's written application? [226.19(a)(1)(i)]										
18. In addition to the disclosures required by 226.18, did the creditor provide the notice indicating the consumer is not required to complete the agreement merely because the consumer has received disclosures or signed a loan application? [226.19(a)(4)]										
19. Did the creditor refrain from imposing a fee on a consumer in connection with the mortgage application before the consumer has received the relevant disclosures required in step 18, except for a bona fide and reasonable fee for obtaining the consumer's credit history, unless the consumer modifies or waives the applicable waiting period due to a bona fide personal financial emergency? [226.19(a)(3)]										

#5—Closed-End Credit File Review Worksheet											
Product Type: Name of Borrower: Account Number:	Yes	No	Yes	No	Yes	No	Yes	No	Yes	No	
20. Is the good faith estimate in step 18 delivered or placed in the mail not later than the seventh business day before consummation of the transaction, unless the consumer modifies or waives the applicable waiting period due to a bona fide personal financial emergency? [226.19(a)(2)(i)]											
21. Did the creditor provide corrected disclosures of all changed terms, including the APR, no later than the third business day before consummation, if the APR stated in the good faith estimate is not considered accurate under §226.22 when compared to the APR at consummation? [226.19(a)(2)(ii)]											
22. Unless subject to the exceptions at 226.39(c), for consumer credit transactions secured by the consumer's principal dwelling that were acquired by, or otherwise sold, transferred, or assigned to the creditor who is the new legal owner of the debt (covered person), did the covered person provide a written disclosure notice to the borrower within 30 calendar days of the transaction that includes the following: a. An identification of the loan that was sold, assigned, or otherwise transferred? [226.39(d)] b. Name, address, and telephone number of the covered person? [226.39(d)(1)] c. If there are multiple covered persons, has contact information been provided for each of them, unless one of them has been authorized to receive the consumer's notice of the right to rescind and resolve issues concerning the consumer's payments on the loan? [226.39(d)(1))ii)]											

#5—Closed-End Credit File Review Worksheet										
Product Type: Name of Borrower: Account Number:										
	Yes	No	Yes	No	Yes	No	Yes	No	Yes	No
d. Date of transfer, which may, at the covered person's option, be either the date of acquisition recognized in the books and records of the acquiring party, or the date of transfer recognized in the books and records of the transferring party? [226.39(d)(2)]										
e. Name, address, and telephone number of an agent or party authorized to receive notice of the right to rescind and resolve issues concerning the consumer's payments on the loan, unless the consumer can use the information provided under (b) for this purpose? [226.39(d)(3)]										
f. The location where the transfer of ownership of the debt to the covered person is or may be recorded? [Note: If the transfer of ownership has not been recorded in public records at the time the disclosure is provided, the covered person complies with this paragraph by stating this fact.] [226.39(d)(4)]										
g. At the option of the covered person, any other information regarding the transaction? [226.39(e)]										
Note: if more than one consumer is liable on the obligation, the covered person may mail or deliver the disclosure notice to any consumer who is primarily liable. [226.39(b)(3)]										
23. Is the disclosure notice required by 226.39 provided clearly and conspicuously in writing, in a form that the consumer may keep? [226.39(b)(1)]										

#5—Closed-End Credit File Review Worksheet										
Product Type: Name of Borrower: Account Number:										
	Yes	No	Yes	No	Yes	No	Yes	No	Yes	No
Note: the disclosure notice may be provided to the consumer in electronic form, subject to compliance with the consumer consent and other applicable provisions of the E-Sign Act. [226.39(b)(1)]										
24. If a consumer credit transaction secured by the principal dwelling of a consumer is acquired by a covered person and subsequently sold, assigned, or otherwise transferred to another covered person and a single disclosure notice is provided on behalf of both covered persons, did the disclosure notice satisfy the timing (226.39(b)) and content (226.39(d)) requirements applicable to each covered person? [226.39(b)(4)]										
25. If an acquisition involves multiple covered persons who jointly acquire the consumer credit transaction secured by the principal dwelling of a consumer, was a single disclosure notice provided on behalf of all covered persons? [226.39(b)(5)] Note: If an acquisition involves multiple covered persons who each acquire a partial interest in the loan pursuant to separate and unrelated agreements, each covered person has a duty to ensure that disclosures related to its acquisition are accurate and provided in a timely manner unless an exception in 226.39(c) applies. The parties may, but are not required to, provide a single notice that satisfies the timing and content requirements applicable to each covered person. [Commentary 226.39(b)(5) – 2]										
26. For private education loans, are the application or solicitation disclosures (226.47(a)) provided on or with any application or solicitation? [226.46(d)] Note: The disclosures required by 226.47(a) may be provided to the consumer in electronic										

#5—Closed-End Credit File Review Worksheet										
Product Type: Name of Borrower: Account Number:										
	Yes	No	Yes	No	Yes	No	Yes	No	Yes	No
form on or with an application or solicitation that is accessed by a consumer in electronic form without regard to the consumer consent or other provisions of the E-Sign Act. [226.46(c)(3)]										

27. Do the application and solicitation disclosures for private education loans disclose the following:
 	
a. Accurate interest rate, including:
 	
   1. Rate or range, and if the rate depends in part on a determination of the borrower's creditworthiness or other factors, a statement to that effect?
 	
   2. Whether rate is fixed or variable?
 	
   3. If rate may increase after consummation, any limitations, or lack thereof, and if the limitation is imposed by law, that fact. Also, the creditor must state that the consumer's actual rate may be higher or lower than that disclosed, if applicable?
 	
   4. Whether the rate will typically be higher if the loan is not co-signed or guaranteed? [226.47(a)(1)]
 	
b. Fees and default or late payment costs? [226.47(a)(2)]
 	
c. Repayment terms, including:
 	
   1. Term of the loan, which is the period during which regularly scheduled payments of principal and interest will be due?										

#5—Closed-End Credit File Review Worksheet											
Product Type: Name of Borrower: Account Number:											
	Yes	No	Yes	No	Yes	No	Yes	No	Yes	No	
2. Deferral options, or if consumer does not have the option to defer, that fact?											
3. For each available deferral option applicable, information as to:											
a) Whether interest will accrue during deferral period?											
b) If interest accrues, whether payment of interest may be deferred and added to the principal balance?											
c) A statement that, if the consumer files bankruptcy, the consumer may still be required to repay the loan? [226.47(a)(3)]											
d. Cost estimates, based on an example of the total cost of the loan, calculated using:											
1. The highest interest rate and including all applicable finance charges?											
2. An amount financed of $10,000, or $5,000, if the creditor offers loans less than $10,000?											
3. Calculated for each payment option? [226.47(a)(4)]											
e. Eligibility (e.g., any age or school enrollment eligibility requirements)? [226.47(a)(5)]											
f. Alternatives to private education loans, including:											

#5—Closed-End Credit File Review Worksheet										
Product Type: Name of Borrower: Account Number:										
	Yes	No	Yes	No	Yes	No	Yes	No	Yes	No
1. A statement that the consumer may qualify for Federal student loans?										
2. The interest rates available for each program available under title IV of the Higher Education Act of 1965, and whether the rate is variable or fixed?										
3. A statement that the consumer may obtain additional information regarding student federal financial assistance from the school or U.S. Department of Education, including an appropriate Web site?										
4. A statement that a covered educational institution may have school specific educational loan benefits and terms not detailed in the loan disclosure forms? [226.47(a)(6)]										
g. A statement that if the loan is approved, that the loan will be available for 30 days and the terms will not change, except for changes to the interest rate in the case of a variable rate and other changes permitted by law? [226.47(a)(7)]										
h. A statement that before consummation, the borrower must complete a self-certification form obtained from the student's institution of higher education? [226.47(a)(8)]										
28. For private education loans, are the approval disclosures provided before consummation on or with any notice of approval provided to the consumer? [226.46(d)(2)]										
29. Do the approval disclosures for private education loans disclose the information required under 226.18 and the following:										

#5—Closed-End Credit File Review Worksheet										
Product Type: Name of Borrower: Account Number:										
	Yes	No	Yes	No	Yes	No	Yes	No	Yes	No
a. Interest rate, information, including:										
1. Interest rate applicable to the loan?										
2. Whether the interest rate is variable or fixed?										
3. If the interest rate may increase after consummation, any limitations on the rate adjustments, or lack thereof? [226.47(b)(1)]										
b. Fees and default or late payment costs, including:										
1. An itemization of the fees or range of fees required to obtain the loan?										
2. Any fees, changes to the interest rate, and adjustments to principal based on the consumer's defaults or late payments? [226.47(b)2)]										
c. Repayment terms, including:										
1. Principal amount?										
2. Term of the loan?										
3. A description of the payment deferral option chosen by the consumer, if applicable, and any other payment deferral options that the consumer may elect at a later time?										
4. Any payments required while the student is enrolled at the educational institution, based on the deferral option										

#5—Closed-End Credit File Review Worksheet										
Product Type: Name of Borrower: Account Number:										
	Yes	No	Yes	No	Yes	No	Yes	No	Yes	No
chosen by the consumer?										
5. Amount of any unpaid interest that will accrue while the student is enrolled in school, based upon the deferral option chosen by the consumer?										
6. A statement that if the consumer files for bankruptcy, that the consumer may still be required to pay back the loan?										
7. An estimate of the total amount of payments calculated based upon:										
i. The interest rate applicable to the loan (compliance with §226.18(h) constitutes compliance with this requirement)?										
ii. The maximum possible rate of interest for the loan, or, if a maximum rate cannot be determined, a rate of 25%?										
iii. If a maximum rate cannot be determined, the estimate of the total amount for repayment must include a statement that there is no maximum rate and that the total amount for repayment disclosed is an estimate?										
8. The maximum monthly payment based on the maximum rate of interest for the loan, or, if a maximum rate of interest cannot be determined, a rate of 25%. If a maximum cannot be determined, a statement that there is no maximum rate and that the monthly payment amount disclosed is an estimate and will be										

#5—Closed-End Credit File Review Worksheet										
Product Type: Name of Borrower: Account Number:										
	Yes	No	Yes	No	Yes	No	Yes	No	Yes	No
higher if the applicable interest rate increases? [226.47(b)(3)]										
d. Alternatives to private education loans, including:										
1. A statement that the consumer may qualify for Federal student loans?										
2. The interest rates available for each program available under title IV of the Higher Education Act of 1965, and whether the rate is variable or fixed?										
3. A statement that the consumer may obtain additional information regarding student federal financial assistance from his school or U.S. Department of Education, including an appropriate Web site? [226.47(b)(4)]										
e. A statement that the consumer may accept the terms of the loan until the acceptance period under section §226.48(c)(1) has expired. The statement must include:										
1. The specific date on which the acceptance period expires, based on the date upon which the consumer receives the disclosures required under this subsection for the loan?										
2. The method or methods by which the consumer may communicate the acceptance (written, oral, or by electronic means?)										
3. A statement that except for changes to the interest rate and other changes										

#5—Closed-End Credit File Review Worksheet										
Product Type: Name of Borrower: Account Number:										
	Yes	No	Yes	No	Yes	No	Yes	No	Yes	No
permitted by law, the rates and the terms of the loan may not be changed by the creditor during the 30 day acceptance period? [226.47(b)(5)] Note: The disclosures required by 226.47(b) may be provided to the consumer in electronic form, subject to compliance with the consumer consent and other applicable provisions of the E-Sign Act. [226.46(c)(3)]										
30. For private education loans, are the final approval disclosures provided after the consumer accepts the loan and at least three business days prior to disbursing the private education loan funds? [226.46(d)(3)]										
31. In addition to the disclosures required under 226.18, do the final disclosures for private education loans disclose the following: a. Interest rate, including: 1. Interest rate applicable to the loan? 2. Whether the interest rate is variable or fixed? 3. If the interest rate may increase after consummation, any limitations on the rate adjustments, or lack thereof? [226.47(c)(1)] b. Fees and default or late payment costs, including: 1. An itemization of the fees or range of fees required to obtain the loan?										

#5—Closed-End Credit File Review Worksheet										
Product Type: Name of Borrower: Account Number:	Yes	No	Yes	No	Yes	No	Yes	No	Yes	No
2. Any fees, changes to the interest rate, and adjustments to principal based on the consumer's defaults or late payments? [226.47(c)(2)]										
c. Repayment terms, including:										
1. Principal amount?										
2. Term of the loan?										
3. A description of the payment deferral option chosen by the consumer, if applicable, and any other payment deferral options that the consumer may elect at a later time?										
4. Any payments required while the student is enrolled at the educational institution, based on the deferral option chosen by the consumer?										
5. Amount of any unpaid interest that will accrue while the student is enrolled in school, based upon the deferral option chosen by the consumer?										
6. A statement that if the consumer files for bankruptcy, that the consumer may still be required to pay back the loan?										
7. An estimate of the total amount of payments calculated based upon:										
i. The interest rate applicable to the loan (compliance with §226.18(h)										

#5—Closed-End Credit File Review Worksheet										
Product Type: Name of Borrower: Account Number:	Yes	No	Yes	No	Yes	No	Yes	No	Yes	No
constitutes compliance with this requirement)?										
ii. The maximum possible rate of interest for the loan, or, if a maximum rate cannot be determined, a rate of 25%?										
iii. If a maximum rate cannot be determined, the estimate of the total amount for repayment must include a statement that there is no maximum rate and that the total amount for repayment disclosed is an estimate?										
8. The maximum monthly payment based on the maximum rate of interest for the loan, or, if a maximum rate of interest cannot be determined, a rate of 25%. If a maximum cannot be determined, a statement that there is no maximum rate and that the monthly payment amount disclosed is an estimate and will be higher if the applicable interest rate increases? [226.47(c)(3)]										
d. In a text more conspicuous than any other required disclosure, except for the finance charge, the interest rate, and the creditor's identify the following disclosures:										
1. A statement that the consumer has the right to cancel the loan, without penalty, at any time before the midnight of the third business day following the date on which the consumer receives the final loan disclosures. The statement must include the specific date on which the										

#5—Closed-End Credit File Review Worksheet										
Product Type: Name of Borrower: Account Number:	Yes	No	Yes	No	Yes	No	Yes	No	Yes	No
cancellation period expires and that the consumer may cancel by that date?										
2. A statement that the loan proceeds will not be disbursed until the cancellation period expires?										
3. The method or methods by which the consumer may cancel?										
4. If the creditor permits cancellation by mail, the statement specifying that the consumer's mailed request will be deemed timely if placed in the mail not later than the cancellation date specified on the disclosures? [226.47(c)(4)] Note: The disclosures required by 226.47(c) may be provided to the consumer in electronic form, subject to compliance with the consumer consent and other applicable provisions of the E-Sign Act. [226.46(c)(3)]										
32. Has the creditor retained evidence of compliance with regulation Z for two years after the date disclosures were required to be made or action was required to be taken? [226.25(a)]										

Worksheet #6—
Closed-End Credit—Adjustable Rate Mortgage File Review

Use this worksheet when reviewing variable rate loans or ARMs with maturity greater than one year secured by the principal dwelling of the borrower. To complete, review applicable loan files and place a check in each applicable box. Determine the accuracy of the disclosures by comparing them to the contract and other bank documents. This worksheet can be used for reviewing audit work papers, evaluating bank policies, performing expanded procedures, and training as appropriate. Only complete those sections of the worksheet that specifically relate to the issue being reviewed, evaluated or tested, and retain those completed sections in the work papers.

When reviewing audit or evaluating bank policies, a "No" answer indicates a possible exception/deficiency and should be explained in the work papers. When performing expanded procedures, a "No" answer indicates a violation and should be explained in the work papers. If a line item is not applicable within the area you are reviewing, indicate "NA."

Underline the applicable use: Audit   Bank Policies   Expanded Procedures

#6—Closed-End Credit—Adjustable Rate Mortgage File Review Worksheet										
Name of Borrower: Account Number:	Yes	No	Yes	No	Yes	No	Yes	No	Yes	No
1. Did the bank provide timely early disclosures for residential mortgage transactions subject to RESPA? [226.19(a)(1)] Note: Closed-end disclosures may be provided to the consumer in electronic form, subject to compliance with the consumer consent and other applicable provisions of the E-Sign Act. [226.17(a)(1) and 226.39(b)(1)]										
2. Was the booklet entitled "Consumer Handbook on ARMs" or a substitute provided? [226.19(b)(1)] Note: The disclosures required by 226.19(b) may be provided to the consumer in electronic form without regard to the consumer consent or other provisions of the E-Sign Act in the circumstances set forth in those sections. [226.17(a)(1) and 226.19(c)]										
3. Does the contract contain an independent index or combination of indices [12 CFR 34.22] if the transaction is an ARM under 12 CFR 34.20 or an ARM under 226.19(b)?										
4. For mortgage transactions subject to RESPA secured by the consumer's dwelling, does the creditor provide a good faith estimate of the										

#6—Closed-End Credit—Adjustable Rate Mortgage File Review Worksheet										
Name of Borrower: Account Number:	Yes	No	Yes	No	Yes	No	Yes	No	Yes	No
disclosures required by 226.18 within three business days after receiving the consumer's written application? [226.19(a)(1)]										
5. In addition to the disclosures required by 226.18, did the creditor provide the notice indicating the consumer is not required to complete the agreement merely because the consumer has received disclosures or signed a loan application? [226.19(a)(4)]										
6. Did the creditor refrain from imposing a fee on a consumer in connection with the mortgage application before the consumer has received the relevant disclosures required in step 4, except for a bona fide and reasonable fee for obtaining the consumer's credit history, unless the consumer modifies or waives the applicable waiting period due to a bona fide personal financial emergency? [226.19(a)(1)]										
7. Is the good faith estimate in step 4 delivered or placed in the mail not later than the seventh business day before consummation of the transaction? [226.19(a)(2)]										
8. Did the creditor provide corrected disclosures of all changed terms, including the APR, that the consumer received no later than the third business day before consummation, if the APR stated in the good faith estimate is not considered accurate under §226.22 when compared to the APR at consummation? [226.19(a)(2)(ii)]										
9. Unless subject to the exceptions at 226.39(c), for consumer credit transactions secured by the consumer's principal dwelling that were acquired by, or otherwise sold, transferred, or assigned to, the creditor who is the new legal owner of the debt (covered person), did the covered person provide a written disclosure notice to the borrower within 30 calendar days of the transaction that includes the following: a. An identification of the loan that was sold, assigned, or otherwise transferred? [226.39(d)]										

#6—Closed-End Credit—Adjustable Rate Mortgage File Review Worksheet										
Name of Borrower: Account Number:	Yes	No	Yes	No	Yes	No	Yes	No	Yes	No
b. Name, address, and telephone number of the covered person? [226.39(d)(1)]										
c. If there are multiple covered persons, has contact information been provided for each of them, unless one of them has been authorized to receive the consumer's notice of the right to rescind and resolve issues concerning the consumer's payments on the loan? [226.39(d)(1))ii)]										
d. Date of transfer, which may, at the covered person's option, be either the date of acquisition recognized in the books and records of the acquiring party, or the date of transfer recognized in the books and records of the transferring party? [226.39(d)(2)]										
e. Name, address, and telephone number of an agent or party authorized to receive notice of the right to rescind and resolve issues concerning the consumer's payments on the loan, unless the consumer can use the information provided under (b) for this purpose? [226.39(d)(3)]										
f. The location where the transfer of ownership of the debt to the covered person is or may be recorded? [Note: If the transfer of ownership has not been recorded in public records at the time the disclosure is provided, the covered person complies with this paragraph by stating this fact.] [226.39(d)(4)]										
g. At the option of the covered person, any other information regarding the transaction? [226.39(e)]										

#6—Closed-End Credit—Adjustable Rate Mortgage File Review Worksheet										
Name of Borrower: Account Number:	Yes	No	Yes	No	Yes	No	Yes	No	Yes	No
Note: if more than one consumer is liable on the obligation, the covered person may mail or deliver the disclosure notice to any consumer who is primarily liable. [226.39(b)(3)]										
10. Is the disclosure notice required by 226.39 provided clearly and conspicuously in writing, in a form that the consumer may keep? [226.39(b)(1)] Note: the disclosure notice may be provided to the consumer in electronic form, subject to compliance with the consumer consent and other applicable provisions of the E-Sign Act. [226.39(b)(1)]										
11. If a consumer credit transaction secured by the principal dwelling of a consumer is acquired by a covered person and subsequently sold, assigned, or otherwise transferred to another covered person and a single disclosure notice is provided on behalf of both covered persons, did the disclosure notice satisfy the timing (226.39(b)) and content (226.39(d)) requirements applicable to each covered person? [226.39(b)(4)]										
12. If an acquisition involves multiple covered persons who jointly acquire the consumer credit transaction secured by the principal dwelling of a consumer, was a single disclosure notice provided on behalf of all covered persons? [226.39(b)(5)] Note: If an acquisition involves multiple covered persons who each acquire a partial interest in the loan pursuant to separate and unrelated agreements, each covered person has a duty to ensure that disclosures related to its acquisition are accurate and provided in a timely manner unless an exception in 226.39(c) applies. The parties may, but are not required to, provide a single notice that satisfies the timing and content requirements applicable to each covered person. [Commentary 226.39(b)(5) – 2]										

#6—Closed-End Credit—Adjustable Rate Mortgage File Review Worksheet										
Name of Borrower: Account Number:	Yes	No	Yes	No	Yes	No	Yes	No	Yes	No
Subsequent Disclosures										
13. Were subsequent disclosures mailed in accordance with timing requirements? [226.20(c)] and do they provide the: a. Current and prior interest rates (verify accuracy of rates used)? [226.20(c)(1)] b. Index values on which interest rates are based (verify accuracy of indexes used)? [226.20(c)(2)] c. Extent to which the creditor has foregone an interest rate increase (only if carryover exists)? [226.20(c)(3)] d. Contractual effects of the adjustment, including the new payment amount and a statement of the loan balance? [226.20(c)(4)] e. Payment required to avoid negative amortization? [226.20(c)(5)]										
14. Has the creditor retained evidence of compliance with regulation Z for two years after the date disclosures were required to be made or action was required to be taken? [226.25(a)]										

Worksheet #7—
Right of Rescission File Review

Use this worksheet when reviewing the right to rescission for both closed- and open-end loans subject to Regulation Z that are secured by the consumer's principal dwelling. Requirements for closed- and open-end loans are found in 12 CFR 226.23 and 12 CFR 226.15, respectively. (Note: Loans not subject to rescission include business purpose credit, refinancings in which no new money is advanced, and residential mortgage transactions.) To complete, review applicable loan files and place a check in each applicable box. If applicable, test rescission waivers.

This worksheet can be used for reviewing audit work papers, evaluating bank policies, performing expanded procedures, and training as appropriate. Only complete those sections of the worksheet that specifically relate to the issue being reviewed, evaluated or tested, and retain those completed sections in the work papers.

When reviewing audit or evaluating bank policies, a "No" answer indicates a possible exception/deficiency and should be explained in the work papers. When performing expanded procedures, a "No" answer indicates a violation and should be explained in the work papers. If a line item is not applicable within the area you are reviewing, indicate "NA."

Underline the applicable use: Audit   Bank Policies   Expanded Procedures

#7—Right of Rescission File Review Worksheet										
Product Type: Name of Borrower: Loan/Account #: Type of Credit (closed or open):	Yes	No	Yes	No	Yes	No	Yes	No	Yes	No
1. Was the appropriate number of copies furnished to each person entitled to rescind including one copy to each consumer entitled to rescind if the notice is delivered in electronic form in accordance with the consumer consent and other applicable provisions of the E-Sign Act? [226.23(b)(1) or 226.15(b)]										
2. Does the rescission notice identify the transaction? [226.23(b)(1) or 226.15(b)]										
3. Does the rescission notice disclose: a. The retention or acquisition of a security interest in the consumer's principal dwelling? [226.23(b)(1)(i) or 226.15(b)(1)] b. The consumer's right to rescind? [226.23(b)(1)(ii) or 226.15(b)(2)]										

#7—Right of Rescission File Review Worksheet										
Product Type: Name of Borrower: Loan/Account #: Type of Credit (closed or open):	Yes	No	Yes	No	Yes	No	Yes	No	Yes	No

c. How to exercise the right to rescind?
     [226.15(b)(1)(iii) or 226.23(b)(3)]
 	
   d. The effects of rescission?
     [226.23(b)(1)(iv) or 226.15(b)(4)]
 	
   e. The date the rescission period expires?
     [226.23(b)(1)(v) or 226.15(b)(5)]										

4. Was funding delayed (except into escrow) until the rescission period expired? [226.23(c) or 226.15(c)]										
5. Are waivers of the right to rescind appropriate? [226.23(e) or 226.15(e)]										
6. Internal controls: Does the consumer sign and date the notice to acknowledge receipt? Note: A "no" answer is not a violation of law.										
7. Has the creditor retained evidence of compliance with regulation Z for two years after the date disclosures were required to be made or action was required to be taken? [226.25(a)]										

Worksheet #8—
Open-End Not Home-Secured Credit Forms Review

Use this worksheet when reviewing general and account-opening disclosures for open-end not home-secured credit forms, including applicable electronic forms. To complete, review the forms and place a check in each applicable box. Determine the accuracy of the disclosures by comparing them to the contract and other bank documents. Forms that include or involve current transactions, such as change-in-terms notices, periodic billing statements, rescission notices, and billing error communications, are verified for accuracy when the file review worksheets are completed. This worksheet can be used for reviewing audit work papers, evaluating bank policies, performing expanded procedures, and training as appropriate. Only complete those sections of the worksheet that specifically relate to the issue being reviewed, evaluated or tested, and retain those completed sections in the work papers.

When reviewing audit or evaluating bank policies, a "No" answer indicates a possible exception/deficiency and should be explained in the work papers. When performing expanded procedures, a "No" answer indicates a violation and should be explained in the work papers. If a line item is not applicable within the area you are reviewing, indicate "NA."

Underline the applicable use: Audit   Bank Policies   Expanded Procedures

#8—Open-End Not Home-Secured Credit Forms Review Worksheet										
Product Type:	Yes	No	Yes	No	Yes	No	Yes	No	Yes	No
General Disclosures										
1. Did the creditor make the disclosures clearly and conspicuously and, unless subject to an exception listed at 226.5(a)(1)(ii)(A) or (B), in a form that the consumer may keep? [226.5(a)(1)] Note: Generally, the disclosures required by subpart B may be provided to the consumer in electronic form, subject to compliance with the consumer consent and other applicable provisions of the E-Sign Act. [226.5(a)(iii)] However, disclosures that need not be provided in writing under 226.5(a)(1)(ii)(A) may be provided in writing, orally, or in electronic form. If the consumer requests the service in electronic form, such as on the creditor's Web site, the specified disclosures may be provided in electronic form without regard to the consumer consent or other provisions of the E-Sign Act. [Commentary 226.5(a)(1)(ii)A)]										
2. Is the terminology used in providing the disclosures required by the open-end credit provisions of Regulation Z (226.5) consistent? [226.5(a)(2)(i)]										

#8—Open-End Not Home-Secured Credit Forms Review Worksheet										
Product Type:										
	Yes	No	Yes	No	Yes	No	Yes	No	Yes	No
3. If disclosures are required to be presented in a tabular format pursuant to 226.5(a)(3), is the term penalty APR used as applicable; and does the creditor refrain from using the term fixed, or a similar term, to describe such rate unless the creditor also specifies a time period that the rate will be fixed and the rate will not increase during that period, or if no such time period is provided, the rate will not increase while the plan is open? [226.5(a)(2)(iii]										
Account-Opening Disclosures										
4. Are the disclosures required in steps 5–9, steps 11–16, and steps 18–25 in the form of a table with headings, content, and format substantially similar to any of the applicable tables in G-17 in appendix G, including proper font and bolded text where applicable? [226.6(b)(1)(i)] Note: Refer to the model forms for examples. Bold text is not used for the amount of any periodic fee disclosed per 226.6(b)(2) that is not an annualized amount; and other annual percentage rates or fee amounts disclosed in the table. [226.6(b)(1)(i)]										
5. Is each periodic rate that may be used to compute the finance charge on an outstanding balance for purchases, a cash advance, or a balance transfer, expressed as an APR, disclosed; when more than one rate applies for a category of transactions, did the creditor disclose the range of balances to which each rate is applicable; and is the APR for purchases disclosed pursuant to this paragraph in at least 16-point type, except for a penalty rate that may apply upon the occurrence of one or more specific events? [226.6(b)(2)(i)]										
6. If the rate is a variable rate, did the creditor also disclose the fact that the rate may vary and how the rate is										

#8—Open-End Not Home-Secured Credit Forms Review Worksheet										
Product Type:	Yes	No	Yes	No	Yes	No	Yes	No	Yes	No
determined (i.e., identify the type of index or formula used in setting the rate)? [226.6(b)(2)(i)(A)]										
7. If the rate is an introductory rate, did the creditor disclose the rate that would otherwise apply to the account; where the rate is not tied to an index or formula, did the creditor disclose the rate that applies after the introductory rate expires; and for a variable rate account, did the creditor disclose a rate based on the applicable index or formula in accordance with the accuracy requirements? [226.6(b)(2)(i)(B)]										
8. If the initial rate is temporary and is higher than the rate that will apply after the temporary rate expires, did the creditor disclose the premium initial rate; and is the premium rate for purchases in at least 16-point type? [226.6(b)(2)(i)(C)]										
9. If the rate is a penalty rate, did the creditor disclose, as part of the APR disclosure: the rate that may apply, a brief description of the event or events that may result in the increased rate, and a brief description of how long the increased rate will remain in effect? [226.6(b)(2)(i)(D)(1)]										
10. If the creditor discloses in the table an introductory rate, as that term is defined in 226.16(g)(2)(ii), did the creditor briefly disclose directly beneath the table the circumstances under which the introductory rate may be revoked, and the rate that will apply after the introductory rate is revoked? [226.6(b)(2)(i)(D)(2)]										

#8—Open-End Not Home-Secured Credit Forms Review Worksheet										
Product Type:	Yes	No	Yes	No	Yes	No	Yes	No	Yes	No
11. If the creditor imposes an APR that varies by state or based on the consumer's creditworthiness and provides required disclosures in person at the time the open-end plan is established in connection with financing the purchase of goods or services, did the creditor either: a. Disclosure the specific APR applicable to the consumer's account or the range of the APRs? b. Refrain from listing APRs for multiple states in the account opening table? [226.6(b)(2)(i)(E)]										
12. Did the creditor disclose: a. Any introductory rate? b. Any rate that would apply upon expiration of a premium initial rate? [226.6(b)(2)(i)(F))] Note: If the amount of any fee required to be disclosed under 226.6(b)(2) is determined on the basis of a percentage of another amount, the percentage used and the identification of the amount against which the percentage is applied may be disclosed instead of the amount of the fee. [226.6(b)(1)(iv)]										
13. Did the creditor disclose any annual or periodic fee that may be imposed for the issuance or availability of an open-end plan (including any fee based on account activity or inactivity); how frequently the fee will be imposed; and the annualized amount of the fee; and any one-time fee? [226.6(b)(2)(ii)]										
14. Did the creditor disclose any fixed finance charge and a brief description of that charge? [226.6(b)(2)(iii)]										

#8—Open-End Not Home-Secured Credit Forms Review Worksheet										
Product Type:	Yes	No	Yes	No	Yes	No	Yes	No	Yes	No
15. Did the creditor disclose any transaction charge imposed by the creditor for use of the open-end plan for purchases? [226.6(b)(2)(iv)]										
16. Did the creditor disclose the grace period or if no grace period is provided did the creditor disclose that fact; if the grace period varies did the creditor disclose the range of days; in disclosing in the tabular format a grace period that applies to all features on the account, did the creditor include the phrase "How to Avoid Paying Interest" as the heading for the row describing the grace period; and if a grace period is not offered on all features of the account, did the creditor include the phrase "Paying Interest" as the heading for the row describing this fact? [226.6(b)(2)(v)]										
17. Did the creditor disclose the name of the balance computation method that is used to determine the balance on which the finance charge is computed for each feature, or an explanation of the method used if it is not listed, along with a statement that an explanation of the methods required by 226.6(b)(4)(i)(D) is provided with the account-opening disclosures? And is this information placed directly below the table? [226.6(b)(2)(vi)]										
18. Did the creditor disclose any fee imposed for an extension of credit in the form of cash or its equivalent? [226.6(b)(2)(vii)]										
19. Did the creditor disclose any fee imposed for a late payment? [226.6(b)(2)(viii)]										
20. Did the creditor disclose any fee imposed for exceeding the credit limit? [226.6(b)(2)(ix)]										
21. Did the creditor disclose any fee imposed to transfer a balance? [226.6(b)(2)(x)]										

#8—Open-End Not Home-Secured Credit Forms Review Worksheet										
Product Type:	Yes	No	Yes	No	Yes	No	Yes	No	Yes	No
22. Did the creditor disclose any fee imposed for a returned payment? [226.6(b)(2)(xi)]										
23. Did the creditor disclose fees for required insurance, debt cancellation or debt suspension coverage and a cross reference to any additional information provided about the insurance or coverage, as applicable? [226.6(b)(2)(xii)]										
24. Did the creditor disclose, as applicable, the available credit remaining after fees or security deposit is debited to the account? [226.6(b)(2)(xiii)]										
25. For issuers of credit cards that are not charge cards, did the creditor disclose a reference to the Web site established by the Board and a statement that consumers may obtain on the Web site information about shopping for and using credit cards? [226.6(b)(2)(xiv)]										
26. Did the creditor disclose a statement that information about the consumers' right to dispute transactions is included in the account-opening disclosures, and is this statement placed directly below the table? [226.6(b)(2)(xv)]										
27. To the extent applicable, did the creditor disclose, for charges imposed, the circumstances under which the charge may be imposed, including the amount of the charge or explanation of how the charge is determined; and did the creditor include a statement of when finance charges begin to accrue, including an explanation of whether or not any time period exists within which any credit extended may be repaid without incurring a finance charge? [226.6(b)(3)(i)]										

#8—Open-End Not Home-Secured Credit Forms Review Worksheet										
Product Type:										
	Yes	No	Yes	No	Yes	No	Yes	No	Yes	No

28. Did the creditor disclose, as applicable, for each periodic rate that may be used to calculate interest:
 	
  a. The rate (expressed as a periodic rate and a corresponding APR)?
 	
  b. The range of balances to which the rate is applicable?
 	
  c. The type of transaction to which the periodic rate applies?
 	
  d. An explanation of the method used to determine the balance to which the rate is applied? [226.6(b)(4)(i)]										

29. Did the creditor disclose, as applicable, for interest rate changes that are tied to increases in an index or formula specifically set forth in the account agreement:
 	
  a. The fact that the annual percentage rate may increase?
 	
  b. How the rate is determined, including the margin?
 	
  c. The circumstances under which the rate may increase?
 	
  d. The frequency with which the rate may increase?
 	
  e. Any limitation on the amount the rate may change?
 	
  f. The effect(s) of an increase? [226.6(b)(4)(ii)]										

#8—Open-End Not Home-Secured Credit Forms Review Worksheet										
Product Type:	Yes	No	Yes	No	Yes	No	Yes	No	Yes	No
30. Did the creditor disclose, as applicable, for interest rate changes that are specifically set forth in the account agreement and not tied to increases in an index or formula: a. The initial rate (expressed as a periodic rate and a corresponding APR)? b. How long the initial rate will remain in effect and the specific events that cause the initial rate to change? c. The rate (expressed as a periodic rate and a corresponding APR) that will apply when the initial rate is no longer in effect and any limitation on the time period the new rate will remain in effect? d. The balances to which the new rate will apply? e. The balances to which the current rate at the time of the change will apply? [226.6(b)(4)(iii))]										
31. Did the creditor provide the applicable disclosures if the creditor offers optional credit insurance, or debt cancellation or debt suspension coverage? [226.6(b)(5)(i)]										
32. Did the creditor disclose the fact it has or will acquire a security interest in the property purchased under the plan, or in other property identified by item or type? [226.6(b)(5)(ii)]										
33. Did the creditor disclose a statement that outlines the consumer's rights and the creditor's responsibilities, substantially similar to Model Form G-3(A) in appendix G? [226.6(b)(5)(iii)]										

#8—Open-End Not Home-Secured Credit Forms Review Worksheet										
Product Type:										
	Yes	No	Yes	No	Yes	No	Yes	No	Yes	No
Note: Disclosures required by 226.6(b)(3) through (b)(5) that are not otherwise required to be in the table and other information may be presented with the account agreement or account-opening disclosure statement, provided such information appears outside the required table. [226.6(b)(1)(i)]										
34. If applicable, did the creditor that provided the account-opening disclosures in person at the time the plan was established, in connection with financing the purchase of goods or services, and that imposed fees (see 226.6(b)(2)(vii) through (b)(2)(xi)) that vary by state in the account-opening table disclose either A) the specific fee applicable to the consumer's account, or B) the range of the fees and a statement that the amount of the fee varies by state and refers the consumer to the account agreement or other disclosure provided with the account-opening table, where the amount of the fee applicable to the consumer's account is disclosed? And did the creditor refrain from listing fees for multiple states in the account-opening summary table? [226.6(b)(1)(iii)]										
35. Are the 226.6(a) disclosures for an added feature or credit device with different finance charge terms provided before the consumer uses the feature or device? [226.9(b)(2)].										
36. Has the creditor retained evidence of compliance with regulation Z for two years after the date disclosures were required to be made or action was required to be taken? [226.25(a)]										

Worksheet #9—
Open-End Home-Secured Credit Forms Review

Use this worksheet when reviewing open-end home-secured forms (including HELOC, and reverse mortgages if applicable) for general, application, and account-opening disclosures, including electronic disclosures. To complete, review the forms and place a check in each applicable box. Determine the accuracy of the disclosures by comparing them to the contract and other bank documents. Forms that include or involve current transactions, such as change-in-terms notices, periodic billing statements, rescission notices, and billing error communications, are verified for accuracy when the file review worksheets are completed. This worksheet can be used for reviewing audit work papers, evaluating bank policies, performing expanded procedures, and training as appropriate. Only complete those sections of the worksheet that specifically relate to the issue being reviewed, evaluated or tested, and retain those completed sections in the work papers.

When reviewing audit or evaluating bank policies, a "No" answer indicates a possible exception/deficiency and should be explained in the work papers. When performing expanded procedures, a "No" answer indicates a violation and should be explained in the work papers. If a line item is not applicable within the area you are reviewing, indicate "NA."

Underline the applicable use: Audit   Bank Policies   Expanded Procedures

#9—Open-End Home-Secured Credit Forms Review Worksheet										
Product Type:	Yes	No	Yes	No	Yes	No	Yes	No	Yes	No
1. Did the creditor make the disclosures clearly and conspicuously and, unless subject to an exception listed at 226.5(a)(1)(ii)(A) or (B), in a form that the consumer may keep? [226.5(a)(1)] Note: Generally, the disclosures required by Subpart B may be provided to the consumer in electronic form, subject to compliance with the consumer consent and other applicable provisions of the E-Sign Act. However, the disclosures required by 226.5a, 226.5b, and 226.16 may be provided to the consumer in electronic form without regard to the consumer consent or other provisions of the E-Sign Act in the circumstances set forth in those sections. [226.5(a)(1)(iii)]										
2. Is the terminology used in providing the disclosures required by the open-end provisions of Regulation Z (226.5) consistent? [226.5(a)(2)(i)]										

#9—Open-End Home-Secured Credit Forms Review Worksheet										
Product Type:	Yes	No	Yes	No	Yes	No	Yes	No	Yes	No
3. For home-equity plans subject to 226.5b, are the terms finance charge and annual percentage rate, when required to be disclosed with a corresponding amount or percentage rate, more conspicuous than any other required disclosure? [226.5(a)(2)(ii)] Note: The terms need not be more conspicuous when used for periodic statement disclosures under 226.7(a)(4) and for advertisements under 226.16.										
4. If disclosures are required to be presented in a tabular format pursuant to 226.5(a)(3), is the term penalty APR used as applicable? [226.5(a)(2)(iii]										
5. Are disclosures segregated, clear, and conspicuous? [226.5b(a)(1)]										
6. Do the required disclosures of paragraph (d)(1) through (4)(ii) precede the other disclosures? [226.5b(a)(2)]										
7. Is a home equity brochure provided? [226.5b(e)]										
8. Does the disclosure state: a. That the consumer should retain a copy of the disclosures? [226.5b(d)(1)] b. The time by which to apply to obtain the specific terms disclosed? [226.5b(d)(2)(i)] c. That terms are subject to change before the plan opens, if applicable? [226.5b(d)(2)(i)] d. That the consumer may receive a refund of all application fees if terms change prior to opening? [226.5b(d)(2)(ii)] e. That the consumer's dwelling secures the HELOC and that the loss of the dwelling may occur? [226.5b(d)(3)]										

#9—Open-End Home-Secured Credit Forms Review Worksheet										
Product Type:	Yes	No	Yes	No	Yes	No	Yes	No	Yes	No
f. The creditor's right to change, freeze, or terminate the account? [226.5b(d)(4)(i)]										
g. That information about conditions for adverse action is available on request? [226.5b(d)(4)(ii)]										
h. Payment terms? [226.5b(d)(5)]										
i. A recent APR and that the APR does not include costs other than interest for fixed rate plans? [226.5b(d)(6)]										
j. An itemization of fees to open, use, or maintain the plan and when such fees are payable? [226.5b(d)(7)]										
k. An estimate of total fees imposed by third parties to open the account? [226.5b(d)(8)]										
l. That the consumer may receive a good faith itemization of third-party fees? [226.5b(d)(8)]										
m. That negative amortization may occur and could increase the principal balance and reduce the consumer's equity? [226.5b(d)(9)]										
n. Transaction requirements under the plan? [226.5b(d)(10)]										
o. That a tax advisor should be consulted? [226.5b(d)(11)]										
Variable Rate HELOC Disclosure Requirements—[226.5b(d)(12)(i)–(xii)]										
9. Does the disclosure state, as applicable:										
a. That the APR, payment, or term may change? [226.5b(d)(12)(i)]										

#9—Open-End Home-Secured Credit Forms Review Worksheet										
Product Type:	Yes	No	Yes	No	Yes	No	Yes	No	Yes	No
b. That the APR excludes costs other than interest? [226.5b(d)(12)(ii)]										
c. The index and its source? [226.5b(d)(12)(iii)]										
d. How the APR will be determined? [226.5b(d)(12)(iv)]										
e. That the consumer should request information on the current index value, margin, discount or premium, and APR? [226.5b(d)(12)(v)]										
f. That the initial APR is discounted and the duration of the discount, if applicable? [226.5b(d)(12)(vi)]										
g. The frequency of APR changes? [226.5b(d)(12)(vii)]										
h. The rules relating to changes in the index, APR, and payment amount? [226.5b(d)(12)(viii)]										
i. The lifetime rate cap and any annual (or more frequent) caps, or a statement that there is no annual limitation and a statement of the maximum APR that may be imposed under each payment option? [226.5b(d)(12)(ix)]										
j. The minimum payment requirement, using the maximum APR, and the earliest date the maximum APR may be imposed? [226.5b(d)(12)(x)]										
k. A historical example, based on a $10,000 balance, reflecting all significant plan terms? [226.5b(d)(12)(xi)]										

#9—Open-End Home-Secured Credit Forms Review Worksheet										
Product Type:	Yes	No	Yes	No	Yes	No	Yes	No	Yes	No
l. That rate information will be provided on or with each periodic statement? [226.5b(d)(12)(xii)]										
Limitations on Home Equity Plans										
10. Is the APR based on an independent index for variable rate accounts? [226.5b(f)(1)(i)]										
11. Is the index available to the public? [226.5b(f)(1)(ii)]										
12. Are accounts terminated and repayment of the entire balance due only under the following conditions: a. There is fraud or material misrepresentation by the consumer in connection with the plan at any time, including during the application process, the draw period, or any repayment period? b. The consumer fails to meet the plan's repayment terms? c. The consumer takes action or fails to act in a manner that adversely affects the bank's security for the plan or any right in the security? [226.5b(f)(2)(iii)] Note: Regulation O requires, and Regulation Z permits, a demand feature in executive officer plans.										
13. Are the terms of an account only changed under the following circumstances: a. A specified change occurs when a specific event takes place, as provided for in the initial agreement? b. The index or margin is changed because the original index is no longer available?										

#9—Open-End Home-Secured Credit Forms Review Worksheet										
Product Type:										
	Yes	No	Yes	No	Yes	No	Yes	No	Yes	No
c. The consumer specifically agrees to a specified change in writing at the time of the change?										
d. Any change unequivocally will benefit the consumer?										
e. Changes made to the terms are insignificant? [226.5b(f)(3)(i)–(v)]										
14. Is the credit limit reduced, or are additional extensions of credit prohibited, only under the following circumstances:										
a. The value of the dwelling securing the plan declines significantly?										
b. The consumer's financial circumstances change materially?										
c. The consumer defaults on any material obligation under the agreement?										
d. Government action restricts an APR increase?										
e. The bank's security interest is adversely affected because of government action to the extent that the security value is less than 120 percent of the credit line?										
f. The bank is notified by a regulatory agency that continued advances constitute an unsafe and unsound practice? [226.5b(f)(3)(vi)]										

#9—Open-End Home-Secured Credit Forms Review Worksheet										
Product Type:	Yes	No	Yes	No	Yes	No	Yes	No	Yes	No
Account-Opening Disclosures										
15. Does the creditor disclose, as applicable, the circumstances under which a finance charge will be imposed and an explanation of how it will be determined, including a statement of when finance charges begin to accrue; an explanation of whether or not any grace period exists? [226.6(a)(1)(i)]										
16. Does the creditor disclose each periodic rate that may be used to compute the finance charge, the range of balances to which it is applicable, and the corresponding APR? [226.6(a)(1)(ii)] If a variable rate applies, does the creditor also disclose the circumstances under which the rate may increase; any limitations on the increase, and the effects of an increase? [226.6(a)(1)(ii)] When different periodic rates apply to different types of transactions, does the creditor disclose the types of transactions to which the periodic rates apply? [226.6(a)(1)(ii)]										
17. Does the creditor disclose an explanation of the method used to determine the balance on which the finance charge may be computed? [226.6(a)(1)(iii)]										
18. Does the creditor disclose an explanation of how the amount of any finance charge will be determined, including a description of how any finance charge other than the periodic rate will be determined? [226.6(a)(1)(iv)]										
19. Is there a statement of the amount of other charges or an explanation of how the charge will be determined? [226.6(a)(2)]										
20. Are conditions for terminating the HELOC plan, for prohibiting additional credit, for reducing the credit limit, and										

#9—Open-End Home-Secured Credit Forms Review Worksheet										
Product Type:	Yes	No	Yes	No	Yes	No	Yes	No	Yes	No
for implementing changes provided? [226.6(a)(3)(i)]										
21. Are the payment terms for the HELOC plan provided per 226.5b(d) (if terms for draw and repayment period are different, the terms for each must be disclosed, as applicable), including: a. The length of the draw period and any repayment period? b. An explanation of how the minimum periodic payment will be computed? c. The timing of periodic payments? d. If the periodic payment repays less than the balance or does not reduce principal (e.g., interest only payments), a statement of that fact and that a balloon payment may or will result, as applicable? [226.6(a)(3)(ii)]										
22. For the HELOC, is there a statement, if applicable, that negative amortization might occur, and that it increases the principal balance and reduces the consumer's equity in the dwelling? [226.6(a)(3)(iii)]										
23. Is there a statement of transaction requirements for the HELOC? [226.6(a)(3)(iv)]										
24. Is there a statement about tax implication and consulting a tax advisor for the HELOC? [226.6(a)(3)(v)]										
25. Is there a statement that the APR does not include costs other than interest for the HELOC? [226.6(a)(3)(vi)]										
26. Unless the disclosures provided with the application were in a form the consumer could keep and included a representative payment example for the category of payment option chosen by the consumer, are the following										

#9—Open-End Home-Secured Credit Forms Review Worksheet										
Product Type:	Yes	No	Yes	No	Yes	No	Yes	No	Yes	No
disclosures provided for variable rate HELOCs? [226.6(a)(3)(vii)]: a. The rules relating to changes to the index, APR, changes in the payment amount, including information on payment limitations and carryover? b. The minimum payment required (for both the draw and repayment periods) when the maximum APR is in effect for a $10,000 balance and the earliest date the maximum APR may be imposed? c. An example based on a $10,000 balance, reflecting all significant plan terms and showing how the APR and the minimum periodic payment amount would have been affected during the most recent 15 years by changes in the index? d. A statement that rate information will be provided on or with each periodic statement? e. An example based on a $10,000 balance and a recent APR showing the minimum periodic payment, any balloon payment, and the time it would take to repay the $10,000 balance making only the minimum payment while obtaining no additional credit? [226.6(a)(3)(vii)]										
27. Has the fact that the creditor has or will acquire a security interest in the property purchased or other property identified by item or type been disclosed? [226.6(a)(4)]										
28. Is there a statement detailing consumer-billing rights and creditor's responsibilities under 226.12(c) and 226.13 included and is it substantially similar to the statement in Model Form G-3, or at the creditor's option, G-3A in appendix G? [226.6(a)(5)]										

#9—Open-End Home-Secured Credit Forms Review Worksheet										
Product Type:	Yes	No	Yes	No	Yes	No	Yes	No	Yes	No
29. Is the maximum interest rate disclosed (variable rate)? [226.30(b)]										
Subsequent Disclosure Requirements [226.9]										
30. Does the bank furnish the annual statement of billing rights? [226.9(a)(1)] Or is an alternative summary statement provided with each periodic statement? [226.9(a)(2)]										
31. Has the creditor retained evidence of compliance with regulation Z for two years after the date disclosures were required to be made or action was required to be taken? [226.25(a)]										

Worksheet #10—
Credit and Charge Card Forms Review

Use this worksheet when reviewing credit and charge card forms for general applications as well as creditor initiated direct mail applications, preapproved solicitations and electronic applications. To complete, review the forms and place a check in each applicable box. Determine the accuracy of the disclosures by comparing them to the contract and other bank documents. Forms that include or involve current transactions, such as change-in-terms notices, periodic billing statements, rescission notices, and billing error communications, are verified for accuracy when the file review worksheets are completed. This worksheet can be used for reviewing audit work papers, evaluating bank policies, performing expanded procedures, and training as appropriate. Only complete those sections of the worksheet that specifically relate to the issue being reviewed, evaluated or tested, and retain those completed sections in the work papers.

When reviewing audit or evaluating bank policies, a "No" answer indicates a possible exception/deficiency and should be explained in the work papers. When performing expanded procedures, a "No" answer indicates a violation and should be explained in the work papers. If a line item is not applicable within the area you are reviewing, indicate "NA."

Underline the applicable use: Audit   Bank Policies   Expanded Procedures

#10—Credit and Charge Card Forms Review Worksheet										
Product Identification: Product Type:	Yes	No	Yes	No	Yes	No	Yes	No	Yes	No
Application and Solicitation Disclosures										
1. Were the solicitation or application disclosures made clearly and conspicuously on or with a solicitation or an application? [226.5a(a)(1)]										
2. For the disclosures in 226.5a(b)(1) through (5) (except for (b)(1)(iv)(B)) and (b)(7) through (15), did the creditor make the disclosures required for 226.5a(c), (d)(2), (e)(1) and (f) in the form of a table with headings, content, and format substantially similar to the applicable tables found in G-10 in appendix G? [226.5a(a)(2)(i)] Note: For an application or a solicitation that is accessed by the consumer in electronic form, the disclosures required under this section may be provided to the consumer in electronic form on or with the application or solicitation. [226.5a(a)(2)(v)]										
3. Does the table required by 226.5a(a)(2)(i) contain only the information required or permitted by that section? If the creditor provides other information, does such information appear outside the table? [226.5a(a)(2)(ii)]										

#10—Credit and Charge Card Forms Review Worksheet										
Product Identification: Product Type:	Yes	No	Yes	No	Yes	No	Yes	No	Yes	No
4. Are the disclosures required by 226.5a(b)(1)(iv)(B) and (b)(6) placed directly beneath the table required by 226.5a(a)(2)(i)? [225.5a(a)(2)(iii)]										
5. When a tabular format is required, are the following disclosures in bold text? a. APR required to be disclosed pursuant to paragraph (b)(1) of this section? b. Introductory rate required to be disclosed pursuant to paragraph (b)(1)(ii) of this section? c. Rate that will apply after a premium initial rate expires required to be disclosed under paragraph (b)(1)(iii) of this section? d. Fee or percentage amounts or maximum limits on fee amounts required to be disclosed pursuant to paragraphs (b)(2), (b)(4), (b)(8) through (b)(13)? [226.5a(a)(2)(iv)] Note: Bold text shall not be used for the amount of any periodic fee disclosed pursuant to 226.5a(b)(2) that is not an annualized amount; and other APRs or fee amounts disclosed in the table. [226.5a(a)(2)(iv)]										
6. Does the card issuer disclose each periodic rate that may be used to compute the finance charge on an outstanding balance for purchases, a cash advance, or a balance transfer, expressed as an APR; when more than one rate applies for a category of transactions, is the range of balances to which each rate is applicable also disclosed; and except for oral disclosures of the APR for purchases or a penalty rate that may apply upon the occurrence of one or more specific events, is the APR for purchases disclosed pursuant to 226.5a(b)(1) in at least 16-point type? [226.5a(b)(1)]										
7. If a rate is a variable rate, does the card issuer disclose the fact that the rate may vary and how the rate is determined; does the card issuer identify the type of index or formula that is used in setting										

#10—Credit and Charge Card Forms Review Worksheet										
Product Identification: Product Type:	Yes	No	Yes	No	Yes	No	Yes	No	Yes	No
the rate; are the value of the index and the amount of the margin that are used to calculate the variable rate not disclosed in the table; and are any applicable limitations on rate increases or decreases not included in the table? [226.5a(b)(1)(i)]										
8. If the initial rate is an introductory rate, does the card issuer disclose in the table the introductory rate, the time period during which the introductory rate will remain in effect, and the term "introductory" or "intro" in immediate proximity to the introductory rate; and does the card issuer disclose, as applicable, either the variable or fixed rate that would otherwise apply to the account? [226.5a(b)(1)(ii)]										
9. If the initial rate is temporary and is higher than the rate that will apply after the temporary rate expires, does the card issuer disclose the premium initial rate and the time period during which the premium initial rate will remain in effect; is the premium initial rate for purchases in at least 16-point type; and does the issuer disclose in the table the rate that will apply after the premium initial rate expires, in at least 16-point type? [226.5a(b)(1)(iii)]										
10. If a rate may increase as a penalty for one or more events specified in the account agreement, such as a late payment or an extension of credit that exceeds the credit limit, does the card issuer disclose the increased rate that may apply, a brief description of the event or events that may result in the increased rate, and a brief description of how long the increased rate will remain in effect? [226.5a(b)(1)(iv)(A)]										
11. If the issuer discloses an introductory rate in the table or in any written or electronic promotional materials accompanying applications or solicitations (and subject to paragraph (c) or (e) of §226.5a), does the issuer briefly disclose, directly beneath the table, the circumstances, if any, under which the introductory rate may be revoked, and the type of rate that will apply after the introductory rate is revoked? [226.5a(b)(1)(iv)(B)]										
12. If a rate cannot be determined at the time disclosures are given because the rate depends, at										

#10—Credit and Charge Card Forms Review Worksheet										
Product Identification: Product Type:	Yes	No	Yes	No	Yes	No	Yes	No	Yes	No
least in part, on a later determination of the consumer's creditworthiness, does the card issuer disclose the specific rates or the range of rates that could apply and a statement that the rate for which the consumer may qualify at account opening will depend on the consumer's creditworthiness, and other factors if applicable? [226.5a(b)(1)(v)] Note: If the rate that depends, at least in part, on a later determination of the consumer's creditworthiness is a penalty rate, as described in (b)(1)(iv), the card issuer at its option may disclose the highest rate that could apply, instead of disclosing the specific rates or the range of rates that could apply. [226.5a(b)(1)(v)]										
13. Does the card issuer refrain from listing APR rates for multiple states in the table? Note: Issuers imposing APRs that vary by state may, at the issuers option, disclose in the table the specific APR applicable to the consumer's account; or the range of the APRs, if the disclosure includes a statement that the APR varies by state and refers the consumer to a disclosure provided with the table where the APR applicable to the consumer's account is disclosed. [226.5a(b)(1)(vi)]										
14. Does the card issuer disclose any annual or other periodic fee, expressed as an annualized amount, or any other fee that may be imposed for the issuance or availability of a credit or charge card, including any fee based on account activity or inactivity? [226.5a(b)(2)]										
15. Does the card issuer disclose any fixed finance charge that could be imposed during a billing cycle, as well as a brief description of that charge; any minimum interest charge if it exceeds $1.00 that could be imposed during a billing cycle; and a brief description of the charge? [226.5a(b)(3)]										
16. Does the creditor disclose any transaction charge imposed for the use of the card for purchases? [226.5a(b)(4)]										

#10—Credit and Charge Card Forms Review Worksheet										
Product Identification: Product Type:	Yes	No	Yes	No	Yes	No	Yes	No	Yes	No
17. Does the issuer disclose the grace period and any conditions on the availability of the grace period; if no grace period is provided, is this fact disclosed; if the grace period varies, does the issuer disclose the range of days, the minimum number of days, or the average number of days in the grace period; in disclosing in the tabular format a grace period that applies to all types of purchases, is the phrase "How to Avoid Paying Interest on Purchases" used as the heading for the row describing the grace period; and if a grace period is not offered on all types of purchases, in disclosing this fact in the tabular format, is the phrase "Paying Interest" used as the heading for the row describing this fact? [226.5a(b)(5)]										
18. Does the creditor disclose the name of the balance computation method that is used to determine the balance on which the finance charge is computed, or an explanation of the method used if it is not listed? [226.5a(b)(6)] Note: Disclosures required by 226.5a(b)(6) must be placed directly beneath the table.										
19. Does the creditor disclose a statement that charges incurred by use of the charge card are due when the periodic statement is received? [226.5a(b)(7)]										
20. Does the creditor disclose any fee imposed for an extension of credit in the form of cash or its equivalent? [226.5a(b)(8)]										
21. Does the creditor disclose any fee imposed for a late payment? [226.5a(b)(9)]										
22. Does the creditor disclose any fee imposed for exceeding the credit limit? [226.5a(b)(10)]										
23. Does the creditor disclose any fee imposed to transfer a balance? [226.5a(b)(11)]										
24. Does the creditor disclose any fee imposed for a returned payment? [226.5a(b)(12)]										
25. Does the creditor disclose any fee for insurance, debt cancellation or suspension coverage if these are required as part of the plan? [226.5a(b)(13)]										

#10—Credit and Charge Card Forms Review Worksheet										
Product Identification: Product Type:	Yes	No	Yes	No	Yes	No	Yes	No	Yes	No
26. If the total of required fees for the issuance or availability of credit and/or security deposit debited to the account at account opening equals or exceeds 15 percent of the minimum credit limit for the account, does the creditor disclose, as applicable, the available credit remaining after the fees and/or security deposit are debited to the account? [226.5a(b)(14)]										
27. For issuers of credit cards that are not charge cards, does the creditor disclose a reference to the Web site established by the Board and a statement that the consumers may obtain on the Web site information about shopping for and using credit cards? [226.5a(b)(15)]										
28. Has the creditor retained evidence of compliance with regulation Z for two years after the date disclosures were required to be made or action was required to be taken? [226.25(a)]										

Worksheet #11—
Open-End Credit File Review

Use this worksheet when reviewing all open-end credit. To complete, review loan files and place a check in each applicable box. Determine the accuracy of the disclosures by comparing them to the contract and other bank documents. This worksheet can be used for reviewing audit work papers, evaluating bank policies, performing expanded procedures, and training as appropriate. Only complete those sections of the worksheet that specifically relate to the issue being reviewed, evaluated or tested, and retain those completed sections in the work papers.

When reviewing audit or evaluating bank policies, a "No" answer indicates a possible exception/deficiency and should be explained in the work papers. When performing expanded procedures, a "No" answer indicates a violation and should be explained in the work papers. If a line item is not applicable within the area you are reviewing, indicate "NA."

Underline the applicable use: Audit   Bank Policies   Expanded Procedures

#11—Open-End Credit File Review Worksheet—General and Subsequent Disclosures, Payments, Balances, Terminations, Renewals, Unauthorized Charges, and Billing Errors										
Product Type: **Name of Borrower:** **Account #:**	Yes	No	Yes	No	Yes	No	Yes	No	Yes	No
1. Is the timing of disclosures provided in accordance with all sections of 226.5(b)(1)?										
2. If the creditor collected an application fee excludable from the finance charge before providing account-opening disclosures and the consumer rejected the plan after receiving account-opening disclosures, was the consumer under no obligation to pay such an application fee, or if the fee was paid, was it refunded? [226.5(b)(1)(v)]										
3. Are periodic statements provided for each billing cycle in which the account has a debit or credit balance of more than $1 or a finance charge was imposed? [226.5(b)(2)(i)]										
4. Does the disclosure reflect the terms of the legal obligation between the parties, and if any necessary information for accurate disclosure is unknown, is the disclosure based on the best information reasonably										

#11—Open-End Credit File Review Worksheet—General and Subsequent Disclosures, Payments, Balances, Terminations, Renewals, Unauthorized Charges, and Billing Errors										
Product Type: **Name of Borrower:** **Account #:**	Yes	No	Yes	No	Yes	No	Yes	No	Yes	No
available and states clearly that the disclosure is an estimate? [226.5(c)]										
5. Does the bank indicate, for an added credit feature or credit device, that the feature or device is for use in obtaining credit under the terms previously disclosed? [226.9(b)(1)]										
6. Except for checks that access a credit card account, are the 226.6(a)(1) or 226.6(b)(3)(ii)(A) disclosures for an added feature or credit device with different finance charge terms provided before the consumer uses the feature or device? [226.9(b)(2)]										
7. If checks that can be used to access a credit card account are provided more than 30 days after account-opening disclosures under 226.6(b) are mailed or delivered, or are provided within 30 days of the account-opening disclosures and the finance charge terms for the checks differ from the finance charge terms previously disclosed, did the creditor disclose on the front of the page containing the checks the following terms in the form of a table with the headings, content, and form substantially similar to Sample G–19 in appendix G to this part: a. If a promotional rate applies to the checks, the promotional rate and the time period during which the promotional rate will remain in effect; the type of rate that will apply after the promotional rate expires; the APR that will apply after the promotional rate expires; if a variable-rate account, an APR based on the applicable index or formula in accordance with the										

#11—Open-End Credit File Review Worksheet—General and Subsequent Disclosures, Payments, Balances, Terminations, Renewals, Unauthorized Charges, and Billing Errors										
Product Type: Name of Borrower: Account #:	Yes	No	Yes	No	Yes	No	Yes	No	Yes	No
accuracy requirements set forth in paragraph (b)(3)(ii) of this section; the date, if any, by which the consumer must use the checks in order to qualify for the promotional rate; if the creditor will honor checks used after such date but will apply an APR other than the promotional rate, does the creditor disclose this fact and the type of APR that will apply if the consumer uses the checks after such date? [226.9(b)(3)(i)(A)]										
b. If no promotional rate applies to checks that can be used to access accredit card account, the type of rate that will apply to the checks and the applicable APR; and, if a variable-rate account, an APR based on the applicable index or formula in accordance with the accuracy requirements set forth in 226.9(b)(3)(ii)? [226.9(b)(3)(i)(B)]										
c. Transaction fees applicable to checks disclosed under 226.6(b)(2)(iv)? [226.9(b)(3)(i)(C)]										
d. When disclosing whether there is a grace period, did the creditor use the phrase "How to Avoid Paying Interest on Check Transactions" as the row heading when a grace period applies to credit extended by the use of checks? When disclosing the fact that no grace period exists, did the creditor use the phrase "Paying Interest" as the row heading? [226.9(b)(3)(i)(D)]										

#11—Open-End Credit File Review Worksheet—General and Subsequent Disclosures, Payments, Balances, Terminations, Renewals, Unauthorized Charges, and Billing Errors										
Product Type: Name of Borrower: Account #:	Yes	No	Yes	No	Yes	No	Yes	No	Yes	No
8. Are written advance notices of any significant changes in account terms or increase in the required minimum payment provided at least 45 days prior to the effective date of the change, unless an exception applies? [226.9(c)(2)(i)]										
9. If the creditor increases any component of a charge on a credit card account or introduces a new charge required to be disclosed under 226.6(b)(3) that is not a significant charge, did the creditor either comply with the 45 day notice requirement or provide notice of the amount of the charge before the consumer agrees to or becomes obligated to pay the charge, at a time or in a manner that a consumer would be likely to notice the disclosure of the charge, either in writing or orally? [226.9(c)(2)(iii)]										
10. Does the written change-in-terms notice include, in the proper format, the following: a. A summary of the changes, any increase in the required minimum payment, and the security interest being acquired? [226.9(c)(2)(iv)(A)(1)] b. A statement that changes are being made to the account? [226.9(c)(2)(iv)(A)(2) c. For accounts other than credit card accounts under an open-end (not home-secured) consumer credit plan subject to §226.9(c)(2)(iv)(B), a statement indicating that the										

#11—Open-End Credit File Review Worksheet—General and Subsequent Disclosures, Payments, Balances, Terminations, Renewals, Unauthorized Charges, and Billing Errors										
Product Type: Name of Borrower: Account #:	Yes	No	Yes	No	Yes	No	Yes	No	Yes	No
consumer has the right to opt-out of the changes, if applicable, and a reference to the opt-out right provided in the notice? [226.9(c)(2)(iv)(A)(3)]										
d. The date the changes will become effective? [226.9(c)(2)(iv)(A)(4)]										
e. If applicable, a statement that the consumer may find additional information about the summarized changes, and other changes, in the notice? [226.9(c)(2)(iv)(A)(5)]										
f. In the case of a rate change, other than a penalty rate, a statement that if a penalty rate currently applies to the consumer's account, the new rate described in the notice will not apply to the consumer's account until the consumer's account balances are no longer subject to the penalty rate? [226.9(c)(2)(iv)(A)6)]										
g. If the change in terms being disclosed is an increase in the APR, the balances to which the increased rate will apply; and if applicable, a statement identifying the balances to which the current rate will apply as of the effective date of the change? [226.9(c)(2)(iv)(A)7)]										
h. If the change in terms being disclosed is an increase in an APR for a credit card account under an										

#11—Open-End Credit File Review Worksheet—General and Subsequent Disclosures, Payments, Balances, Terminations, Renewals, Unauthorized Charges, and Billing Errors										
Product Type: Name of Borrower: Account #:	Yes	No	Yes	No	Yes	No	Yes	No	Yes	No
open-end (not home-secured) consumer credit plan, a statement of no more than four principal reasons for the rate increase, listed in their order of importance? [226.9(c)(2)(iv)(A)(8)] Note: The disclosed reasons must accurately describe the principal factors actually considered by the card issuer in increasing the rate. [Commentary 226.9(c)(2)(iv) - 11]										
11. Except in the case of an increase in the required minimum periodic payment, a change in the APR, a change in the balance computation method necessary to comply with section 226.54, an increase in a fee resulting from reevaluation of a determination made under 226.52(b)(1)(i) or a regulatory adjustment to the safe harbor provision at 226.52(b)(1)(ii), or when the change results from the creditor not receiving the required minimum periodic payment within 60 days after the due date for that payment, did the creditor provide: a. A statement that the consumer has the right to reject the change or changes prior to the effective date of the changes, unless the consumer fails to make a required minimum periodic payment within 60 days after the due date for payment? b. Instructions for rejecting the change or changes, and a toll-free telephone number that the										

#11—Open-End Credit File Review Worksheet—General and Subsequent Disclosures, Payments, Balances, Terminations, Renewals, Unauthorized Charges, and Billing Errors										
Product Type: Name of Borrower: Account #:	Yes	No	Yes	No	Yes	No	Yes	No	Yes	No
consumer may use to notify the creditor of the rejection? c. If applicable, a statement that if the consumer rejects the change or changes, the consumer's ability to use the account for further advances will be terminated or suspended? [226.9(c)(2)(iv)(B)]										
12. If the significant change required to be disclosed is an increase in an APR or fee or charge required to be disclosed under 226.6(b)(2)(ii), (b)(2)(iii), or (b)(2)(xii) based upon the consumer's failure to make a minimum periodic payment within 60 days from the due date for that payment, does the 45-day notice include the following information: a. A statement of the reason for the increase? b. That the increase will cease to apply to transactions that occurred prior to or within 14 days of provision of the notice, if the creditor receives six consecutive required minimum periodic payments on or before the payment due date beginning with the first payment due following the effective date of the increase? [226.9(c)(2)(iv)(C)]										
13. Is the summary of changes described in 226.9(c)(2)(iv)(A)(1) in a tabular format (except for a summary of any increase in the required minimum periodic payment), with headings and format substantially similar to any of the account-opening tables found in										

#11—Open-End Credit File Review Worksheet—General and Subsequent Disclosures, Payments, Balances, Terminations, Renewals, Unauthorized Charges, and Billing Errors										
Product Type: Name of Borrower: Account #:	Yes	No	Yes	No	Yes	No	Yes	No	Yes	No
G–17 in Appendix G; does the table disclose the changed term and information relevant to the change, if that relevant information is required by 226.6(b)(1) and (b)(2); and are the new terms described in the same level of detail as required when disclosing the terms under 226.6(b)(2) (Account opening)? [226.9(c)(2)(iv)(D)(1)]										
14. If a notice required by 226.9 (c)(2)(i) (change in terms) is included on or with a periodic statement, is the information described in 226.9(c)(2)(iv)(A)(1) disclosed on the front of any page of the statement, and does it immediately follow the information described in paragraph (c)(2)(iv)(A)(2) through (c)(2)(iv)(A)(8) and, if applicable, paragraphs (c)(2)(iv)(B) and (c)(2)(iv)(C), and is it substantially similar to the format shown in Sample G–20 or G–21 in Appendix G? [226.9(c)(2)(iv)(D)(2)]										
15. If a notice required by 226.9(c)(2)(i) (change in terms) is not included on or with a periodic statement, is the information described in 226.9(c)(2)(iv)(A)(1), at the creditor's option, disclosed on the front of the first page of the notice or segregated on a separate page from other information given with the notice? The summary of changes may be on more than one page, and may use both the front and reverse sides, but if so, does the table begin on the front of the first page of the notice and is there a reference on the first page indicating that the table continues on the following page? [226.9(c)(2)(iv)(D)(3)]										

#11—Open-End Credit File Review Worksheet—General and Subsequent Disclosures, Payments, Balances, Terminations, Renewals, Unauthorized Charges, and Billing Errors										
Product Type: Name of Borrower: Account #:	Yes	No	Yes	No	Yes	No	Yes	No	Yes	No
16. For change-in-terms notices, unless an exception listed at 226.9(c)(2)(v) applies, is the summary of changes at 226.9(c)(iv)(A)(1) immediately following the information described in 226.9(c)(2)(iv)(A)(2) through (c)(2)(iv)(A)(7) and, if applicable, paragraphs (c)(2)(iv)(A)(8), (c)(2)(iv)(B) and (c)(2)(iv)(C), substantially similar to the format shown in Sample G–20 or G–21 in appendix G? [226.9(c)(2)(iv)(D)(3)]										
17. Was a notice of a decrease in the credit limit provided in writing or orally at least 45 days before an over-the-limit fee or penalty rate is imposed as a result of a consumer exceeding the newly decreased credit limit; and does the notice state that the credit limit on the account has been or will be decreased? [226.9(c)(2)(vi)]										
18. Are any applicable renewal disclosures provided at least 30 days or one billing cycle, whichever is less, before the mailing or delivery of the periodic statement on which the renewal fee is initially charged to the account; and if the card issuer has changed or amended any term of the account required to be disclosed under 226.6(b)(1) and (b)(2) that has not previously been disclosed to the consumer has the notice been provided at least 30 days prior to the scheduled renewal date of the consumer's credit or charge card? [226.9(e)(1)]										
19. Does the renewal disclosure contain the disclosures required by 226.5a(b)(1) through (b)(7)? [226.9(e)(1)(i)]										

#11—Open-End Credit File Review Worksheet—General and Subsequent Disclosures, Payments, Balances, Terminations, Renewals, Unauthorized Charges, and Billing Errors										
Product Type: Name of Borrower: Account #:	Yes	No	Yes	No	Yes	No	Yes	No	Yes	No
20. Does the renewal disclosure include how and when the cardholder may terminate the credit to avoid paying the renewal fee? [226.9(e)(1)(ii)]										
21. If the renewal disclosure is provided on the back of a periodic statement, has the card issuer included a reference to those disclosures on the front of the statement? [226.9(e)(2)]										
22. Are credit insurance disclosures provided when the insurance provider is changed within 30 days before the change in provider occurs; and does the insurance notice include: any resulting increase in the rate, any substantial decrease in coverage, and a statement that the cardholder may discontinue the insurance? [226.9(f)(1)]										
23. If the provider of insurance changes, did the issuer provide the cardholder with a written notice no later than 30 days after the change that includes the following: name and address of the new insurance provider; copy of the new policy or group certificate containing the basic terms of the insurance, including the rate to be charged; and a statement that the cardholder may discontinue the insurance? [226.9(f)(2)] Note: The notices required by 226.9(f)(1) and (f)(2) may be combined provided they meet timing requirement of 226.9(f)(1).										
24. For plans other than home-equity plans subject to the requirements of 226.5b, unless the exception at 226.9(g)(4) applies, did the creditor provide a written notice to each consumer who may be affected when:										

#11—Open-End Credit File Review Worksheet—General and Subsequent Disclosures, Payments, Balances, Terminations, Renewals, Unauthorized Charges, and Billing Errors										
Product Type: Name of Borrower: Account #:	Yes	No	Yes	No	Yes	No	Yes	No	Yes	No
a. A rate is increased because of the consumer's delinquency or default; [226.9(g)(1)(i)] or b. A rate is increased as a penalty for one or more events specified in the account agreement, such as making a late payment or obtaining an extension of credit that exceeds the credit limit? [226.9(g)(1)(ii)] c. Was the written notice provided at least 45 days prior to the effective date of an increase in the rate because of delinquency, default, or as a penalty for a specified event, like late payment or an extension of credit in excess of the credit limit, and was the notice provided after the occurrence of the triggering event? [226.9(g)(2)]										
25. If a notice required by 226.9(g)(1) (increase in rates due to delinquency or default or as a penalty) is included on or with a periodic statement, was the disclosure provided in the form of a table and provided on the front of any page of the periodic statement? [226.9(g)(3)(ii)]										
26. If the notice described in 226.9(c)(2)(iv) (significant changes in account terms) is provided on the same statement, is the increase in rates disclosure above that notice? [226.9(g)(3)(ii)(A)]										
27. If a notice required by 226.9(g)(1) is not included on or with a periodic statement, is the information described in paragraph 226.9(g)(3)(i) disclosed										

#11—Open-End Credit File Review Worksheet—General and Subsequent Disclosures, Payments, Balances, Terminations, Renewals, Unauthorized Charges, and Billing Errors										
Product Type: **Name of Borrower:** **Account #:**	Yes	No	Yes	No	Yes	No	Yes	No	Yes	No
on the front of the first page of the notice; and is only information related to the increase in the rate to a penalty rate included with the notice? [226.9(g)(3)(ii)(B)] Note: This notice may be combined with a notice described in paragraph 226.9(c)(2)(iv) or 226.9(g)(4).										
28. Does the written notice include the following: a. A statement that the delinquency or default rate or penalty rate, as applicable, has been triggered? b. Date upon which the delinquency or default rate will apply? c. Circumstances under which the delinquency or default rate, as applicable, will cease to apply, or if it will remain in effect indefinitely? d. Statement indicating to which balances the delinquency or default rate or penalty rate will be applied? e. If applicable, a description of any balances to which the current rate will continue to apply as of the effective date of the rate increase, unless a consumer fails to make a minimum periodic payment within 60 days from the due date for that payment? f. For a credit card account under an open-end (not home-secured) consumer credit plan, a statement of no more than four principal reasons for the rate increase, listed										

#11—Open-End Credit File Review Worksheet—General and Subsequent Disclosures, Payments, Balances, Terminations, Renewals, Unauthorized Charges, and Billing Errors										
Product Type: Name of Borrower: Account #:	Yes	No	Yes	No	Yes	No	Yes	No	Yes	No
in their order of importance? [226.9(g)(3)(i)(A)] Note: The disclosed reasons must accurately describe the principal factors actually considered by the card issuer in increasing the rate. [Commentary 226.9(g) - 7]										
29. If the rate increase required to be disclosed is an increase pursuant to 226.55(b)(4) based on the consumer's failure to make a minimum periodic payment within 60 days from the due date for that payment, does the notice also contain a statement that the increase will cease to apply to transactions that occurred prior to or within 14 days of provision of the delinquency or penalty notice, if the creditor receives six consecutive required minimum periodic payments on or before the payment due date, beginning with the first payment due following the effective date of the increase? [226.9(g)(3)(i)(B)]										
30. If applicable, is a written notice provided 45 days in advance of imposing a penalty rate as a result of a consumer obtaining an extension of credit that exceeds the credit limit that includes: a. A statement that the credit limit on the account has been or will be decreased? b. A statement indicating the date on which the penalty rate will apply, if the outstanding balance exceeds the credit limit as of that date?										

#11—Open-End Credit File Review Worksheet—General and Subsequent Disclosures, Payments, Balances, Terminations, Renewals, Unauthorized Charges, and Billing Errors										
Product Type: Name of Borrower: Account #:	Yes	No	Yes	No	Yes	No	Yes	No	Yes	No
c. A statement that the penalty rate will not be imposed on the date, if the outstanding balance does not exceed the credit limit as of that date?										
d. The circumstances under which the penalty rate, if applied, will cease to apply to the account, or that the penalty rate, if applied, will remain in effect for a potentially indefinite time period?										
e. A statement indicating to which balances the penalty rate may be applied?										
f. If applicable, a description of any balances to which the current rate will continue to apply as of the effective date of the rate increase, unless the consumer fails to make a minimum periodic payment within 60 days from the due date for that payment? [226.9(g)(4)(i)(A)] Note: If the above notice is provided, the creditor is not required to provide the notice under 226.9(g)(1).										
31. Did the creditor refrain from increasing the rate applicable to the consumer's account to the penalty rate if the outstanding balance did not exceed the credit limit on the date set forth in the notice? [226.9(g)(4)(ii)]										
32. Is the information provided pursuant to 226.9(g)(4)(i) in the form of a table and provided on the front of any page of the periodic statement; or on the front of the first page of the notice? [226.9(g)(4)(iii)]										

#11—Open-End Credit File Review Worksheet—General and Subsequent Disclosures, Payments, Balances, Terminations, Renewals, Unauthorized Charges, and Billing Errors										
Product Type: Name of Borrower: Account #:	Yes	No	Yes	No	Yes	No	Yes	No	Yes	No
Note: Only the information related to the reduction in credit limit may be included with the notice, except that this notice may be combined with a notice described in 226.9(c)(2)(iv) or 226.9(g(1).										
33. When the consumer is given the right to reject a significant change to an account term, was the consumer given the option to reject the change by notifying the creditor of the rejection before the effective date of the change? [226.9(h)(1)]										
34. If the creditor was notified of the rejection of a significant change to an account term, did the creditor: a. Not apply the change or increase to the account? b. Not impose a fee or charge or treat the account as in default solely as a result of the rejection? c. Not require repayment of the balance of the account using a method that is LESS beneficial to the consumer than one of the following methods: 1. The method of repayment for the account on the date on which the creditor was notified of the rejection? 2. An amortization period of not less than five years, beginning no earlier than the date on which the creditor was notified of the rejection?										

#11—Open-End Credit File Review Worksheet—General and Subsequent Disclosures, Payments, Balances, Terminations, Renewals, Unauthorized Charges, and Billing Errors										
Product Type: Name of Borrower: Account #:	Yes	No	Yes	No	Yes	No	Yes	No	Yes	No
3. A required minimum periodic payment that includes a percentage of the balance that is equal to no more than twice the percentage required on the date on which the creditor was notified of the rejection? [226.9(h)(2)] Note: 226.9(h) does not apply if the creditor has not received the consumer's required minimum periodic payment within 60 days after the due date for that payment and the creditor has provided timely change in terms disclosures. [226.9(h)(3)]										
35. Are payments credited to a consumer's account as of the date of receipt, except when a delay in crediting does not result in a finance charge or other charge? [226.10(a)]										
36. If a creditor specifies requirements for payments, are they reasonable and do they allow most consumers to make conforming payments? [226.10(b)(1)]										
37. If the creditor sets a cut-off time for payments to be received by mail, by electronic means, by telephone, or in person, is the cut-off time 5 p.m. or later on the payment due date at the location specified by the creditor for the receipt of such payments? [226.10(b)(2)(ii)]										
38. For in-person payments at a financial institution branch or office that accepts such payments, does the card issuer not impose a cut-off time earlier than the close of business for any such payments made in person at any branch or office of the card issuer at which such payments are accepted (unless the close of business of the										

#11—Open-End Credit File Review Worksheet—General and Subsequent Disclosures, Payments, Balances, Terminations, Renewals, Unauthorized Charges, and Billing Errors										
Product Type: Name of Borrower: Account #:	Yes	No	Yes	No	Yes	No	Yes	No	Yes	No
branch or office is earlier than 5 p.m.)? [226.10(b)(3)(i)]										
39. If a creditor specifies, on or with the periodic statement, requirements for the consumer to follow in making payments, but accepts a payment that does not conform to the requirements, is the payment credited within five days of receipt? [226.10(b)(4)]										
40. If a creditor fails to credit a payment as required and imposes a finance or other charge, does the creditor credit the charge(s) to the consumer's account during the next billing cycle? [226.10(c)]										
41. If (due to a weekend or holiday, for example) a creditor does not receive or accept payments by mail on the due date for payments, does the creditor treat as timely a payment received on the next business day? [226.10(d)(1)]										
42. Does the creditor not impose a separate fee to allow consumers to make a payment by any method, such as mail, electronic, or telephone payments, unless such payment method involves an expedited service by a customer service representative of the creditor? [226.10(e)]										
43. If a card issuer makes a material change in the address for receiving payments or procedures for handling payments, and such change causes a material delay in the crediting of a payment to a consumer's account during the 60-day period following the date on which such change took effect, does the card issuer not impose any late fee or finance charge for a late payment on the credit card account										

#11—Open-End Credit File Review Worksheet—General and Subsequent Disclosures, Payments, Balances, Terminations, Renewals, Unauthorized Charges, and Billing Errors										
Product Type: **Name of Borrower:** **Account #:**	Yes	No	Yes	No	Yes	No	Yes	No	Yes	No
during the 60-day period following the date on which the change took effect? [226.10(f)]										
44. If the account's credit balance is in excess of $1, does the bank credit the amount to the consumer's account and either refund any part of the remaining credit balance within seven business days from receiving a written request from the consumer; or if no written request is received and the credit remains for more than six months, make a good faith effort to refund the amount of the credit to the consumer by cash, check, money order, or credit to a deposit account of the consumer? [226.11(a)]										
45. Did the creditor refrain from terminating an account prior to its expiration date solely because the consumer did not incur a finance charge? [226.11(b)(1)]										
46. Except for the account of a deceased consumer if a joint accountholder remains on the account, has the card issuer adopted reasonable written policies and procedures designed to ensure that an administrator of an estate of a deceased accountholder can determine the amount of and pay any balance on the account in a timely manner? [226.11(c)(1)(i)]										
47. Upon request by the administrator of an estate, does the card issuer provide the administrator with the amount of the balance on a deceased consumer's account in a timely manner, i.e., within 30 days of receiving the request? [226.11(c)(2)(i)]										

#11—Open-End Credit File Review Worksheet—General and Subsequent Disclosures, Payments, Balances, Terminations, Renewals, Unauthorized Charges, and Billing Errors										
Product Type: Name of Borrower: Account #:	Yes	No	Yes	No	Yes	No	Yes	No	Yes	No
48. After receiving a request from the administrator of an estate for the amount of the balance on a deceased consumer's account, does the card issuer not impose any fees on the account (such as a late fee, annual fee, or over the-limit fee) or increase any annual percentage rate, except as provided by 226.55(b)(2) (i.e., due to the operation of an index)? [226.11(c)(3)(i)]										
49. If payment in full of the disclosed balance, pursuant to paragraph 226.11(c)(2), is received within 30 days after disclosure, does the card issuer waive or rebate any additional finance charge due to a periodic interest rate? [226.11(c)(3)(ii)]										
50. Are credit cards issued only upon request or as a renewal or substitute for an accepted credit card? [226.12(a)]										
51. Is liability for unauthorized credit card use limited to a maximum of $50? [226.12(b)(1)]										
52. Are disputes handled properly? Also, determine if the bank reports the disputed amount withheld by the consumer as delinquent only if the disputed amount remains unpaid after the dispute has been settled or judgment has been rendered against the consumer. [226.12(c)]										
53. Is offsetting credit card indebtedness prohibited? [226.12(d)(1)]										
54. Are billing errors resolved within two complete billing cycles (in no event more than 90 days)? [226.13(c)(2)]										

#11—Open-End Credit File Review Worksheet—General and Subsequent Disclosures, Payments, Balances, Terminations, Renewals, Unauthorized Charges, and Billing Errors										
Product Type: Name of Borrower: Account #:	Yes	No	Yes	No	Yes	No	Yes	No	Yes	No
55. Has the creditor retained evidence of compliance with regulation Z for two years after the date disclosures were required to be made or action was required to be taken? [226.25(a)]										

Worksheet #12—
Home Equity Line of Credit File Review

Use this worksheet when reviewing HELOCs. To complete, review loan files and place a check in each applicable box. Determine the accuracy of the disclosures by comparing them to the contract and other bank documents. This worksheet can be used for reviewing audit work papers, evaluating bank policies, performing expanded procedures, and training as appropriate. Only complete those sections of the worksheet that specifically relate to the issue being reviewed, evaluated or tested, and retain those completed sections in the work papers.

When reviewing audit or evaluating bank policies, a "No" answer indicates a possible exception/deficiency and should be explained in the work papers. When performing expanded procedures, a "No" answer indicates a violation and should be explained in the work papers. If a line item is not applicable within the area you are reviewing, indicate "NA."

Underline the applicable use: Audit   Bank Policies   Expanded Procedures

#12—Home Equity Line of Credit File Review Worksheet										
Name of Borrower: Account Number:	Yes	No	Yes	No	Yes	No	Yes	No	Yes	No
1. Are the disclosures and brochure given at the time an application is provided to the consumer or within three business days of receipt in the case of applications contained in magazines or other publications or if the application is received through a broker or by telephone? [226.5b(b)] Note: Generally, the disclosures required by Subpart B may be provided to the consumer in electronic form, subject to compliance with the consumer consent and other applicable provisions of the E-Sign Act. However, the disclosures required by 226.5b may be provided to the consumer in electronic form without regard to the consumer consent or other provisions of the E-Sign Act in the circumstances set forth in those sections. [226.5(a)(iii)]										
2. Does the bank indicate, for an added credit feature or credit device, that the feature or device is for use in obtaining credit under the terms previously disclosed? [226.9(b)(1)]										
3. Except for checks that access a credit card account, are the 226.6(a)										

#12—Home Equity Line of Credit File Review Worksheet										
Name of Borrower: **Account Number:**	Yes	No	Yes	No	Yes	No	Yes	No	Yes	No
disclosures for an added feature or credit device with different finance charge terms provided before the consumer uses the feature or device? [226.9(b)(2)]										
4. Did the creditor mail or deliver written notice of a change in any term required to be disclosed under 226.6(a) or an increase in the required minimum periodic payment at least 15 days prior to the effective date of the change? [226.9(c)(1)(i)] Note: This notice is not required when the change involves a reduction of any component of a finance or other charge or when the change results from an agreement involving a court proceeding? [226.9(c)(1)(ii)]										
5. If the creditor prohibits additional extensions of credit or reduces the credit limit, did the creditor mail or deliver notice of the action not later than three business days after such action is taken and does the notice contain the specific reasons for the action? [226.9(c)(1)(iii)]										
6. Are all fees refunded when the consumer rejects the plan because a disclosed term changes before the plan is opened? [226.5b(g)]										
7. Does the bank collect only refundable fees, if any, from the consumer before the end of three business days from delivering the disclosures (six days from the date of mailing, if mailed)? [226.5b(h)]										
8. Has the bank refunded any fees that it collected from the consumer before it delivered the required disclosures if the consumer rejected the plan within three business days after receiving the disclosures (even if there is no change in the disclosed terms)? [226.5b(h)]										

#12—Home Equity Line of Credit File Review Worksheet										
Name of Borrower: Account Number:	Yes	No	Yes	No	Yes	No	Yes	No	Yes	No
9. Are payments credited to a consumer's account as of the date of receipt, except when a delay in crediting does not result in a finance charge or other charge? [226.10(a)]										
10. If a creditor specifies requirements for payments, are they reasonable and do they allow most consumers to make conforming payments? [226.10(b)(1)]										
11. If the creditor sets a cut-off time for payments to be received by mail, by electronic means, by telephone, or in person, is the cut-off time 5 p.m. or later on the payment due date at the location specified by the creditor for the receipt of such payments? [226.10(b)(2)(ii)]										
12. If a creditor specifies, on or with the periodic statement, requirements for the consumer to follow in making payments, but accepts a payment that does not conform to the requirements, is the payment credited within five days of receipt? [226.10(b)(4)]										
13. If a creditor fails to credit a payment as required and imposes a finance or other charge, does the creditor credit the charge(s) to the consumer's account during the next billing cycle? [226.10(c)]										
14. If (due to a weekend or holiday, for example) a creditor does not receive or accept payments by mail on the due date for payments, does the creditor treat as timely a payment received on the next business day? [226.10(d)(1)]										
15. If the account's credit balance is in excess of $1, does the bank credit the amount to the consumer's account and either refund any part of the remaining credit balance within seven business days from receiving a written request from the consumer; or if no written										

#12—Home Equity Line of Credit File Review Worksheet										
Name of Borrower: Account Number:	Yes	No	Yes	No	Yes	No	Yes	No	Yes	No
request is received and the credit remains for more than six months, make a good faith effort to refund the amount of the credit to the consumer by cash, check, money order, or credit to a deposit account of the consumer? [226.11(a)]										
16. Did the creditor not terminate an account prior to its expiration date solely because the consumer did not incur a finance charge? [226.11(b)(1)]										
17. Unless subject to the exceptions at 226.39(c), for consumer credit transactions secured by the consumer's principal dwelling that were acquired by, or otherwise sold, transferred, or assigned to the creditor who is the new legal owner of the debt (covered person), did the covered person provide a written disclosure notice to the borrower within 30 calendar days of the transaction that includes the following: a. An identification of the loan that was sold, assigned, or otherwise transferred? [226.39(d)] b. Name, address, and telephone number of the covered person? [226.39(d)(1)] c. If there are multiple covered persons, has contact information been provided for each of them, unless one of them has been authorized to receive the consumer's notice of the right to rescind and resolve issues concerning the consumer's payments on the loan? [226.39(d)(1))ii)]										

#12—Home Equity Line of Credit File Review Worksheet										
Name of Borrower: Account Number:	Yes	No	Yes	No	Yes	No	Yes	No	Yes	No
d. Date of transfer, which may, at the covered person's option, be either the date of acquisition recognized in the books and records of the acquiring party, or the date of transfer recognized in the books and records of the transferring party? [226.39(d)(2)]										
e. Name, address, and telephone number of an agent or party authorized to receive notice of the right to rescind and resolve issues concerning the consumer's payments on the loan, unless the consumer can use the information provided under (b) for this purpose? [226.39(d)(3)]										
f. The location where the transfer of ownership of the debt to the covered person is or may be recorded? [Note: If the transfer of ownership has not been recorded in public records at the time the disclosure is provided, the covered person complies with this paragraph by stating this fact.] [226.39(d)(4)]										
g. At the option of the covered person, any other information regarding the transaction? [226.39(e)]										
Note: if more than one consumer is liable on the obligation, the covered person may mail or deliver the disclosure notice to any consumer who is primarily liable. [226.39(b)(3)]										

#12—Home Equity Line of Credit File Review Worksheet										
Name of Borrower: Account Number:	Yes	No	Yes	No	Yes	No	Yes	No	Yes	No
18. Is the disclosure notice required by 226.39 provided clearly and conspicuously in writing, in a form that the consumer may keep? [226.39(b)(1)] Note: the disclosure notice may be provided to the consumer in electronic form, subject to compliance with the consumer consent and other applicable provisions of the E-Sign Act. [226.39(b)(1)]										
19. If a consumer credit transaction secured by the principal dwelling of a consumer is acquired by a covered person and subsequently sold, assigned, or otherwise transferred to another covered person and a single disclosure notice is provided on behalf of both covered persons, did the disclosure notice satisfy the timing (226.39(b)) and content (226.39(d)) requirements applicable to each covered person? [226.39(b)(4)]										
20. If an acquisition involves multiple covered persons who jointly acquire the consumer credit transaction secured by the principal dwelling of a consumer, was a single disclosure notice provided on behalf of all covered persons? [226.39(b)(5)] Note: If an acquisition involves multiple covered persons who each acquire a partial interest in the loan pursuant to separate and unrelated agreements, each covered person has a duty to ensure that disclosures related to its acquisition are accurate and provided in a timely manner unless an exception in 226.39(c) applies. The parties may, but are not required to, provide a single notice that satisfies the timing and content requirements applicable to each covered person. [Commentary 226.39(b)(5) – 2]										

#12—Home Equity Line of Credit File Review Worksheet										
Name of Borrower: Account Number:	Yes	No	Yes	No	Yes	No	Yes	No	Yes	No
21. Has the creditor retained evidence of compliance with regulation Z for two years after the date disclosures were required to be made or action was required to be taken? [226.25(a)]										

Worksheet #13—
Special Rules for Certain Home Mortgage Transactions
(High-Cost Mortgages, Reverse Mortgages,
Higher-Priced Mortgages, and Credit Secured by
Consumer's Principal Dwelling)
File Review

Use this worksheet when reviewing HOEPA, reverse mortgage, higher-priced mortgage loans, and certain credit secured by a consumer's principal dwelling. To complete, review loan files and place a check in each applicable box. This worksheet can be used for reviewing audit work papers, evaluating bank policies, performing expanded procedures, and training as appropriate. Only complete those sections of the worksheet that specifically relate to the issue being reviewed, evaluated or tested, and retain those completed sections in the work papers.

When reviewing audit or evaluating bank policies, a "No" answer indicates a possible exception/deficiency and should be explained in the work papers. When performing expanded procedures, a "No" answer indicates a violation and should be explained in the work papers. If a line item is not applicable within the area you are reviewing, indicate "NA."

Underline the applicable use: Audit   Bank Policies   Expanded Procedures

#13—Special Rules for Certain Home Mortgage Transactions File Review Worksheet										
Product Type: Name of Borrower: Account Number:	Yes	No	Yes	No	Yes	No	Yes	No	Yes	No
1. Are required disclosures provided to consumers in addition to, not in lieu of, the disclosures contained in other subparts of Regulation Z? [226.31(a)]										
2. Are disclosures clear, conspicuous, in writing and in a form the consumer may keep? [226.31(b)] Note: The disclosures required by Subpart E (226.31 - .39) may be provided to the consumer in electronic form, subject to compliance with the consumer consent and other applicable provisions of the E-Sign Act. [226.31(b)]										
3. Do the disclosures reflect the terms of the legal obligation between the parties? [226.31(d)]										

#13—Special Rules for Certain Home Mortgage Transactions File Review Worksheet										
Product Type: Name of Borrower: Account Number:	Yes	No	Yes	No	Yes	No	Yes	No	Yes	No
4. If the transaction involves more than one creditor, did only one creditor provide the disclosures? And where the obligation involves multiple consumers, were the disclosures provided to any consumer who is primarily liable on the obligation? And for rescindable transactions, were the disclosures provided to each consumer who has the right to rescind? [226.31(e)]										
5. Is the APR accurately calculated and disclosed in accordance with the requirements and within the tolerances allowed in section 226.22? [226.31(g)]										
HOEPA Mortgages [226.32]										
6. Are disclosures provided at least 3 business days prior to consummation? [226.31(c)(1)]										
7. Are new disclosures provided when terms change prior to consummation? [226.31(c)(1)(i)]										
8. Does the bank disclose the following: a. Notices? [226.32(c)(1)] b. APR? [226.32(c)(2)] c. Regular payment and any balloon payment? [226.32(c)(3)] d. Variable rate? [226.32(c)(4)] e. Amount borrowed? [226.32(c)(5)]										
9. Are these terms absent from the mortgage transaction: a. Balloon payment (if term is less than five years) other than bridge										

#13—Special Rules for Certain Home Mortgage Transactions File Review Worksheet										
Product Type: Name of Borrower: Account Number:	Yes	No	Yes	No	Yes	No	Yes	No	Yes	No
loans of less than one year? [226.32(d)(1)]										
b. Negative amortization? [226.32(d)(2)]										
c. Advance payments of more than two periodic payments? [226.32(d)(3)]										
d. Increased interest rate after default? [226.32(d)(4)]										
e. Refund calculation by method less favorable than the actuarial method for rebates of interest arising from loan acceleration due to default? [226.32(d)(5)]										
f. Prepayment penalties (unless an exception in section 32(d)(7) exists)? [226.32(d)(6)]										
g. Due-on-demand clause (unless conditions are met)? [226.32(d)(8)]										
10. Does the bank:										
a. Pay a contractor under a home improvement contract from mortgage proceeds only as allowed in 226.34(a)(1)?										
b. Sell or assign a mortgage only when furnishing the required notice to assignee? [226.34(a)(2)]										
c. Refinance a loan subject to section 32 or an original refinance of a loan subject to										

#13—Special Rules for Certain Home Mortgage Transactions File Review Worksheet										
Product Type: Name of Borrower: Account Number:	Yes	No	Yes	No	Yes	No	Yes	No	Yes	No
section 32 only after one year? [226.34(a)(3)] d. Only make the loan if the consumer has the ability to repay based on the consumer's current income, reasonably expected income, employment, assets other than the collateral, current obligations, and mortgage-related obligations. [226.34(a)(4)] e. Verify the consumer's repayment ability and current obligations? [226.34(a)(4)(ii) and (iii)]										
11. Are waivers of the waiting period appropriate, and do they reflect the signature of all the consumers entitled to the waiting period? [226.31(c)(1)(iii)]										
12. Has the creditor avoided structuring the loan as an open-end plan to evade the Regulation Z requirements? [226.34(b)]										
Reverse Mortgages (Open- and Closed-End) [226.33]										
13. Are disclosures provided at least three business days prior to: a. Consummation for closed-end loans? [226.31(c)(2)(i)] b. First transaction under an open-end credit plan? [226.31(c)(2)(ii)]										
14. Are disclosures substantially similar to the Appendix K model form, and include: a. Notice? [226.33(b)(1)]										

#13—Special Rules for Certain Home Mortgage Transactions File Review Worksheet										
Product Type: Name of Borrower: Account Number:	Yes	No	Yes	No	Yes	No	Yes	No	Yes	No
b. Total annual loan cost rates? [226.33(c)(1)–(6)] c. Itemization of pertinent information? [226.33(b)(3)] d. Explanation of table? [226.33(b)(4)]										
Higher-Priced Mortgages (226.35)										
15. Is the loan without a prepayment penalty unless: a. It is otherwise permitted by law, including 226.32(d)(7)? b. It will not apply after the two-year period following consummation? c. The source of prepayment funds is a refinancing by the creditor or an affiliate of the creditor? d. The amount of the periodic payment of principal or interest or both may not change during the four-year period following consummation? e. The consumer's verified total monthly debt payments (at consummation), including amounts owed under the mortgage, does not exceed 50 percent of the consumer's monthly gross income? [226.35(b)(2) and 226.35(b)(2) commentary]										
16. Has an escrow account been established before consummation for										

#13—Special Rules for Certain Home Mortgage Transactions File Review Worksheet										
Product Type: Name of Borrower: Account Number:	Yes	No	Yes	No	Yes	No	Yes	No	Yes	No
property taxes and premiums for mortgage-related insurance if the loan is secured by a first lien on a principal dwelling? [226.35(b)(3)]										
17. Does the creditor refrain from basing the consumer's ability to repay on the collateral without regard to repayment ability, including the consumer's current and expected income, current obligations, mortgage related obligations, assets other than the collateral, and employment? [226.35(b)(1)]										
18. Has the creditor verified amounts of income or assets that it relies on to determine repayment ability, including expected income or assets, by the consumer's IRS Form W-2, tax returns, payroll receipts, financial records, or other third party documents that provide reasonably reliable evidence of the consumer's income or assets? [226.35(b)(1)]										
19. Has the creditor avoided structuring the loan as an open-end plan to evade the Regulation Z requirements? See commentary to section 34(b). [226.35(b)(4)]										
Credit Secured by the Consumer's Principal Dwelling (226.36 and 226.39)										
20. Has the creditor, mortgage broker, or an affiliate thereof avoided direct or indirect coercion or influence on an appraiser to misstate or misrepresent the value of the consumer's principal dwelling? [226.36(b)(1)] Note: Section 226.36 does not apply to HELOCs that are subject to 226.5b. [226.36(d)]										
21. If the creditor knew, at or before loan consummation, that a violation of the										

#13—Special Rules for Certain Home Mortgage Transactions File Review Worksheet										
Product Type: Name of Borrower: Account Number:	Yes	No	Yes	No	Yes	No	Yes	No	Yes	No
appraiser coercion prohibition occurred, did the creditor act with reasonable diligence to determine that the appraisal in question does not materially misstate or misrepresent the value of the consumer's principal dwelling? [226.36(b)(2)]										
22. Does the loan servicer credit a conforming payment to the consumer's loan account as of the date of receipt, except when a delay in crediting does not result in any charge to the consumer or reporting of negative information to a consumer reporting agency? [226.36(c)(1)(i)] Note: The servicer shall credit the payment as of 5 days after receipt when it accepts a payment that does not conform with written requirements specified for making payments. [226.36(c)2]										
23. Has the loan servicer refrained from imposing any late fee or delinquency charge in connection with a payment, when the only delinquency was attributable to late fees or delinquency charges assessed on an earlier payment, and the payment is otherwise a full payment for the applicable period and is paid on its due date or within any applicable grace period? [226.36(c)(1)(ii)]										
24. Does the loan servicer provide an accurate statement of the total outstanding balance that would be required to satisfy the obligation in full as of a specific date within a reasonable time after receiving the request? [226.36(c)(1)(iii)]										

#13—Special Rules for Certain Home Mortgage Transactions File Review Worksheet										
Product Type: Name of Borrower: Account Number:	Yes	No	Yes	No	Yes	No	Yes	No	Yes	No
Note: Under most circumstances, a reasonable time is within 5 business days, unless refinance application volume is unusually high.										
25. Unless subject to the exceptions at 226.39(c), for consumer credit transactions secured by the consumer's principal dwelling that were acquired by, or otherwise sold, transferred, or assigned to the creditor who is the new legal owner of the debt (covered person), did the covered person provide a written disclosure notice to the borrower within 30 calendar days of the transaction that includes the following: a. An identification of the loan that was sold, assigned, or otherwise transferred? [226.39(d)] b. Name, address, and telephone number of the covered person? [226.39(d)(1)] c. If there are multiple covered persons, has contact information been provided for each of them, unless one of them has been authorized to receive the consumer's notice of the right to rescind and resolve issues concerning the consumer's payments on the loan? [226.39(d)(1))ii)] d. Date of transfer, which may, at the covered person's option, be either the date of acquisition recognized in the books and records of the acquiring party, or										

#13—Special Rules for Certain Home Mortgage Transactions File Review Worksheet										
Product Type: Name of Borrower: Account Number:	Yes	No	Yes	No	Yes	No	Yes	No	Yes	No
the date of transfer recognized in the books and records of the transferring party? [226.39(d)(2)] e. Name, address, and telephone number of an agent or party authorized to receive notice of the right to rescind and resolve issues concerning the consumer's payments on the loan, unless the consumer can use the information provided under (b) for this purpose? [226.39(d)(3)] f. The location where the transfer of ownership of the debt to the covered person is or may be recorded? [Note: If the transfer of ownership has not been recorded in public records at the time the disclosure is provided, the covered person complies with this paragraph by stating this fact.] [226.39(d)(4)] g. At the option of the covered person, any other information regarding the transaction? [226.39(e)] Note: If more than one consumer is liable on the obligation, the covered person may mail or deliver the disclosure notice to any consumer who is primarily liable. [226.39(b)(3)]										
26. Is the disclosure notice required by 226.39 provided clearly and conspicuously in writing, in a form that the consumer may keep? [226.39(b)(1)] Note: The disclosure notice may be provided to the consumer in electronic										

#13—Special Rules for Certain Home Mortgage Transactions File Review Worksheet										
Product Type: Name of Borrower: Account Number:	Yes	No	Yes	No	Yes	No	Yes	No	Yes	No
form, subject to compliance with the consumer consent and other applicable provisions of the E-Sign Act. [226.39(b)(1)]										
27. If a consumer credit transaction secured by the principal dwelling of a consumer is acquired by a covered person and subsequently sold, assigned, or otherwise transferred to another covered person and a single disclosure notice is provided on behalf of both covered persons, did the disclosure notice satisfy the timing (226.39(b)) and content (226.39(d)) requirements applicable to each covered person? [226.39(b)(4)]										
28. If an acquisition involves multiple covered persons who jointly acquire the consumer credit transaction secured by the principal dwelling of a consumer, was a single disclosure notice provided on behalf of all covered persons? [226.39(b)(5)] Note: If an acquisition involves multiple covered persons who each acquire a partial interest in the loan pursuant to separate and unrelated agreements, each covered person has a duty to ensure that disclosures related to its acquisition are accurate and provided in a timely manner unless an exception in 226.39(c) applies. The parties may, but are not required to, provide a single notice that satisfies the timing and content requirements applicable to each covered person. [Commentary 226.39(b)(5) – 2]										
29. Has the creditor retained evidence of compliance with regulation Z for two years after the date disclosures were required to be made or action was required to be taken? [226.25(a)]										

Worksheet #14—
Periodic Billing Statements

Use for all open-end credit products for forms review by product type and sample review by loan name. To complete, review applicable forms and place a check in each applicable box. Review two consecutive periodic billing statements for each major type of open-end credit product offered. Determine if disclosures were calculated accurately and are consistent with the initial disclosure statement furnished in connection with the accounts (or any subsequent change in terms notice) and the underlying contractual terms governing the product(s). This worksheet can be used for reviewing audit work papers, evaluating bank policies, performing expanded procedures, and training as appropriate. Only complete those sections of the worksheet that specifically relate to the issue being reviewed, evaluated or tested, and retain those completed sections in the work papers.

When reviewing audit or evaluating bank policies, a "No" answer indicates a possible exception/deficiency and should be explained in the work papers. When performing expanded procedures, a "No" answer indicates a violation and should be explained in the work papers. If a line item is not applicable within the area you are reviewing, indicate "NA."

Underline the applicable use:　　　Audit　　　Bank Policies　　　Expanded Procedures

#14—Periodic Billing Statements Worksheet										
Product Type: Name of Borrower: Account Number:	Yes	No	Yes	No	Yes	No	Yes	No	Yes	No
1.　Are periodic billing statements provided if at the end of a billing cycle the account has a debit or credit balance of $1 or more or if a finance charge has been imposed? [226.5(b)(2)(i)]										
Periodic Billing Statements Worksheet for Home-Equity Plans Subject to 226.5b										
Note: For home-equity plans subject to 226.5b, a creditor may instead, at its option, comply with any of the requirements of 226.7(b); however, any creditor that chooses not to provide a disclosure under paragraph 226.7(a)(7) must comply with paragraph 226.7(b)(6).										
2.　Is the beginning outstanding balance provided? [226.7(a)(1)]										
3.　Are transactions identified and accurate? [226.7(a)(2) and 226.8]										
4.　Are the dates and amounts of credits to account disclosed accurately? [226.7(a)(3)]										
5.　Are the periodic rate(s) and APR(s) stated and accurate? If it is a variable rate plan, is the fact that the periodic rate(s) may vary disclosed? [226.7(a)(4) and footnote 15]										

#14—Periodic Billing Statements Worksheet										
Product Type: Name of Borrower: Account Number:	Yes	No	Yes	No	Yes	No	Yes	No	Yes	No
6. If different rates apply to different types of transactions, except for promotional rates in periods in which they are actually applied, are the types of transactions to which the periodic rates apply disclosed? [226.7(a)(4)]										
7. Is the amount of balance subject to the periodic rate and an explanation of how the balance is determined disclosed? [226.7(a)(5)] Note: When a balance is determined without first deducting all credits and payments made during the billing cycle, that fact and the amount of the credits and payments shall be disclosed.										
8. Is any "finance charge" amount (using that term) disclosed and accurate? [226.7(a)(6)]										
9. Are the components of the finance charge imposed during the billing cycle individually itemized and identified? [226.7(a)(6)(i)]										
10. Are the amounts of any other charges debited to the account itemized, identified by type, and accurately disclosed? [226.7(a)(6)(ii)]										
11. Is the APR (using that term) disclosed and accurate? [226.7(a)(7)]										
12. Does the periodic statement disclose the date by which or the time period within which the new balance or any portion of the new balance must be paid to avoid additional finance charges? [226.7(a)(8)]										
13. Does the periodic statement include the address for notice of billing errors? [226.7(a)(9)] Note: Alternatively, the address may be provided on the billing rights statement permitted by 226.9(a)(2)										
14. Are the account balance and closing date disclosed and accurate? [226.7(a)(10)]										
Periodic Billing Statements for Open-End Not Home-Secured Plans										
15. Have reasonable procedures been adopted to ensure periodic statements for credit cards are mailed or delivered at least 21 days prior to the										

#14—Periodic Billing Statements Worksheet										
Product Type: Name of Borrower: Account Number:	Yes	No	Yes	No	Yes	No	Yes	No	Yes	No
payment due date and the date on which any grace period expires? [226.5(b)(2)(ii)]										
16. Is the beginning outstanding balance provided? [226.7(b)(1)]										
17. Are transactions identified and disclosed accurately? [226.7(b)(2) and 226.8]										
18. Are the dates and amounts of credits to account disclosed accurately? [226.7(b)(3)]										
19. Are the periodic rate(s) and APR(s), along with the range of balances to which they apply, stated and accurate? If it is a variable rate plan, is the fact that the periodic rate may vary disclosed? [226.7(b)(4)]										
20. If different rates apply to different types of transactions, except for promotional rates in periods in which they are actually applied, are the types of transactions to which the periodic rates apply disclosed? [226.7(b)(4)]										
21. Is the amount of balance to which a periodic rate was applied and an explanation of how that balance was determined, using the term "Balance Subject to Interest Rate," included? [226.7(b)(5)] Note: when a balance is determined without first deducting all credits and payments made during the billing cycle, that fact and the amount of the credits and payments shall be disclosed.										
22. Does the periodic statement include the amounts of any charges imposed as part of a plan as stated in 226.6(b)(3) (account-opening charges), grouped together, in proximity to transactions identified under 226.7(b)(2), substantially similar to Sample G-18(A) in appendix G? [226.7(b)(6)]										
23. Are finance charges attributable to periodic interest rates, using the term "Interest Charge," grouped together under the heading "Interest Charged" and itemized and totaled by type of transaction; and is the total finance charges attributable to periodic interest rates, using the term "Total Interest," disclosed for the statement										

#14—Periodic Billing Statements Worksheet										
Product Type: Name of Borrower: Account Number:	Yes	No	Yes	No	Yes	No	Yes	No	Yes	No
period and calendar year-to-date using a format substantially similar to Sample G-18A? [226.7(b)(6)(i)]										
24. Are charges imposed as part of the plan, other than charges attributable to periodic interest rates, grouped together under the heading "Fees," identified consistent with the feature or type, and itemized; and are total charges, using the term "Fees," disclosed for the statement period and calendar year-to-date, using a format substantially similar to Sample G–18(A)? [226.7(b)(6)(ii)]										
25. If the creditor provides a change-in-terms notice required by 226.9(c), or a rate increase notice required by 226.9(g), on or with the periodic statement, has the creditor disclosed the information in 226.9(c)(2)(iv)(A) and (c)(2)(iv)(B) (if applicable) or 226.9(g)(3)(i) on the periodic statement in accordance with the format requirements in 226.9(c)(2)(iv)(D), and 226.9(g)(3)(ii). See Forms G–18(F) and G–18(G)? [226.7(b)(7)]										
26. Is the grace period disclosed? Note: If a grace period is provided, a creditor may, at its option and without disclosure, impose no finance charge if payment is received after the time period's expiration. [226.7(b)(8)]										
27. Does the periodic statement include the address for notice of billing errors? [226.7(b)(9)] Note: The address may be provided on the billing rights statement permitted by 226.9(a)(2)]										
28. Are the account balance and closing date disclosed and accurate and is the new balance disclosed in accordance with the format requirements of 226.7(b)(13)? [226.7(b)(10)]										
29. Except for periodic statements provided solely for charge card accounts and for a charged-off account where payment of the entire account balance is due immediately, do periodic statements for credit cards include:										

#14—Periodic Billing Statements Worksheet										
Product Type: Name of Borrower: Account Number:	Yes	No	Yes	No	Yes	No	Yes	No	Yes	No
a. Due date for a payment, which must be the same day of the month for each billing cycle? [226.7(b)(11)(i)(A)] b. Amount of any late payment fee and any increased periodic rate(s) expressed as an APR that may be imposed because of the late payment? [226.7(b)(11)(i)(B)] c. If a range of fees may be assessed, either the range of fees or the highest fees that could apply and an indication that the fee imposed could be lower? [226.7(b)(11)(i)(B)] d. If the rate may be increased for more than one feature or balance, either the range of rates or the highest rate that could apply? [226.7(b)(11)(i)(B)]										
30. Is the due date disclosed on the front of the first page of the periodic statement; are the amount of the late payment fee and the increased APR stated in close proximity to the due date; are the ending balance and repayment disclosures (required by 226.7(b)(12) disclosed closely proximate to the minimum payment due; and are the due date, late payment fee and APR, ending balance, minimum payment due, and repayment disclosures grouped together? [226.7(b)(13)]										
31. For accounts with an outstanding balance subject to a deferred interest (or similar program), is the date by which that outstanding balance must be paid in full to avoid finance charges disclosed on the front of each applicable periodic statement? [226.7(b)(14)]										
32. Is the deferred interest disclosure substantially similar to Sample G-18(H) in Appendix G? [226.7(b)(14)]										
33. Except for those credit cards for which negative or no amortization occurs when calculating the minimum repayment payment estimate as										

#14—Periodic Billing Statements Worksheet										
Product Type: Name of Borrower: Account Number:										
	Yes	No	Yes	No	Yes	No	Yes	No	Yes	No
described in Appendix M1, do periodic statements for a credit card account under an open-end (not home-secured) consumer credit plan provide the following disclosures on each periodic statement?										
a. The following statement with a bold heading: "Minimum Payment Warning: If you make only the minimum payment each period, you will pay more in interest and it will take you longer to pay off your balance? [226.7(b)(12)(i)(A)]										
b. The minimum payment repayment estimate? [226.7(b)(12)(i)(B)]										
Note: If the minimum payment repayment estimate is less than 2 years, the card issuer must disclose the estimate in months. Otherwise, the estimate must be disclosed in years and rounded to the nearest whole year.										
c. The minimum payment total cost estimate rounded to the nearest whole dollar? [226.7(b)(12)(i)(C)]										
d. A statement that the minimum payment repayment estimate and the minimum payment total cost estimate are based on the current outstanding balance shown on the periodic statement; and a statement that the minimum payment repayment estimate and the minimum payment total cost estimate are based on the assumption that only minimum payments are made and no other amounts are added to the balance? [226.7(b)(12)(i)(D)]										
e. A toll-free telephone number where the consumer may obtain from the card issuer information about credit counseling services? [226.7(b)(12)(i)(E)]										

#14—Periodic Billing Statements Worksheet										
Product Type: Name of Borrower: Account Number:	Yes	No	Yes	No	Yes	No	Yes	No	Yes	No
f. Except when the minimum payment repayment estimate is three years or less; and the estimated monthly payment for repayment in 36 months is less than the minimum payment required for that billing cycle; and a billing cycle where an account has both a balance in a revolving feature where the required minimum payments for this feature will not amortize that balance in a fixed amount of time specified in the account agreement and a balance in a fixed repayment feature where the required minimum payment for this fixed repayment feature will amortize that balance in a fixed amount of time specified in the account agreement which is less than 36 months, are the following disclosures provided:										
i. The estimated monthly payment for repayment in 36 months rounded to the nearest whole dollar? [226.7(b)(12)(i)(F)(1)(i)]										
ii. A statement that the card issuer estimates that the consumer will repay the outstanding balance shown on the periodic statement in 3 years if the consumer pays the estimated monthly payment each month for 3 years? [226.7(b)(12)(i)(F)(1)(ii)]										
iii. The total cost estimate for repayment in 36 months rounded to the nearest whole dollar? [226.7(b)(12)(i)(F)(1)(iii)] and										
iv. The savings estimate for repayment in 36 months rounded to the nearest whole dollar? [226.7(b)(12)(i)(F)(1)(iv)]										

#14—Periodic Billing Statements Worksheet										
Product Type: Name of Borrower: Account Number:										
	Yes	No	Yes	No	Yes	No	Yes	No	Yes	No
34. For non-amortizing or negatively amortizing credit card accounts under an open-end (not home-secured) consumer credit plan, does the card issuer provide the following disclosures on each periodic statement:										
a. "Minimum Payment Warning: Even if you make no more charges using this card, if you make only the minimum payment each month we estimate you will never pay off the balance shown on this statement because your payment will be less than the interest charged each month?" [226.7(b)(12)(ii)(A)]										
b. "If you make more than the minimum payment each period, you will pay less in interest and pay off your balance sooner?" [226.7(b)(12)(ii)(B)]										
c. The estimated monthly payment for repayment in 36 months rounded to the nearest whole dollar? [226.7(b)(12)(ii)(C]										
d. A statement that the card issuer estimates that the consumer will repay the outstanding balance shown on the periodic statement in 3 years if the consumer pays the estimated monthly payment each month for 3 years? [226.7(b)(12)(ii)(D)]?										
e. A toll-free telephone number where the consumer may obtain from the card issuer information about credit counseling services? [226.7(b)(12)(ii)(E))										
Note: Regarding steps 33 and 34, the repayment disclosures in 226.7(b)(12) that must be included on periodic statements do not apply to:										
a. Charge card accounts that require payment of outstanding balances in full at the end of each billing cycle.										

#14—Periodic Billing Statements Worksheet										
Product Type: Name of Borrower: Account Number:	Yes	No	Yes	No	Yes	No	Yes	No	Yes	No
b. A billing cycle immediately following two consecutive billing cycles in which the consumer paid the entire balance in full, had a zero outstanding balance or had a credit balance. c. A billing cycle where paying the minimum payment due for that billing cycle will pay the entire outstanding balance on the account for that billing cycle. [226.7(b)(12)(v)]										
35. For periodic statement repayment disclosures required to be disclosed by 226.7(b)(12), are the disclosures made in accordance with the format requirements of §226.7(b)(13) and similar to the samples provided in Appendix G of Regulation Z? [226.7(b)(13)]										
36. Does the card issuer provide (to the extent available from the United States Trustee or a bankruptcy administrator) through the disclosed toll-free telephone number the name, street address, telephone number, and Web site address for at least three organizations that have been approved by the United States Trustee or a bankruptcy administrator to provide credit counseling services in either the state in which the billing address for the account is located or the state specified by the consumer? [226.7(b)(12)(iv)(A)]										
37. Is the credit counseling information discussed in step 36 updated annually for consistency with the information available from the United States Trustee or a bankruptcy administrator? [226.7(b)(12)(iv)(B)]										
38. Has the creditor retained evidence of compliance with regulation Z for two years after the date disclosures were required to be made or action was required to be taken? [226.25(a)]										

#14—Periodic Billing Statements Worksheet										
Product Type: Name of Borrower: Account Number:	Yes	No	Yes	No	Yes	No	Yes	No	Yes	No
Billing Rights Statement										
39. Is the billing rights statement provided at least once each calendar year, or with each periodic statement in a form similar to that in appendix G? [226.9(a)]										

Worksheet #15—
High-Cost Mortgages [Section 226.32]

Use this worksheet when you want to determine whether certain mortgage loans are subject to section 226.32. To complete, review applicable loan files and place a check in each applicable box. For loans that are subject to section 226.32, use Worksheet #13 to document that disclosures were provided appropriately. You can insert an "N/A" if the line item is not applicable. If used, this worksheet should be completed and made part of the work papers.

This worksheet can be used for reviewing audit work papers, evaluating bank policies, performing expanded procedures, and training as appropriate. Only complete those sections of the worksheet that specifically relate to the issue being reviewed, evaluated or tested, and retain those completed sections in the work papers.

Underline the applicable use: Audit   Bank Policies   Expanded Procedures

#15—High-Cost Mortgage Worksheet		
Borrower Name:	Loan Number:	
Coverage		
	Yes	No
1. Does the consumer's principal dwelling secure the loan? [226.2(a)(19) and 226.32(a)(1)]		
If No, Stop here		
2. Is the loan for the following: a. Residential Mortgage Transaction? [226.2(a)(24)] b. Reverse Mortgage Transaction? [226.33] c. Open-end Credit Plan—Subpart B? [Note prohibition against structuring loans as open-end plans to evade 226.32 and 226.34(b)]		
If the answer is Yes to Box a, b, or c, STOP HERE. If No, continue to Test 1.		
TEST 1—CALCULATION OF APR		
1. Disclosed APR		
2. Treasury Security Yield of Comparable Maturity Obtain the Treasury Constant Maturities Yield from the FRB's Statistical Release, H-15— "Selected Interest Rates" (the "Business" links will display daily yields). Use the yield that has the most comparable maturity to the loan term and is from the 15th day of the month that immediately precedes the month of the application. If the 15th is not a business day, use the yield for the business day immediately preceding the 15th. If the loan term is exactly halfway between two published security maturities, use the lower of the two yields. Note: Creditors may use the FRB's Selected Interest Rates or the actual auction results. See Staff Commentary to Regulation Z for further details. [section 226.32(a)(1)(i)] Visit the Web site for the yield: www.federalreserve.gov/releases/H15/data.htm		

3. Treasury Security Yield of Comparable Maturity (Box 2)
    Plus: 8 percentage points for first-lien loan; or
              10 percentage points for subordinate-lien loan		

#15—High-Cost Mortgage Worksheet			
Borrower Name:	Loan Number:		
		Yes	No
Is Box 1 greater than Box 3 in test 1?			
If Yes, the transaction is a high-cost mortgage. If No, continue to Test 2, points and fees.			
Test 2—CALCULATION OF POINTS AND FEES			
Step 1: Identify all Charges Paid by the Consumer at or before Loan Closing			
A. Finance Charges—section 226.4(a) and (b) (Interest, including per-diem interest, and time price differential are excluded from these amounts.)			
		Fee	Subtotals
Loan Points			
Mortgage Broker Fees			
Loan Service Fees			
Required Closing Agent/Third-Party Fees			
Required Credit Insurance			
Private Mortgage Insurance			
Life of Loan Charges (flood, taxes, etc.)			
Any Other Fees Considered Finance Charges			
Subtotal			
B. Certain Non-Finance Charges – section 226.4(c)(7)—Include fees paid by consumers only if the amount of the fee is unreasonable or if the creditor receives direct or indirect compensation from the charge or the charge is paid to an affiliate of the bank. (See the examples under section 226.32(b)(1)(ii) of the commentary for further explanation.)			
Title Examination			
Title Insurance			
Property Survey			
Document Preparation Charge			
Credit Report			
Appraisal			
Fee for "Initial" Flood Hazard Determination			
Pest Inspection			
Any Other Fees Not Considered Finance Charges			
Subtotal			
C. Premiums or Other Charges for Optional Credit Life, Accident, Health, or Loss-of-Income Insurance, or Debt Cancellation Coverage			
D. Total Points and Fees: Add Subtotals for A, B, and C			
Step 2: Determine the Total Loan Amount for Cost Calculation [226.32(a)(1)(ii)]			
A. Determine the Amount Financed [226.18(b)] Principal Loan Amount			
Plus: Other Amounts Financed by the Lender (not already included in the principal and not part of the finance charge)			

#15—High-Cost Mortgage Worksheet			
Borrower Name:	Loan Number:		
Less: Prepaid Finance Charges [section 226.2(a)(23)]			
Equals: Amount Financed			
B. Deduct costs included in the points and fees under section 226.32(b)(1)(iii) and (iv) (Step 1, Box B and Box C) that are financed by the creditor.			
C. Total Loan Amount (Step 2, Box A minus Box B)			
Step 3: Perform High-Fee Cost Calculation			
A. Eight Percent of the Total Loan Amount (Step 2, Box C)			
B. Annual Adjustment Amount—[section 226.32(a)(1)(ii)] (use the dollar amount corresponding to the year of the loan's origination)			
C. Total Points and Fees (Step 1, Box D)			
		Yes	No
In Step 3, does Box C exceed the greater of Box A or Box B?			
If Yes, the transaction is a high-cost mortgage. If No, the transaction is not a high-cost mortgage under Test 2, "Points and Fees."			

Worksheet #16—
Special Credit Card Rules

Use for all card issuers that issue credit cards under a credit card account under an open-end (not home-secured) consumer credit plan. To complete, review applicable policies, practices, notices, agreements, and transactions, as applicable and place a check in each applicable box. This worksheet can be used for reviewing audit work papers, evaluating bank policies, performing expanded procedures, and training as appropriate. Only complete those sections of the worksheet that specifically relate to the issue being reviewed, evaluated or tested, and retain those completed sections in the work papers.

When reviewing audit or evaluating bank policies, a "No" answer indicates a possible exception/deficiency and should be explained in the work papers. When performing expanded procedures, a "No" answer indicates a violation and should be explained in the work papers. If a line item is not applicable within the area you are reviewing, indicate "NA."

Underline the applicable use: Audit   Bank Policies   Expanded Procedures

#16—Special Credit Card Rules					
Product Type: Borrower's Name: Account Number:	Yes No	Yes No	Yes No	Yes No	Yes No
Ability to Make the Required Minimum Payments					
1. Does the card issuer not open a credit card account for a consumer, or increase any credit limit applicable to such account, unless the card issuer considers the ability of the consumer to make the required minimum periodic payments under the terms of the account based on the consumer's income or assets and current obligations? [226.51(a)(1)(i)]					
2. Does the card issuer establish and maintain reasonable written policies and procedures to consider a consumer's income or assets and current obligations; and do these policies and procedures to consider a consumer's ability to make the required payments including a consideration of at least one of the following: a. The ratio of debt obligations to income? b. The ratio of debt obligations to assets? c. The income the consumer will have after paying debt obligations? [226.51(a)(1)(ii)]					
3. Does the card issuer not issue a credit card to a consumer who does not have any income or					

#16—Special Credit Card Rules										
Product Type: Borrower's Name: Account Number:										
	Yes	No	Yes	No	Yes	No	Yes	No	Yes	No
assets; and does the creditor not issue a credit card without reviewing any information about a consumer's income, assets, or current obligations? [226.51(a)(1)(ii)]										
4. Does the card issuer use a reasonable method for estimating the minimum periodic payments the consumer would be required to pay under the terms of the account? [226.51(a)(2)(i)]										

5. Does the card issuer's estimate of the minimum periodic payment use the following method to receive the benefit of the safe harbor?
 	
a. The card issuer assumes utilization, from the first day of the billing cycle, of the full credit line that the issuer is considering offering to the consumer?
 	
b. The card issuer uses a minimum payment formula employed by the issuer for the product the issuer is considering offering to the consumer or, in the case of an existing account, the minimum payment formula that currently applies to that account, provided that:
 	
    i) If the applicable minimum payment formula includes interest charges, the card issuer estimates those charges using an interest rate that the issuer is considering offering to the consumer for purchases or, in the case of an existing account, the interest rate that currently applies to purchases?
 	
    ii) If the applicable minimum payment formula includes mandatory fees, the card issuer must assume that such fees have										

#16—Special Credit Card Rules										
Product Type: Borrower's Name: Account Number:										
	Yes	No	Yes	No	Yes	No	Yes	No	Yes	No
been charged to the account? [226.51(a)(2)(ii)]										
6. If the card issuer opens a credit card account for a consumer less than 21 years old, does the issuer require that such consumers: a. Submit a written application b. Possess an independent ability to make the required minimum periodic payments on this credit card or provide a signed agreement of a cosigner, guarantor, or joint applicant who is at least 21 years old who will be either jointly or secondarily liable for any debt on the account incurred by the consumer before the consumer has attained the age of 21, and financial information indicating such cosigner, guarantor, or joint applicant has the ability to make the required minimum periodic payments on such debts, consistent with 226.51(a)? [226.51(b)(1)]										
7. If a credit card account has been opened for a consumer less than 21 years old with a cosigner, guarantor, or joint applicant pursuant to 226.51(b)(1), does the issuer not increase the credit limit on such account before the consumer attains the age of 21 unless the cosigner, guarantor, or joint accountholder who assumed liability at account opening agrees in writing to assume liability on the increase? [226.51(b)(2)]										
Limitations on Fees										
8. During the first year after the opening of a credit card account, did the card issuer refrain from requiring the consumer to pay covered fees in excess of the 25 percent of the credit limit at the time of the account opening? [226.52(a)]										

#16—Special Credit Card Rules										
Product Type: Borrower's Name: Account Number:	Yes	No	Yes	No	Yes	No	Yes	No	Yes	No
9. Does the card issuer refrain from imposing a fee for violating the terms or other requirements of a credit card account under an open-end (not home-secured) consumer credit plan, unless the dollar amount of the fee is consistent with 226.52(b)(1) and (b)(2)? [226.52(b)]										
10. If the issuer relies on the cost-determination review to impose a fee for a particular violation (e.g., late payment), has the issuer: a. Determined that the fee represents a reasonable proportion of the total costs incurred by the issuer as a result of that type of violation? b. Reevaluated this determination at least once every 12 months? c. Imposed the lower fee within 45 days after completing the reevaluation if the result of the reevaluation indicates that a lower fee represents a reasonable proportion of the total costs incurred by the issuer as a result of that type of violation? d. Complied with the notice requirements of 226.9, before imposing the higher fee, if the result of the reevaluation indicates that a higher fee represents a reasonable proportion of the total costs incurred by the issuer as a result of that type of violation? [226.52(b)(1)(i)] Note: Refer to the commentary for 226.52(b)] for a list of factors to be considered in the cost determination review by the issuer.										
11. If the issuer is relying on the safe harbor penalty fee provision, has the issuer refrained from imposing a fee for a particular violation										

#16—Special Credit Card Rules										
Product Type: Borrower's Name: Account Number:										
	Yes	No	Yes	No	Yes	No	Yes	No	Yes	No
(i.e., late payment) in excess of the regulatory limits: a. Of $25.00 for the first violation of a particular type, amount adjusted annually? b. Of $35.00 for an additional violation of the same type during the next six billing cycles, amount adjusted annually? c. Of 3 percent of the delinquent balance when a card issuer has not received the required payment for two or more consecutive billing cycles for a charge card account that requires payment of outstanding balances in full at the end of each billing cycle? [226.52(b)(1)(ii)]										
12. Has the card issuer refrained from imposing a fee for violating the terms or other requirements of a credit card account under an open-end (not home-secured) consumer credit plan that exceeds the dollar amount associated with the violation? [226.52(b)(2)(i)(A)]										
13. Has the card issuer refrained from imposing a fee for violating the terms or other requirements of a credit card account under an open-end (not home-secured) consumer credit plan when there is no dollar amount associated with the violation, including: a. Transactions that the card issuer declines to authorize; b. Account inactivity; and c. The closure or termination of an account? [226.52(b)(2)(i)(B)]										
14. Has the card issuer refrained from imposing more than one fee for violating the terms or other requirements of a credit card account under an open-end (not home-secured) consumer credit plan based on a single event or transaction? [226.52(b)(2)(ii)]										

#16—Special Credit Card Rules										
Product Type: Borrower's Name: Account Number:										
	Yes	No	Yes	No	Yes	No	Yes	No	Yes	No
Allocation of Payments in Excess of the Minimum										
15. When a consumer makes a payment in excess of the required minimum periodic payment, does the card issuer allocate the excess amount first to the balance with the highest annual percentage rate, and any remaining portion to the other balances in descending order based on the applicable annual percentage rate? [226.53(a)]										
16. For balances on a credit card account subject to a deferred interest or similar program, did the card issuer allocate any amount paid by the consumer in excess of the required minimum periodic payment consistent with 226.53(a), except that, during the two billing cycles immediately preceding expiration of the deferred interest period, the excess amount must have been allocated first to the balance subject to the deferred interest or similar program and any remaining portion allocated to any other balances; or in the manner requested by the consumer? [226.53(b)]										
Loss of a Grace Period										
17. Did the card issuer refrain from imposing finance charges as a result of the loss of a grace period on a credit card account based on balances for days in billing cycles that precede the most recent billing cycle or any portion of a balance subject to a grace period that was repaid prior to the expiration of the grace period? [226.54(a)] Note: 226.54(a) does not apply to adjustments to finance charges as a result of the resolution of a dispute under 225.12 or 226.13 or adjustments to finance charges as a result of the return of a payment.										
Limitations on Increasing APR, Fees, and Charges										
18. Unless one of the following exceptions applies, did the card issuer not increase an APR or fee or charge required to be disclosed										

#16—Special Credit Card Rules										
Product Type: Borrower's Name: Account Number:	Yes	No	Yes	No	Yes	No	Yes	No	Yes	No
under §226.6(b)(2)(ii) (example: an annual fee), (b)(2)(iii) (fixed finance charge or minimum interest charge), or (b)(2)(xii) (fee for required insurance, debt cancellation, or debt suspension coverage)? [226.55(a)] Exceptions: Temporary rate, variable rate, advance notice, delinquency, workout and temporary hardship arrangement, and Servicemembers Civil Relief Act. [226.55(b)]										

19. If the temporary rate exception applies, did the card issuer:
 	
  a. Not apply an APR to transactions that occurred prior to the period that exceeds the APR that applied to those transactions prior to the period?
 	
  b. Provide the required notice, but not apply an APR to transactions that occurred within 14 days after provision of the notice that exceeds the APR that applied to that category of transactions prior to provision of the notice
 	
  c. Not apply an annual percentage rate to transactions that occurred during the period that exceeds the increased annual percentage rate? [226.55(b)(1)ii)]
 	
Note: To assess whether the temporary rate exception applies, determine whether the card issuer increased the APR upon the expiration of a specified period of six months or longer; and prior to the commencement of that period, the card issuer disclosed in writing to the consumer, in a clear and conspicuous manner, the length of the period and the APR that would apply after expiration of the period.										

20. If the variable rate exception applies, did the card issuer not increase an APR unless the increase in the APR is due to an increase in the index and the APR varies according to an										

#16—Special Credit Card Rules										
Product Type: Borrower's Name: Account Number:										
	Yes	No	Yes	No	Yes	No	Yes	No	Yes	No
index that is not under the card issuer's control and is available to the general public? [226.55(b)(2)] Note: For purposes of qualifying under this exception, an index is considered under the card issuer's control if the card issuer applies a minimum rate or floor below which the rate cannot decrease. However, because there is no disadvantage to consumers, issuers are not prevented from setting a maximum rate or ceiling.										

21. If the advance notice exception applies, did the card issuer:
 	
  a. Not apply that increased APR, fee, or charge to transactions that occurred prior to provision of the notice?
 	
  b. Not apply the increased APR, fee, or charge to transactions that occurred prior to or within 14 days after provision of the notice?
 	
  c. Not increase the APR, fee, or charge during the first year after the account is opened? [226.55(b)(3)]										

22. If the delinquency exception applies, did the card issuer disclose in a clear and conspicuous manner in the required notice a statement of the reason for the increase, and the fact that the increase will cease to apply if the card issuer receives six consecutive required minimum periodic payments on or before the payment due date, beginning with the first payment due following the effective date of the increase? [226.55(b)(4)]										
23. If the delinquency exception applies and the card issuer received six consecutive required minimum periodic payments on or before the payment due date beginning with the first payment due following the effective date of the increase, did the card issuer reduce any										

#16—Special Credit Card Rules										
Product Type: Borrower's Name: Account Number:										
	Yes	No	Yes	No	Yes	No	Yes	No	Yes	No
APR, fee, or charge (increased pursuant to the delinquency exception) to the original APR, fee, or charge that applied prior to the increase with respect to transactions that occurred prior to or within 14 days after provision of the required notice? [226.55(b)(4)(ii)]										
24. If the workout and temporary hardship arrangement exception applies, prior to commencement of the arrangement (except as provided in 226.9(c)(2)(v)(D)) did the card issuer provide the consumer with a clear and conspicuous written disclosure of the terms of the arrangement (including any increases due to the completion or failure of the arrangement); and upon the completion or failure of the arrangement, did the card issuer not apply to any transactions that occurred prior to commencement of the arrangement an APR, fee, or charge that exceeds the APR, fee, or charge that applied to those transactions prior to commencement of the arrangement? [226.55(b)(5)]										
25. If the Servicemembers Civil Relief Act exception applies, did the card issuer increase the APR only after 50 USC app. 527 no longer applied; and did the issuer not apply to any transactions that occurred prior to the decrease an APR that exceeded the APR that applied to those transactions prior to the decrease? [226.55(b)(6)]										
26. For protected balances, did the card issuer not require repayment using a method that is less beneficial to the consumer than one of the following methods: a. The method of repayment for the account before the effective date of the increase? b. An amortization period of not less than five years, beginning no earlier than the effective date of the increase?										

#16—Special Credit Card Rules										
Product Type: Borrower's Name: Account Number:	Yes	No	Yes	No	Yes	No	Yes	No	Yes	No
c. A required minimum periodic payment that includes a percentage of the balance that is equal to no more than twice the percentage required before the effective date of the increase? [226.55(c)]										
Requirements for Over-the-Limit Transactions										
27. Does the card issuer provide a written over-the-limit notice prior to the assessment of any over-the-limit fee or charge on a consumer's account? [226.56(d)(1)(i)]										
28. If a consumer consents to the card issuer's payment of any over-the-limit transaction by oral or electronic means, does the card issuer provide the required written notice immediately prior to obtaining that consent? [226.56(d)(1)(ii)]										
29. Is the written (or if the consumer agrees, electronic) notice confirming the consumer's consent provided no later than the first periodic statement sent after the consumer has consented to the card issuer's payment of over-the-limit transactions? [226.56(d)(2)]										
30. Is the written notice providing the consumer notice of the right to revoke consent following the assessment of an over-the-limit fee or charge provided on the front of any page of each periodic statement that reflects the assessment of an over-the-limit fee or charge on a consumer's account? [226.56(d)(3)]										
31. Does the oral, written, or electronic "opt-in" notice include all of the following applicable items (and not any information not specified in or otherwise permitted): a. The dollar amount of any fees or charges assessed by the card issuer on a consumer's account for an over-the-limit transaction?										

#16—Special Credit Card Rules										
Product Type: Borrower's Name: Account Number:										
	Yes	No	Yes	No	Yes	No	Yes	No	Yes	No
b. Any increased APR(s) that may be imposed on the account as a result of an over-the-limit transaction? c. An explanation of the consumer's right to affirmatively consent to the card issuer's payment of over-the-limit transactions, including the method(s) by which the consumer may consent? [226.56(e)(1)]										
32. Does the written notice informing the consumer of the right to revoke consent following the assessment of an over-the-limit fee or charge describe that right, including the method(s) by which the consumer may revoke consent? [226.56(e)(2)]										
33. If two or more consumers are jointly liable on a credit card account, does the card issuer treat the affirmative consent of any of the joint consumers as affirmative consent for that account and does the card issuer treat a revocation of consent by any of the joint consumers as revocation of consent for that account? [226.56(f)]										
34. If the credit limit was exceeded during the billing cycle, does the card issuer not impose more than one over-the-limit fee or charge on a consumer's credit card account per billing cycle; and does the card issuer not impose an over-the-limit fee or charge on the consumer's credit card account for more than three billing cycles for the same over-the-limit transaction where the consumer has not reduced the account balance below the credit limit by the payment due date for either of the last two billing cycles? [226.56(j)(1)]										
35. Does the card issuer not impose an over-the-limit fee or charge solely because of the card issuer's failure to promptly replenish the consumer's available credit following the crediting of the consumer's payment? [226.56(j)(2)]										

#16—Special Credit Card Rules										
Product Type: Borrower's Name: Account Number:	Yes	No	Yes	No	Yes	No	Yes	No	Yes	No
36. Does the card issuer not condition the amount of a consumer's credit limit on the consumer affirmatively consenting to the card issuer's payment of over-the-limit transactions if the card issuer assesses a fee or charge for such service? [226.56(j)(3)]										
37. Does the card issuer not impose an over-the-limit fee or charge for a billing cycle if a consumer exceeds a credit limit solely because of fees or interest charged by the card issuer (defined as charges imposed as part of the plan under 226.6(b)(3)) to the consumer's account during that billing cycle? [226.56(j)(4)]										
Reporting Rules for College Credit Card Agreements										
38. If the credit card issuer was a party to one or more college credit card agreements in effect at any time during a calendar year, did the card issuer submit to the Board an annual report regarding those agreements in the form and manner prescribed by the Board? [226.57(d)(1)]										
39. Does the annual report include the following: a. Identifying information about the card issuer and the agreements submitted, including the issuer's name, address, and identifying number (such as an RSSD ID number or tax identification number)? b. A copy of any college credit card agreement to which the card issuer was a party that was in effect at any time during the period covered by the report? c. A copy of any memorandum of understanding in effect at any time during the period covered by the report between the card issuer and an institution of higher education or affiliated organization that directly or indirectly relates to the college credit card agreement or that controls or										

#16—Special Credit Card Rules										
Product Type: Borrower's Name: Account Number:										
	Yes	No	Yes	No	Yes	No	Yes	No	Yes	No
directs any obligations or distribution of benefits between any such entities?										
d. The total dollar amount of any payments pursuant to a college credit card agreement from the card issuer to an institution of higher education or affiliated organization during the period covered by the report, and the method or formula used to determine such amounts?										
e. The total number of credit card accounts opened pursuant to any college credit card agreement during the period covered by the report?										
f. The total number of credit card accounts opened pursuant to any such agreement that were open at the end of the period covered by the report? [226.57(d)(2)]										
40. If the card issuer is subject to reporting, does the card issuer submit its annual report for each calendar year to the Board by the first business day on or after March 31 of the following calendar year? (However, card issuers must submit the first report following the effective date of this section, providing information for the 2009 calendar year, to the Board by February 22, 2010.) [226.57(d)(3)]										
Internet Posting of Credit Card Agreements										
41. Unless it meets one of the exceptions in the regulation, does the card issuer make quarterly submissions to the Board, in the form and manner by the Board, that contain: a. Identifying information about the card issuer and the agreements submitted, including the issuer's name, address, and identifying number (such as an RSSD ID number or tax identification number)? b. The credit card agreements that the card issuer offered to the public as of the last										

#16—Special Credit Card Rules										
Product Type: Borrower's Name: Account Number:										
	Yes	No	Yes	No	Yes	No	Yes	No	Yes	No
business day of the preceding calendar quarter that the card issuer has not previously submitted to the Board? c. Any credit card agreement previously submitted to the Board that was amended during the preceding calendar quarter? d. Notification regarding any credit card agreement previously submitted to the Board that the issuer is withdrawing? [226.58(c)(1)]										
42. Did the card issuer send its first credit card agreement submission to the Board no later than February 22, 2010 and did the first submission contain the credit card agreements that the card issuer offered to the public as of December 31, 2009? [226.58(c)(2)]										
43. Did the card issuer send its second credit card agreement submission to the Board no later than August 2, 2010; and did it contain: a. Any credit card agreement that the card issuer offered to the public as of June 30, 2010 that the card issuer has not previously submitted to the Board? b. Any credit card agreement previously submitted to the Board that was amended after December 31, 2009, and on or before June 30, 2010? c. Notification regarding any credit card agreement previously submitted to the Board that the issuer is withdrawing as of June 30, 2010? [226.58(c)(2)]										

#16—Special Credit Card Rules										
Product Type: Borrower's Name: Account Number:										
	Yes	No	Yes	No	Yes	No	Yes	No	Yes	No
44. Except for the first two submissions on February 22, 2010 and August 2, 2010, did the card issuer send its credit card agreement quarterly submissions to the Board no later than the first business day on or after January 31, April 30, July 31, and October 31 of each year? [226.58(c)(1)]										
45. If a credit card agreement that previously has been submitted to the Board is amended, did the card issuer submit the entire amended agreement to the Board by the first quarterly submission deadline after the last day of the calendar quarter in which the change became effective? [226.58(c)(3)]										
46. If a card issuer no longer offers to the public a credit card agreement that previously has been submitted to the Board, did the card issuer notify the Board by the first quarterly submission deadline after the last day of the calendar quarter in which the issuer ceased to offer the agreement? [226.58(c)(4)]										
47. If an issuer that previously qualified for the de minimis exception ceases to qualify, did the card issuer begin making quarterly submissions to the Board no later than the first quarterly submission deadline after the date as of which the issuer ceased to qualify? [226.58(c)(5)(ii)]										
48. If a card issuer that did not previously qualify for the de minimis exception qualifies for the de minimis exception, did the card issuer continue to make quarterly submissions to the Board until the issuer notifies the Board that the card issuer is withdrawing all agreements it previously submitted to the Board?[226.58(c)(5)(iii)]										
49. If an agreement that previously qualified for the private label credit card exception ceases to qualify, did the card issuer submit the agreement to the Board no later than the first quarterly submission deadline after the date as										

#16—Special Credit Card Rules										
Product Type: Borrower's Name: Account Number:	Yes	No	Yes	No	Yes	No	Yes	No	Yes	No
of which the agreement ceased to qualify? [226.58(c)(6)(ii)]										
50. If an agreement that did not previously qualify for the private label credit card exception qualifies for the exception, did the card issuer continue to make quarterly submissions to the Board with respect to that agreement until the issuer notifies the Board that the agreement is being withdrawn? [226.58(c)(6)(iii)]										
51. If an agreement that previously qualified for the product testing exception ceases to qualify, did the card issuer submit the agreement to the Board no later than the first quarterly submission deadline after the date as of which the agreement ceased to qualify? [226.58(c)(7)(ii)]										
52. If an agreement that did not previously qualify for the product testing exception qualifies for the exception, did the card issuer continue to make quarterly submissions to the Board with respect to that agreement until the issuer notifies the Board that the agreement is being withdrawn? [226.58(c)(7)(iii)]										
53. Does each agreement submitted to the Board contain the provisions of the agreement and the pricing information in effect as of the last business day of the preceding calendar quarter? [226.58(c)(8)(i)(A)]										
54. Does each agreement submitted to the Board exclude any personally identifiable information relating to any cardholder, such as name, address, telephone number, or account number? [226.58(c)(8)(i)(B)]										
55. Is each agreement submitted to the Board presented in a clear and legible font? [226.58(c)(8)(i)(D)]										
56. For each agreement submitted to the Board, is the pricing information set forth in a single addendum to the agreement that contains only the pricing information? [226.58(c)(8)(ii)(A)]										

#16—Special Credit Card Rules										
Product Type: Borrower's Name: Account Number:	Yes	No	Yes	No	Yes	No	Yes	No	Yes	No
57. If pricing information varies from one cardholder to another depending on the cardholder's creditworthiness or state of residence or other factors, is the pricing information disclosed either by setting forth all the possible variations or by providing a range of possible variations? [226.58(c)(8)(ii)(B)]										
58. If a rate included in the pricing information is a variable rate, did the issuer identify the index or formula used in setting the rate and the margin? [226.58(c)(8)(ii)(C)]										
59. If rates vary from one cardholder to another, did the issuer disclose such rates by providing the index and the possible margins or range of margins? [226.58(c)(8)(ii)(C)]										
60. Did the issuer refrain from providing provisions of the agreement or pricing information in the form of change-in-terms notices or riders (other than the pricing information addendum and the optional variable terms addendum)? [226.58(c)(8)(iv)]										
61. Were changes in provisions or pricing information integrated into the text of the agreement, the pricing information addendum or the optional variable terms addendum, as appropriate? [226.58(c)(8)(iv)]										
62. Does the card issuer post and maintain on its publicly available Web site the credit card agreements that the issuer is required to submit to the Board? [226.58(d)(1)]										
63. With respect to an agreement offered solely for accounts under one or more private label credit card plans (and the issuer does not post and maintain the agreements on its publicly available Web site), does the issuer post and maintain the agreement on the publicly available Web site of at least one of the merchants where cards issued under each private label credit card plan with 10,000 or more open accounts may be used? [226.58(d)(1)]										
64. Do the agreements posted pursuant to §226.58(d) conform to the form and content										

#16—Special Credit Card Rules	Yes No	Yes No	Yes No	Yes No	Yes No
Product Type: Borrower's Name: Account Number:					
requirements for agreements submitted to the Board specified in §226.58(c)(8)? [226.58(d)(2)]					
65. Are agreements that are posted in an electronic format readily usable by the general public? [226.58(d)(3)]					
66. Are the agreements placed in a location on the issuer's Web site that is prominent and readily accessible by the public and accessible without submission of personally identifiable information? [226.58(d)(3)]					
67. Does the card issuer update the agreements posted on its Web site at least as frequently as the quarterly schedule required for submission of agreements to the Board? [226.58(d)(4)]					
68. For any open credit card account (i.e., the cardholder can obtain extensions or there is an outstanding balance on the account that has not been charged off), does the card issuer either: a. Post and maintain the cardholder's agreement on its Web site? b. Promptly provide a copy of the cardholder's agreement to the cardholder upon the cardholder's request? [226.58(e)(1)] Note: Card issuers may provide credit card agreements in electronic form under 226.58(d) and (e) without regard to the consumer notice and consent requirements of section 101(c) of the E-Sign Act.					
69. If the card issuer makes an agreement available upon request, does the issuer provide the cardholder with the ability to request a copy of the agreement both by:					

#16—Special Credit Card Rules										
Product Type: Borrower's Name: Account Number:	Yes	No	Yes	No	Yes	No	Yes	No	Yes	No
a. Using the issuer's Web site (such as by clicking on a clearly identified box to make the request)? b. Calling a readily available telephone line the number for which is displayed on the issuer's Web site and clearly identified as to purpose? [226.58(e)(1)(ii) and (e)(2)]										
70. If an issuer does not maintain a Web site from which cardholders can access specific information about their individual accounts, does the issuer make agreements available upon request by providing the cardholder with the ability to request a copy of the agreement by calling a readily available telephone line the number for which is: a. Displayed on the issuer's Web site and clearly identified as to purpose? b. Included on each periodic statement sent to the cardholder and clearly identified as to purpose? [226.58(e)(2)]										
71. Does the card issuer send to the cardholder or otherwise make available to the cardholder a copy of the cardholder's agreement in electronic or paper form no later than 30 days after the issuer receives the cardholder's request? [226.58(e)(1)(ii) or (e)(2)]										
72. Do agreements posted on the card issuer's Web site or made available upon the cardholder's request conform to the form and content requirements for agreements submitted to the Board? [226.58(e)(3)(i)]										
73. If the card issuer posts an agreement on its Web site or otherwise provides an agreement to a cardholder electronically, is the agreement posted or provided in an electronic format that is readily usable by the general public and placed in a location that is prominent and readily accessible to the cardholder? [226.58(e)(3)(ii)]										

#16—Special Credit Card Rules										
Product Type: Borrower's Name: Account Number:	Yes	No	Yes	No	Yes	No	Yes	No	Yes	No
74. If agreements posted or otherwise provided contain personally identifiable information relating to the cardholder, such as name, address, telephone number, or account number, does the issuer take appropriate measures to make the agreement accessible only to the cardholder or other authorized persons? [226.58(e)(3)(iii)]										
75. Do agreements posted or otherwise provided set forth the specific provisions and pricing information applicable to the particular cardholder? [226.58(e)(3)(iv)]										
76. For agreements posted or otherwise provided to the cardholder, are the provisions and pricing information complete and accurate as of a date no more than 60 days prior to: a. The date on which the agreement is posted on the card issuer's Web site under §226.58(e)(1)(i)? b. The date the cardholder's request is received under §226.58(e)(1)(ii) or (e)(2)? [226.58(e)(3)(iv)]										
Reevaluation of Rate Increases										
Note: Section 226.59 does not apply to increases in an APR that was previously decreased pursuant to 50 USC app. 527 (Servicemembers Civil Relief Act), provided the increase is made in accordance with 226.55(b)(6), and to accounts that the issuer has charged off in accordance with loan-loss provisions. In addition, the required 226.59(a)(1) review ceases in certain situations as described at 226.59(f). 77. If a card issuer increases an APR that applies to a credit card account under an open-end (not home-secured) consumer credit plan, based on the credit risk of the consumer, market conditions, or other factors, or increased such										

#16—Special Credit Card Rules										
Product Type: Borrower's Name: Account Number:										
	Yes	No	Yes	No	Yes	No	Yes	No	Yes	No
an APR on or after January 1, 2009, and 45 days' advance notice of the APR increase is required pursuant to 226.9(c)(2) or (g), has the card issuer evaluated the factors at 226.59(d) and, based on its review of such factors, reduced the APR applicable to the consumer's account, as appropriate? [226.59(a)(1)]										
78. If a card issuer is required to reduce the APR applicable to an account pursuant to 226.59(a)(1), has the card issuer reduced the APR not later than 45 days after completion of the evaluation? [226.59(a)(2)(i)] Note: Any reduction in an APR required pursuant to 226.59(a)(1) of this section shall apply to any outstanding balances to which the increased APR per 226.59(a)(1) has been applied and new transactions that occur after the effective date of the APR reduction that would otherwise have been subject to the increased APR.										
79. Does the card issuer have reasonable written policies and procedures in place to conduct the 226.59(a)(1) review? [226.59(b)]										
80. Does the card issuer conduct the 226.59(a)(1) review at least once every six months after the APR increase? [226.59(c)]										
81. Except for the first two 226.59(a)(1) reviews for APR increases imposed between January 1, 2009, and February 21, 2010, did the card issuer review either the factors on which the increase in an APR was originally based or the factors that the card issuer currently considers when determining the APRs applicable to similar new credit card accounts under an open-end (not home-secured) consumer credit plan? [226.59(d)(1)]										

#16—Special Credit Card Rules										
Product Type: Borrower's Name: Account Number:	Yes	No	Yes	No	Yes	No	Yes	No	Yes	No
82. When conducting the first two 226.59(a)(1) reviews for APR increases imposed between January 1, 2009, and February 21, 2010, unless the APR increase subject to this review was based solely upon factors specific to the consumer, such as a decline in the consumer's credit risk, the consumer's delinquency or default, or a violation of the terms of the account, did the issuer consider the factors that it currently considers when determining the APR applicable to similar new credit card accounts under an open-end (not home-secured) consumer credit plan? [226.59(d)(2)]										
83. If an issuer increases an APR applicable to a consumer's account pursuant to 226.55(b)(4) (60 day delinquency) and the APR is not subsequently reduced (after 6 consecutive on-time minimum payments), did the card issuer perform the 226.59(a)(1) review and did the first such review occur no later than six months after the sixth payment due date following the effective date of the APR increase? [226.59(e)] Note: The issuer is not required to perform the 226.59(a)(1) review prior to the sixth payment due date after the effective date of the increase.										
84. If a card issuer that acquires credit card accounts from another issuer complies with 226.59 by reviewing the factors described in 226.59(d)(1)(i), does the issuer review the factors considered by the card issuer from which it acquired the accounts? [226.59(g)(1)] Note: This does not apply if the card issuer performs the 226.59(g)(2) review [226.59(g)]										

#16—Special Credit Card Rules										
Product Type: Borrower's Name: Account Number:	Yes	No	Yes	No	Yes	No	Yes	No	Yes	No
85. If, not later than six months after the acquisition of such accounts, a card issuer reviews all of the credit card accounts it acquired in accordance with the factors that it currently considers in determining the rates applicable to its similar new credit card accounts, has the card issuer conducted the 226.59(a)(1) review for rate increases that are imposed as a result of this review, except as provided at 226.59(g)(2)(iii),? [226.59(g)(2)(i)] Note: Except as provided in 226.59(g)(2)(iii), a card issuer that performs the 226.59(g)(2) review is not required to conduct 226.59(a)(1) reviews for any rate increases made prior to the card issuer's acquisition of such accounts. [226.59(g)(2)(ii)]										
86. If, as a result of the card issuer's review of acquired portfolios, an account is subject to, or continues to be subject to, an increased rate as a penalty, or because of the consumer's delinquency or default, has the card issuer complied with the requirements at 226.59(a), i.e., evaluated the factors at 226.59(d) and made any applicable rate reductions? [226.59(g)(2)(iii)]										
87. Has the creditor retained evidence of compliance with regulation Z for two years after the date disclosures were required to be made or action was required to be taken? [226.25(a)]										

Worksheet #17—Reimbursement Review

Use this worksheet to determine if there is noncompliance involving understated finance charges or understated APRs subject to reimbursement under the FFIEC Policy Guide on Reimbursement (Policy Guide). When verifying APR accuracy and reimbursement amounts, use the current version of the OCC's APRWin program, located in the applications section of your computer software (or download from OCC.gov).

#17—Reimbursement Review Worksheet	
Procedure	Date Completed
1. Document the date on which the administrative enforcement of the TILA Policy Guide would apply to closed-end credit for reimbursement purposes by determining the date of the preceding examination of any type. Preceding Examination Date: _____	

2. If the noncompliance involves indirect (third-party paper) disclosure errors and affected consumers have not been reimbursed:
 	
  a. Prepare comments on the need for improved internal controls, for inclusion in the report of examination.
 	
  b. Notify your supervisory office for follow-up with the regulator that has primary responsibility for the original creditor.	

3. If the noncompliance involves direct credit, make an initial determination if the disclosure error resulted from a clear and consistent pattern or practice of violations, gross negligence, or a willful violation that was intended to mislead the consumer. Consider:
 	
  a. If the conduct appears to be grounded in a written or unwritten policy or established practice.
 	
  b. If there is evidence of similar conduct by the bank in more than one transaction. (Note: More than one does not necessarily constitute a pattern or practice.) If there is a common source or cause within the bank's control.
 	
  c. The relationship of the instances of noncompliance to one another (i.e., if they all occurred in the same area of the bank, in the same product line, or by one employee).
 	
  d. The relationship of the number of instances of noncompliance to the bank's total activity. (Note: Depending on the circumstances, violations that involve only a small percentage of a bank's total activity could constitute a pattern or practice.)	

#17—Reimbursement Review Worksheet	
Procedure	Date Completed

4. For violations determined to be a pattern or practice, gross negligence, or willful, perform the following steps:
 	
  a. Calculate the reimbursement for the loans or accounts in an expanded sample of the identified population.
 	
  b. Estimate the total impact on the population based on the expanded sample.
 	
  c. Inform management that reimbursement may be necessary under the law and the Policy Guide, and discuss all substantive facts, including the sample loans and calculations.
 	
  d. Inform management of the bank's options under section 130 of the TILA for avoiding an OCC order to reimburse affected borrowers.	

Coverage Considerations Under Regulation Z

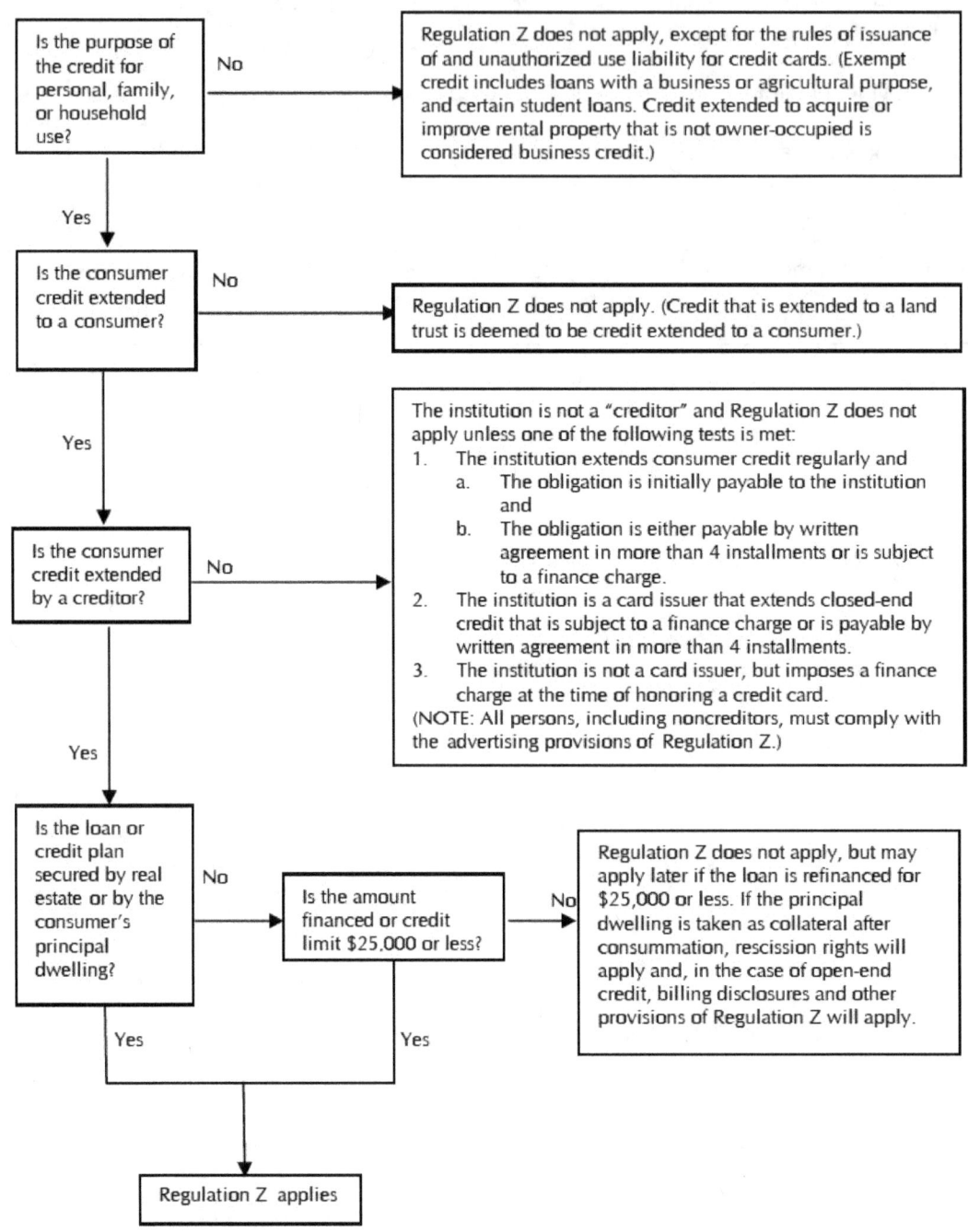

Is the purpose of the credit for personal, family, or household use?

— No → Regulation Z does not apply, except for the rules of issuance of and unauthorized use liability for credit cards. (Exempt credit includes loans with a business or agricultural purpose, and certain student loans. Credit extended to acquire or improve rental property that is not owner-occupied is considered business credit.)

Yes ↓

Is the consumer credit extended to a consumer?

— No → Regulation Z does not apply. (Credit that is extended to a land trust is deemed to be credit extended to a consumer.)

Yes ↓

Is the consumer credit extended by a creditor?

— No → The institution is not a "creditor" and Regulation Z does not apply unless one of the following tests is met:
1. The institution extends consumer credit regularly and
   a. The obligation is initially payable to the institution and
   b. The obligation is either payable by written agreement in more than 4 installments or is subject to a finance charge.
2. The institution is a card issuer that extends closed-end credit that is subject to a finance charge or is payable by written agreement in more than 4 installments.
3. The institution is not a card issuer, but imposes a finance charge at the time of honoring a credit card.
(NOTE: All persons, including noncreditors, must comply with the advertising provisions of Regulation Z.)

Yes ↓

Is the loan or credit plan secured by real estate or by the consumer's principal dwelling?

— No → **Is the amount financed or credit limit $25,000 or less?**

— No → Regulation Z does not apply, but may apply later if the loan is refinanced for $25,000 or less. If the principal dwelling is taken as collateral after consummation, rescission rights will apply and, in the case of open-end credit, billing disclosures and other provisions of Regulation Z will apply.

Yes (from "secured by real estate") ↓ / Yes (from "amount financed") ↓

Regulation Z applies

Finance Charge Chart

Finance Charge = Dollar Cost of Consumer Credit: It includes any charge payable directly or indirectly by the consumer and imposed directly or indirectly by the creditor as a condition of or incident to the extension of credit.

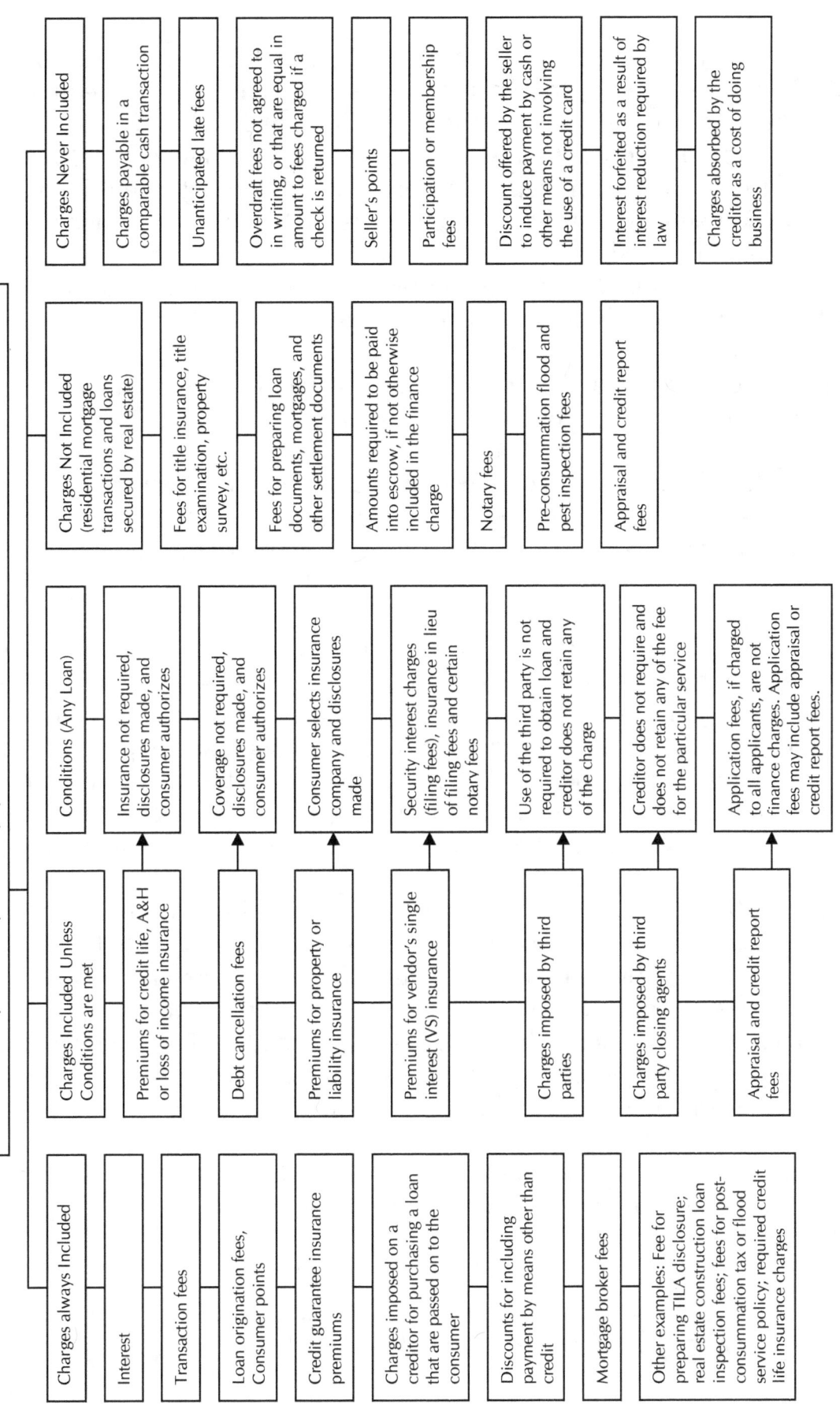

Charges always Included

- Interest
- Transaction fees
- Loan origination fees, Consumer points
- Credit guarantee insurance premiums
- Charges imposed on a creditor for purchasing a loan that are passed on to the consumer
- Discounts for including payment by means other than credit
- Mortgage broker fees
- Other examples: Fee for preparing TILA disclosure; real estate construction loan inspection fees; fees for post-consummation tax or flood service policy; required credit life insurance charges

Charges Included Unless Conditions are met

- Premiums for credit life, A&H or loss of income insurance
- Debt cancellation fees
- Premiums for property or liability insurance
- Premiums for vendor's single interest (VS) insurance
- Charges imposed by third parties
- Charges imposed by third party closing agents
- Appraisal and credit report fees

Conditions (Any Loan)

- Insurance not required, disclosures made, and consumer authorizes
- Coverage not required, disclosures made, and consumer authorizes
- Consumer selects insurance company and disclosures made
- Security interest charges (filing fees), insurance in lieu of filing fees and certain notary fees
- Use of the third party is not required to obtain loan and creditor does not retain any of the charge
- Creditor does not require and does not retain any of the fee for the particular service
- Application fees, if charged to all applicants, are not finance charges. Application fees may include appraisal or credit report fees.

Charges Not Included (residential mortgage transactions and loans secured by real estate)

- Fees for title insurance, title examination, property survey, etc.
- Fees for preparing loan documents, mortgages, and other settlement documents
- Amounts required to be paid into escrow, if not otherwise included in the finance charge
- Notary fees
- Pre-consummation flood and pest inspection fees
- Appraisal and credit report fees

Charges Never Included

- Charges payable in a comparable cash transaction
- Unanticipated late fees
- Overdraft fees not agreed to in writing, or that are equal in amount to fees charged if a check is returned
- Seller's points
- Participation or membership fees
- Discount offered by the seller to induce payment by cash or other means not involving the use of a credit card
- Interest forfeited as a result of interest reduction required by law
- Charges absorbed by the creditor as a cost of doing business

Instructions for the Finance Charge Chart

The finance charge initially includes any charge that is, or will be, connected with a specific loan. Charges imposed by third parties are finance charges if the creditor requires use of the third party or to the extent the creditor retains a portion of the charge. Charges imposed on the consumer by a settlement agent are finance charges only if the creditor requires the particular services for which the settlement agent is charging the borrower and the charge is not otherwise excluded from the finance charge or to the extent the creditor retains a portion of the charge. Immediately below the finance charge definition, the chart presents five captions applicable to determining if a loan-related charge is a finance charge.

The first caption is "charges always included." This category focuses on specific charges given in the regulation or commentary as examples of finance charges.

The second caption, "charges included unless conditions are met," focuses on charges that must be included in the finance charge unless the creditor meets specific disclosure or other conditions to exclude the charges from the finance charge.

The third caption, "conditions," focuses on the conditions that need to be met if the charges identified to the left of the conditions are permitted to be excluded from the finance charge. Although most charges under the second caption may be included in the finance charge at the creditor's option, third party charges and application fees (listed last under the third caption) must be excluded from the finance charge if the relevant conditions are met. However, inclusion of appraisal and credit report charges as part of an application fee that is charged to all applicants is optional.

The fourth caption, "charges not included," identifies fees or charges that are not included in the finance charge under conditions identified by the caption. If the credit transaction is secured by real property or the loan is a residential mortgage transaction, the charges identified in the column, if they are bona fide and reasonable in amount, must be excluded from the finance charge. For example, if a vacant lot or commercial real estate secures a consumer loan, any appraisal fees connected with the loan must not be included in the finance charge.

The fifth caption, "charges never included," lists specific charges provided by the regulation as examples of those that automatically are not finance charges (e.g., fees for unanticipated late payments).

Note: In the first column for the charges always included, transaction fees refer to transaction fees imposed in connection with the credit feature. In the third column for conditions, the condition for both the premiums for credit life, A&H, or loss of income and debt cancellation fees must include affirmative consumer authority. Finally, in the last column of charges never included, over limit fees can be considered as an excludable charge.

Closed-End Credit: Finance Charge Accuracy Tolerances

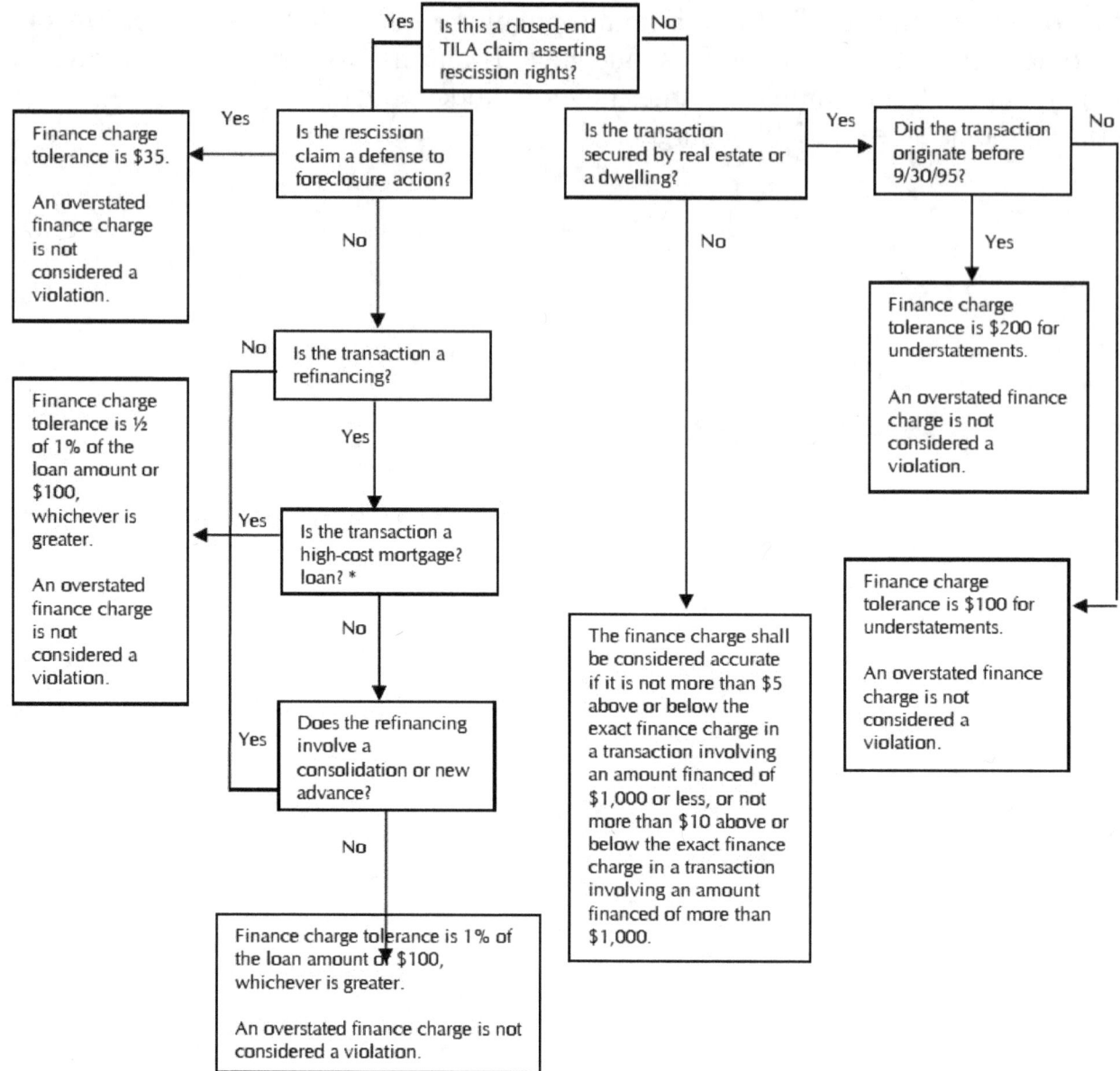

* See 15 USC 1602(aa) and 12 CFR 226.32.

Closed-End Credit: Accuracy and Reimbursement Tolerances for Understated Finance Charges

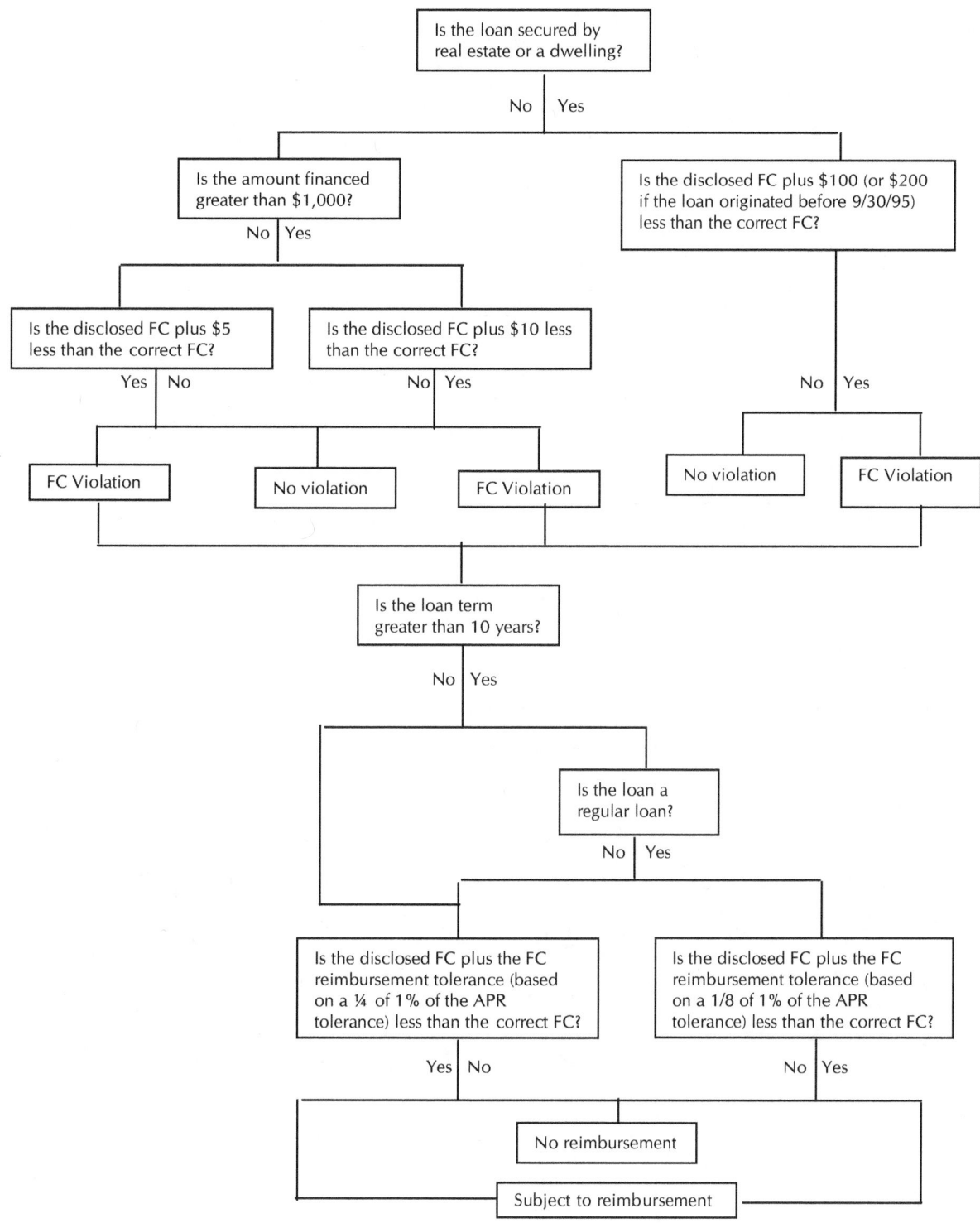

Closed-End Credit: Accuracy Tolerances for Overstated Finance Charges

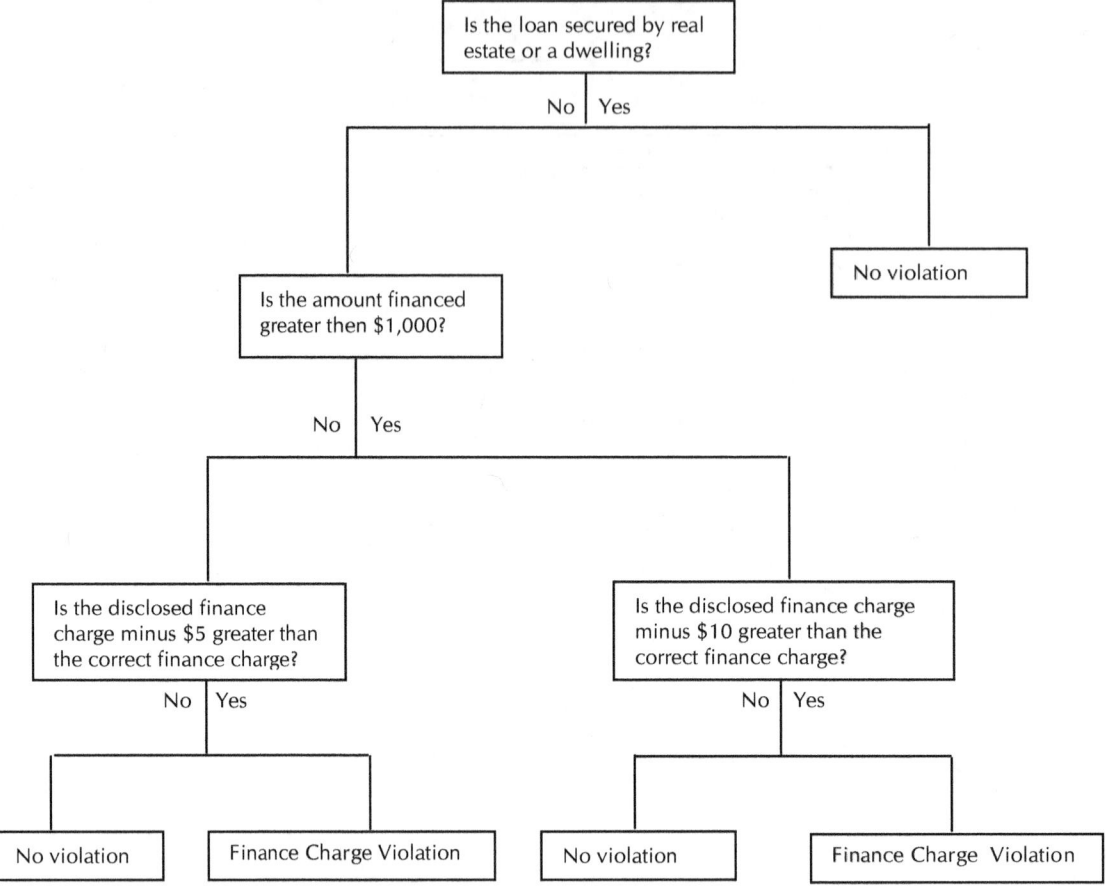

Note: While an overstated Finance Charge is a Regulation Z violation, it is not reimbursable.

Closed-End Credit: Accuracy Tolerances for Overstated APRs

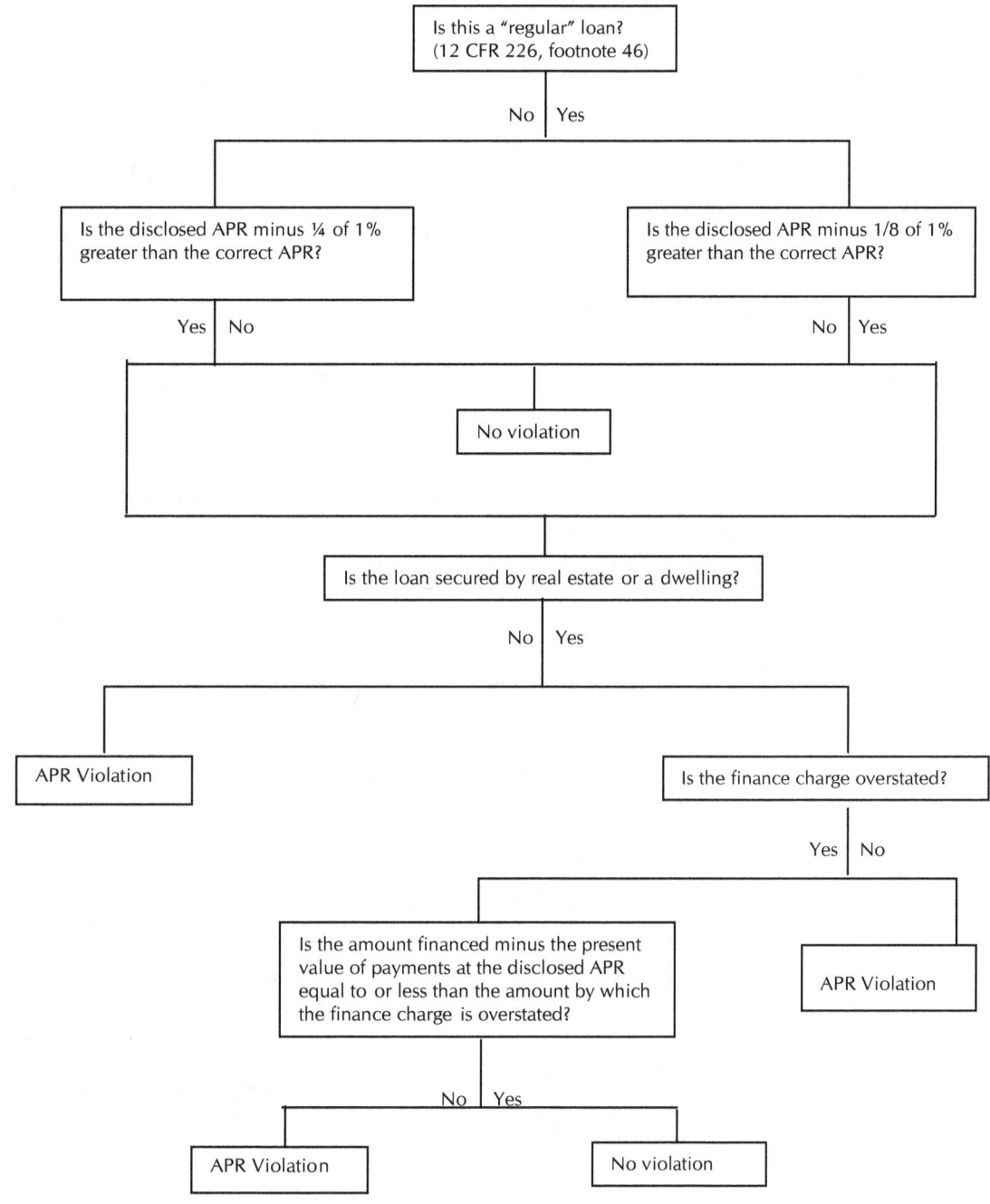

Closed-End Credit: Accuracy and Reimbursement Tolerances for Understated APRs

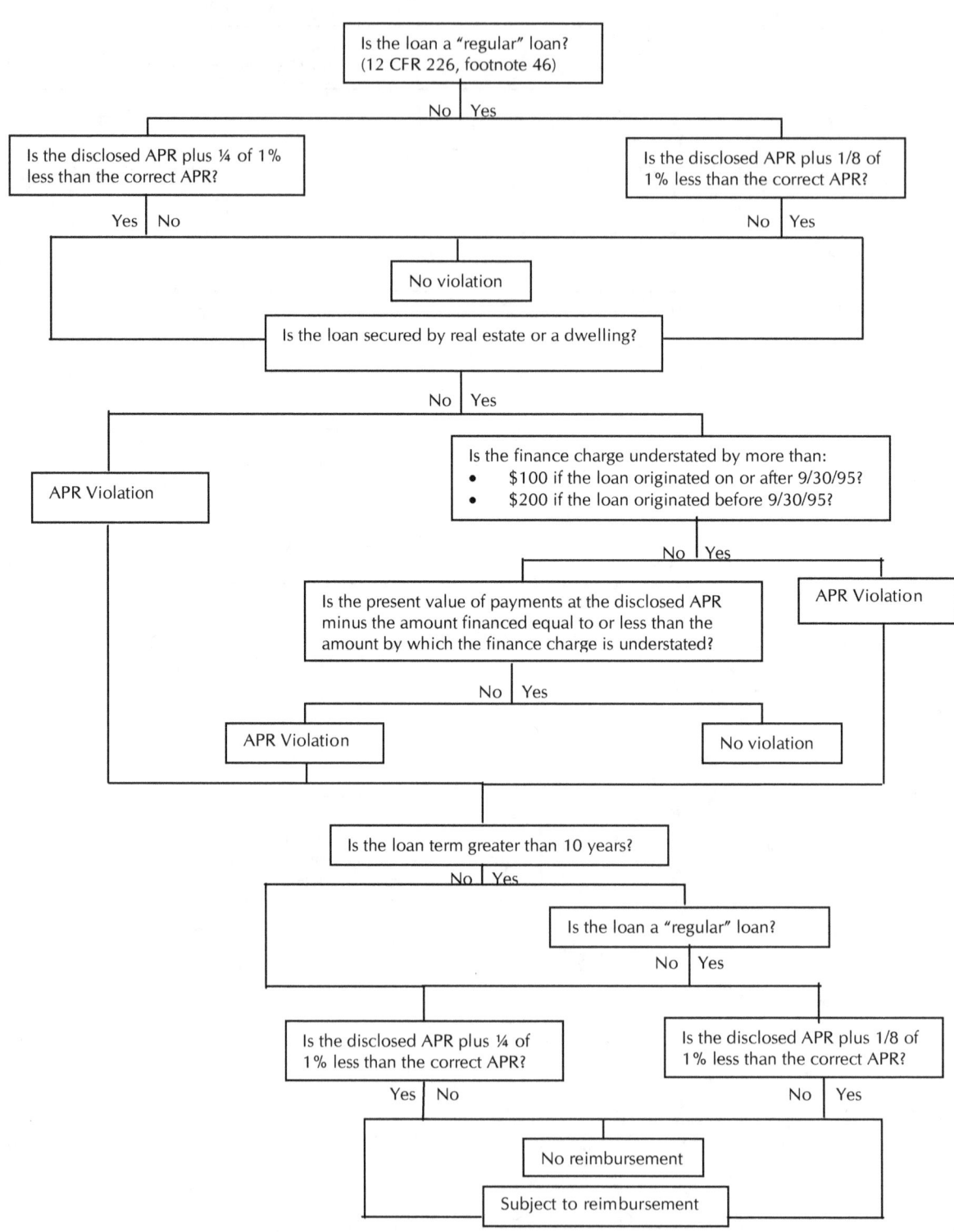

Summary of Coverage Rules for ARMs

OCC's ARM Regulation 12 CFR 34.20

Variable rate loans to purchase or refinance a one- to four-family dwelling and secured by a lien on such a dwelling.

Includes:

- Open-end credit.
- Closed-end credit.
- Consumer-purchase loans.
- Loans to consumers.
- Loans with a business purpose.
- Loans to businesses.
- Loans for second and vacation homes.

Excludes:

- Short-term, fixed rate, nonamortizing loans, even if the creditor is committed to renew (unless the renewal is for the full amortization period).
- Fixed rate demand loans.

Regulation Z ARMs 12 CFR 226.19(b)

Variable rate loans secured by the consumer's principal dwelling.

Includes:

- Loans subject to closed-end credit provisions of Regulation Z.
- Short-term, fixed rate loans, if creditor is committed to renew.
- Loans with maturity greater than one year.

Excludes:

- Business purpose loans.
- Open-end credit (separate open-end HELOC provisions apply).
- Any loans not subject to Regulation Z.
- Loans with maturity of one year or less (unless creditor is committed to renew and total period surpasses one year).
- Second home loans, vacation home loans, short-term bridge loans, short-term construction loans.

Joint Policy Statement on Administrative Enforcement of the Truth in Lending Act—Restitution

The Depository Institutions Deregulation and Monetary Control Act of 1980 (Pub. L. 96-221) was enacted on March 31, 1980. Title VI of that Act, the Truth in Lending Simplification and Reform Act, amends the Truth in Lending Act, 15 USC 1601, et seq. Section 608 of Title VI, effective March 31, 1980, authorizes the federal Truth in Lending enforcement agencies to order creditors to make monetary and other adjustments to the accounts of consumers where an annual percentage rate (APR) or finance charge was inaccurately disclosed. It generally requires the agencies to order restitution when such disclosure errors resulted from a clear and consistent pattern or practice of violations, gross negligence, or a willful violation which was intended to mislead the person to whom the credit was extended. However, the Act does not preclude the agencies from ordering restitution for isolated disclosure errors.

This policy guide summarizes and explains the restitution provisions of the Truth in Lending Act (Act), as amended. The material also explains corrective actions the financial regulatory agencies believe will be appropriate and generally intend to take in those situations in which the Act gives the agencies the authority to take equitable remedial action.

The agencies anticipate that most financial institutions will voluntarily comply with the restitution provisions of the Act as part of the normal regulatory process. If a creditor does not voluntarily act to correct violations, the agencies will use their cease and desist authority to require correction pursuant to: 15 USC 1607 and 12 USC 1818(b) in the cases of the Board of Governors of the Federal Reserve System, the Federal Deposit Insurance Corporation, the Office of the Comptroller of the Currency, and the Office of Thrift Supervision; and 15 USC 1607 and 12 USC 1786(e)(1) in the case of the National Credit Union Administration.

Restitution Provisions

Definitions

Except as provided below, all definitions are those found in the Act and Regulation Z, 12 CFR 226.

1. "Current examination" means the most recent examination begun on or after March 31, 1980, in which compliance with Regulation Z was reviewed.

2. "Lump sum method" means a method of reimbursement in which a cash payment equal to the total adjustment will be made to a consumer.

3. "Lump sum/payment reduction method" means a method of reimbursement in which the total adjustment to a consumer will be made in two stages:

   a. A cash payment that fully adjusts the consumer's account up to the time of the cash payment; and

   b. A reduction of the remaining payment amounts on the loan.

4. "Understated APR" means a disclosed APR that is understated by more than the reimbursement tolerance provided in the Act[8] as follows:

- For loans[9] with an amortization schedule of 10 years or less, a disclosed APR which, when increased by the greater of the APR tolerance specified in the Act[10] and Regulation Z[11] or one-quarter of 1 percent, is less than the actual APR calculated under the Act.[12]

---

[8] 15 USC 1607(e).

[9] For loans consummated after March 31, 1982. For loans consummated prior to that date refer to the Policy Guide dated July 21, 1980 (45 FR 48712) for additional guidance.

[10] 15 USC 1606(c).

[11] 12 CFR 226.14(a) and 226.22(a).

[12] If, however, the loan is closed-end credit secured by real estate or a dwelling and the APR is understated by more than one-quarter of 1 percent, the APR will be considered accurate and not subject to reimbursement if: (1) The finance charge is understated but considered accurate in accordance with the Act and Regulation (i.e., the finance charge is not understated by more than $100 on loans made on or after 9/30/95, or $200 for loans made before that date); and (2) the APR is not understated by more than the dollar equivalent of the finance charge error and the understated APR resulted from the understated finance charge that is considered accurate.

- For loans with an amortization schedule of more than 10 years, a disclosed APR which, when increased by the APR tolerance specified in the Act and Regulation Z (i.e., one-quarter of 1 percent for irregular loans, one-eighth of 1 percent for all other closed-end loans) is less than the actual APR.[13]

5. "Understated finance charge" means a disclosed finance charge which, when increased by the greater of the finance charge dollar tolerance specified in the Act and Regulation Z or a dollar tolerance that is generated by the corresponding APR reimbursement tolerance[14] is less than the finance charge calculated under the Act.

De Minimis Rule

If the amount of adjustment on an account is less than $1.00, no restitution will be ordered. However, the agencies may require a creditor to make any adjustments of less than $1.00 by paying into the United States Treasury, if more than one year has elapsed since the date of the violation.

Corrective Action Period

1. Open-end credit transactions will be subject to an adjustment if the violation occurred within the two-year period preceding the date of the current examination.

---

[13] If, however, the loan is closed-end credit secured by real estate or a dwelling and the APR is understated by more than one-eighth of 1 percent if the transaction is not considered to be an irregular transaction as defined by the Regulation (12 CFR 226.22(a)(3)) or one quarter of 1 percent if the transaction is irregular according to the definition, the APR will be considered accurate and not subject to reimbursement if: (1) the finance charge is understated but considered accurate according to the Actual Regulation (i.e., the finance charge is understated but considered accurate according to the Act and Regulation i.e., the finance charge is not understated by more than $100 on loans made on or after 9/30/95, or $200 for loans made before that date); and (2) the APR is not understated by more than the dollar equivalent of the finance charge error and the understated APR resulted from the understated finance charge that is considered accurate.

[14] The finance charge tolerance for each loan will be generated by the corresponding APR tolerance applicable to that loan. For example, consider a single-payment loan with a one-year maturity that is subject to a one-quarter of 1 percent APR tolerance. If the amount financed is $5,000 and the finance charge is $912.50, the actual APR will be 18.25 percent. The finance charge generated by an APR of 18 percent (applying the one-quarter of one percent APR tolerance to 18.25 percent) for that loan would be $900. The difference between $912.50 and $900 produces a numerical finance charge tolerance of $12.50. If the disclosed finance charge is not understated by more than $12.50, reimbursement would not be ordered.

---

2. Closed-end credit transactions will be subject to an adjustment if the violation resulted from a clear and consistent pattern or practice or gross negligence where:

   a. There is an understated APR on a loan which originated between January 1, 1977, and March 31, 1980.

   b. There is an understated APR or understated finance charge, and the practice giving rise to the violation is identified during the current examination. Loans containing the violation which were consummated since the date of the immediately preceding examination are subject to an adjustment.

   c. There is an understated APR or understated finance charge, the practice giving rise to the violation was identified during a prior examination and the practice is not corrected by the date of the current examination. Loans containing the violation which were consummated since the creditor was first notified in writing of the violation are subject to an adjustment. (Prior examinations include any examinations conducted since July 1, 1969).

3. Each closed-end credit transaction, consummated since July 1, 1969, and containing a willful violation intended to mislead the consumer is subject to an adjustment.

4. For terminated loans subject to 2 above, an adjustment will not be ordered if the violation occurred in a transaction consummated more than two years prior to the date of the current examination.

Calculating the Adjustment

Consumers will not be required to pay any amount in excess of the finance charge or dollar equivalent of the APR actually disclosed on transactions involving:

1. Understated APR violations on transactions consummated between January 1, 1977 and March 31, 1980, or

2. Willful violations which were intended to mislead the consumer.

On all other transactions, applicable tolerances provided in the definitions of understated APR and understated finance charge may be applied in calculating the amount of adjustment to the consumer's account.

Methods of Adjustment

The consumer's account will be adjusted using the lump sum method or the lump sum/payment reduction method, at the discretion of the creditor.

Violations Involving the Non-Disclosure of the APR or Finance Charge

1. In cases where an APR was required to be disclosed but was not, the disclosed APR shall be considered to be the contract rate, if disclosed on the note or the Truth in Lending disclosure statement.

2. In cases where an APR was required to be disclosed but was not, and no contract rate was disclosed, consumers will not be required to pay an amount greater than the actual APR reduced by one-quarter of 1 percentage point, in the case of first lien mortgage transactions, and by 1 percentage point in all other transactions.

3. In cases where a finance charge was not disclosed, no adjustment will be ordered.

Violations Involving the Improper Disclosure of Credit Life, Accident, Health, or Loss of Income Insurance

1. If the creditor has not disclosed to the consumer in writing that credit life, accident, health, or loss of income insurance is optional, the insurance shall be treated as having been required and improperly excluded from the finance charge. An adjustment will be ordered if it results in an understated APR or finance charge. The insurance will remain in effect for the remainder of its term.

2.	If the creditor has disclosed to the consumer in writing that credit life, accident, health, or loss of income insurance is optional, but there is either no signed insurance option or no disclosure of the cost of the insurance, the insurance shall be treated as having been required and improperly excluded from the finance charge. An adjustment will be ordered if it results in an understated APR or finance charge. The insurance will remain in effect for the remainder of its term.

Special Disclosures

Adjustments will not be required for violations involving the disclosures required by sections 106(c) and (d) of the Act, (15 USC 1605(c) and (d)).

Obvious Errors

If an APR was disclosed correctly, but the finance charge required to be disclosed was understated, or if the finance charge was disclosed correctly, but the APR required to be disclosed was understated, no adjustment will be required if the error involved a disclosed value which was 10 percent or less of the amount that should have been disclosed.

Agency Discretion

Adjustments will not be required if the agency determines that the disclosure error resulted from any unique circumstances involving a clearly technical and non-substantive disclosure violation which did not adversely affect information provided to the consumer and which did not mislead or otherwise deceive the consumer.

Safety and Soundness

In some cases, an agency may order, in place of an immediate, full adjustment, either a partial adjustment, or a full adjustment in partial payments over an extended time period that the agency considers reasonable. The agency may do so if it determines that (1) the full, immediate adjustment would have a significantly adverse impact upon the safety and soundness of the creditor, and (2) a partial adjustment, or making partial payments over an extended period of time, is necessary to avoid causing the creditor to become undercapitalized[15].

Exemption from Restitution Orders

A creditor will not be subject to an order to make an adjustment if within 60 days after discovering a disclosure error, whether pursuant to a final written examination report or through the creditor's own procedures, the creditor notifies the person concerned of the error and adjusts the account to ensure that such person will not be required to pay a finance charge in excess of that actually disclosed or the dollar equivalent of the APR disclosed, whichever is lower. This 60-day period for correction of disclosure errors is unrelated to the provisions of the civil liability section of the Act.

---

[15] The term "undercapitalized" will have the meaning as defined in section 38 of the Federal Deposit Insurance Act (12 USC 1831o).

Questions and Answers—Interagen cy Guidance Regarding Joint Interagency Statement of Policy for Administrative Enforcement of the Truth in Lending Act—Reimbursement Issued by the FFIEC on July 11, 1980, and Revised October 1998 (Approved July 22, 1999)

General

1. Q. Do the enforcement standards and accuracy tolerances in the Policy Guide supersede the requirements of the Truth in Lending Act and Regulation Z?

    A. No. The policy guide applies to agency enforcement procedures only. It does not alter a creditor's responsibility to comply fully with all the requirements of the Act and Regulation Z, including finance charge and annual percentage rate (APR) accuracy requirements.

2. Q. When violations are discovered in purchased or assigned loans that are initially payable to an entity other than the financial institution, will the financial institution be ordered to make the necessary adjustments to the accounts of affected consumers?

    A. No, the financial institution is not the creditor, even if the obligation by its terms is payable initially to a third party and simultaneously assigned to the financial institution. The violations will be referred to the creditor's enforcing agency.

3. Q. If the creditor must itemize the amount financed, but fails to disclose or understates the prepaid finance charge, will reimbursement be required?

    A. No, this violation of Regulation Z will require prospective corrective action only, assuming the prepaid finance charges are properly included in the computation of the APR and finance charge.

4. Q. If APR or finance charge disclosures not required by Regulation Z have been made, will reimbursement be required when such optional disclosures are understated?

A. No, however, errors in disclosures not required by Regulation Z for a particular transaction are violations of either 12 CFR 226.5(a)(1) or 12 CFR 226.17(a)(1), both of which require that credit disclosures be made clearly and conspicuously.

Definitions

"Current examination"

1. Q. How should the Policy Guide apply to a situation where an examiner, in an examination in progress discovers that reimbursement had not been undertaken as requested by the enforcement agency following the prior examination? What if the institution states that this examination is the "current examination" thereby requiring it to only make adjustments to those loans found to be in violation and consummated since the prior examination?

   A. TILA does not limit the agencies' authority to require correction of violations detected in earlier examinations and that have not been corrected as of the date of the current examination [see section 108(e)(3)(C)(i) of the Act, found at 15 USC 1607(e)(3)(c)(i)]. In addition, if the practice giving rise to the violations identified in the earlier examination has not been corrected, the institution will be required to make adjustments on any loans containing the violation that were consummated since the date it was first notified in writing of the violation and comply with the corrective action already ordered.

"Understated APR"

1. Q. What is meant by "actual APR" and "annual percentage rate calculated in accordance with the Act," as used in the Policy Guide?

   A. Those terms mean the lowest permissible APR that can be computed, applying all applicable provisions of Regulation Z.

De Minimis Rule

1.   Q. How should the de minimis rule be applied in closed-end credit transactions?

A. The de minimis rule should always be applied to the amount of the adjustment calculated under the "lump sum method" of reimbursement as of the maturity date of the transaction, regardless of which reimbursement method is ultimately used by the creditor.

2.   Q. How should the de minimis rule be applied in open-end credit transactions?

A. The de minimis rule should be applied to the total amount of the adjustment calculated for each consumer's account under the "lump sum method" for the period of time from the date of the current examination back to the date of the first occurrence of the violation. However, the total time period may not exceed the two-year period prior to the date of the current examination.

Corrective Action Period

1.   Q. Have the agencies changed their position on the time period required for taking corrective action for violations involving closed-end credit?

A. Yes. Prior to 1997, the agencies took the position that the statutory phrase "immediately preceding examination" (which serves as the cutoff date for retroactive application of a reimbursement requirement) referred to the most recent examination (prior to the current examination) in which compliance with Regulation Z and the Act was reviewed. Because of decisions reached by the Eighth and Eleventh Circuits of the United States Courts of Appeals, the agencies have adopted a new policy. The agencies by policy now interpret the phrase "immediately preceding examination" to mean an examination of any type conducted for any purpose by a federal regulatory agency with designated administrative enforcement responsibility under the TILA. However, supervisory visitations, inspections, or other reviews that are not considered examinations by the agencies are not considered examinations for purposes of applying the retroactivity limitation. In addition, an examination of an affiliated entity, such as an operating subsidiary or an institution's holding company, is not considered an examination for purposes of determining the corrective action time period under the Act.

2.   Q. What is the effective date of the new policy change regarding the time period for corrective action for violations involving closed-end credit?

A. The policy change regarding the corrective action time period was effective as of August 7, 1997.

3.   Q. Can an institution terminate the remainder of its restitution obligation to a borrower in light of this change in policy?

A. No. The policy change applies to future and pending cases as of the effective date. There will be no change in reimbursement obligations arising in connection with restitution cases that have been previously resolved. Once the institution makes its decision about the restitution method that it will pursue. It is expected to complete its obligations to affected borrowers as agreed.

For example, under the "Lump Sum/Payment Reduction" method of reimbursement, an institution remits to the borrower a lump sum covering excess money paid to the point that restitution is made, and then reduces future payments to cover the remaining restitution obligation. Under the new policy, the agencies will not permit the institution to terminate its remaining restitution obligation by increasing the borrower's payments to the level that were prior to the restitution action.

4.   Q. How will the agencies apply the policy change when "concurrent" examinations are being conducted at a financial institution?

A. Concurrent examinations occur when several different types of examinations begin on the same day or when examinations begin in succession. Concurrent examinations may also begin several weeks or months apart but within the same examination cycle, based on factors such as the availability of working space for the examination teams, or the expressed preferences of the institution's management.

For purposes of applying the policy change regarding the corrective action time period, the agencies consider a concurrent examination to be one event. Assume, for example, the situation where a safety and soundness examination begins on Monday, a trust examination begins on Tuesday, and the compliance examination starts on Wednesday. Assume further that the compliance team identifies a pattern or practice of violations triggering the restitution provisions of the Act. The agencies will consider the immediately preceding examination to be the last completed examination, not the trust examination that begins on Tuesday, or the safety and soundness examination that began on Monday.

Similarly, assume an institution's examination is to be conducted in succession, meaning that the compliance examination would begin after the safety and soundness and/or trust examination on site work in the institution is completed, which could be several months after the start date of the concurrent examination. The agencies will consider those concurrent examinations to be part of the same examination cycle for purposes of the policy.

5. Q. Does the policy change limit or otherwise affect the corrective action time period where a practice identified at a prior examination is not covered by the date of the current examination?

A. No. The Policy Guide and statute provide that if a practice is identified during a current examination and the examiner determines that the practice was identified during a prior examination but is not corrected by the date of the current examination, the corrective action time period is retroactive to the date of the prior examination in which the violation was identified. This will be true even if there have been intervening examinations that did not review for compliance with the Act and Regulation Z. [see section 108(e)(3)(c)(I) found at 15 USC 1107(e)(3)(c)(I)]

6. Q. Are there any differences in application of the policy change when restitution situations involve open-end credit rather than closed-end credit?

A. Yes. The Act provides different corrective action time periods for open-end and closed-end credit. The policy change applies to restitution situations involving closed-end credit. The corrective action time period for open-end credit covers the 24-month period preceding the date of the current examination, regardless of whether another examination intervenes during that period.

7. Q. What is the corrective action period with respect to terminated closed-end loans if an institution elects to comply voluntarily with the restitution provisions of the Policy Guide, absent a current examination?

A. The Policy Guide states that "for terminated loans . . . an adjustment will not be ordered if the violation occurred in a transaction consummated more than two years prior to the date of the current examination." If an institution elects to comply voluntarily with the Policy Guide absent a current examination, the financial institution will have the option of either:

(1) Deferring reimbursement on any terminated loans until its regulatory agency conducts a current examination, or

(2) Reimbursing on any terminated loans falling within the period prior to the discovery of the violation up to the date of the immediately preceding examination. If that time frame is in excess of two years, then reimbursement may be limited to the two-year period prior to the date of discovery of the violation.

8. Q. How will the Policy Guide apply when loans subject to reimbursement are acquired through a merger, consolidation, or in exchange for the assumption of deposit liabilities?

A. In the case of a merger or consolidation, the receiving institution or the consolidated institution is liable for all liabilities of the merged or consolidating institutions, and the Policy Guide will apply.

In the case of loans acquired in exchange for the assumption of deposit liabilities, the Policy Guide will apply to the original creditor.

Calculating the Adjustment

1. Q. How will disclosures containing information properly estimated under 12 CFR 226.5(c), 12 CFR 226.17(c), and appendix D be treated for reimbursement determinations and computations?

    A. If an APR or finance charge is in error for any reason other than a properly made estimate, the determination of whether the error constitutes a reimbursable overcharge should be made using the estimated information as disclosed. At the creditor's option, reimbursement should be based on either:

    (1) The actual amount of loan advances, with consideration given to the amount and the dates payments were made by the borrower, or

    (2) The disclosed amounts or time intervals between advances and between payments.

    The basis selected shall be applied, using the lump sum or lump sum/payment reduction method (at the creditor's discretion), to all loans of the same type subject to reimbursement.

2. Q. If a creditor has failed to reflect private mortgage insurance premiums in the APR or finance charge disclosures, may the institution cancel the insurance after it first reimburses the consumer with a lump sum payment to cover the period up to the date of the reimbursement?

    A. The creditor may elect to cancel the insurance if applicable laws and regulations are not violated. The effect of canceling the insurance will be to reduce the amount of the consumer's future payments, as permitted by the "lump sum payment reduction" method of reimbursement.

3. Q. If a creditor has failed to reflect private mortgage insurance premiums in the APR or finance charge disclosures and restitution is required, but the loan has been sold into the secondary market, how should reimbursement be made?

A. The creditor is responsible for reimbursement, even if the loan has been sold. If its ability to cancel the insurance is limited by terms of the loan sales agreement, the creditor may make payments either to the consumer directly or (if it is agreeable to all parties) to the new owner of the loan. The new owner of the loan would make appropriate adjustments to the account so that the consumer receives the full benefit of the reimbursement.

4. Q. If the creditor failed to include any component of the finance charge (e.g., a loan origination fee) in the APR or finance charge disclosures, may the amount of reimbursement be reduced to account for fees excludable from the finance charge under 12 CFR 226.4(c), which are paid for by such finance charge components?

A. If the borrower has not otherwise paid such excludable fees (e.g., title insurance fees) to the creditor or to a third party, reimbursement may be computed after first deducting from the finance charge those fees qualifying under 12 CFR 226.4(c).

5. Q. A transaction involves a loan with a term of 36 months, a payment schedule where the first 35 payments are calculated using a 30-year amortization and a balloon amount for the final payment. What tolerance should be used when applying the Policy Guide? One-eighth of 1 percent or one-quarter of 1 percent?

A. The application tolerance is based on the amortization of the loan. Because the loan is completely amortized within a three-year period (i.e., the 36-month payment schedule), a tolerance of one-quarter of 1 percent should be used because the amortization period is less than 10 years (15 USC 1607(e)(1)).

6.   Q. How will the policy guide apply if a credit transaction has an interest rate or APR subject to increase and the variable rate feature was not provided on the disclosure statement?

A. If the disclosure statement did not state that the rate would be subject to change, the borrower may be charged only the original APR disclosed. Reimbursement under the policy guide will apply only to the period of time in which the borrower made payments at an increased rate.

7.   Q. How will the policy guide apply if a creditor disclosed that a rate will be prospectively subject to increase, but the APR or the finance charge disclosed or both were originally understated?

A. The policy guide will apply as follows:

(1) If only the APR is understated, reimbursement will be required only for the period of time before the first scheduled change in rate under the variable rate feature in the contract. The term "the first scheduled change in rate" refers to a date on which the rate will change to a level that is unknown or unpredictable at consummation. It does not include changes, such as step rates, that are agreed upon before consummation.

For example, if the loan terms provide for a 9 percent rate for the first year and a 10 percent rate for the second year, followed by a variable rate feature to be invoked at the beginning of the third year, reimbursement will apply only to the initial 24-month period. The lump sum payment reduction adjustment method may be used, using two payment streams for the initial two-year period. Payments after the 24th month would not be affected by the adjustment.

(2) If only the finance charge is understated, reimbursement generally will be required for a period covering the entire life of the loan, consistent with the following:

- If a prepaid finance charge was not included in the disclosed finance charge (such as a loan origination fee paid separately by the consumer at loan closing), the entire loan fee (less the applicable dollar tolerance) must be refunded as a "lump sum" payment.

- If, however, the loan fee was financed (included in the loan amount), the finance charge reimbursement may be prorated on a straight-line basis over the life of the loan and refunded under the lump sum/payment reduction method.

However, a finance charge adjustment will be required only for the period of time before the first scheduled change in rate if the error occurred solely because the interest component of the disclosed finance charge was based on either:

a.   The interest to be earned before the first scheduled change in rate, or

b.   The interest to be earned assuming an initial discounted rate over the life of the loan.

For example, the interest component of the disclosed finance charge might incorrectly reflect only loan interest for the first year on a transaction with variable rate changes scheduled annually. Alternatively, it might incorrectly reflect interest calculated only at an initial discounted variable rate for the full term of the loan. In either case, if the loan terms in the example provide that the variable interest rate is subject to change annually, the finance charge reimbursement will apply only to the initial 12-month period.

The adjustment may be prorated on a straight-line basis over the life of the loan. Reimbursement of prorated amounts covering the period of time after the first scheduled change in rate (after month 12 in this example) would not be required.

(3) If both the APR and finance charge are understated, normally the lump sum finance charge adjustment is compared with the lump sum APR adjustment as of the loan maturity date and the larger adjustment determines which disclosure error is subject to reimbursement. In the case of variable rate transactions,

however, the lump sum APR adjustment used for comparison is calculated for the period of time before the first scheduled change in rate in the manner indicated by (1) above and the finance charge adjustment is calculated in the manner indicated by (2) above.

For example, assume a loan in which both the APR and finance charge are understated on a 30-year, variable rate loan that calls for rate changes annually. If both understatements were caused by the same failure to take into account a prepaid loan origination fee:

- The APR reimbursement amount is the lump sum value for a 12-month period, which is determined by using the lump sum/payment reduction method and appropriate reimbursement tolerances.

- The finance charge reimbursement amount is the lump sum value for a 360-month period, which is determined by subtracting the appropriate reimbursement tolerance from the amount of the loan fee.

The APR adjustment is compared to the finance charge adjustment to determine the larger of the two. In the example, the finance charge adjustment (and not the APR adjustment) would be reimbursable.

8.   Q. If a creditor uses a simple interest rate, which is disclosed as the APR, to compute a monthly payment schedule, and the time interval from the date the finance charge begins to be earned to the date of the first payment is treated as if it were one month, even though that period is greater than one month and is not a "minor irregularity" under 12 CFR 226.17(c)(4), is enforcement action necessary if the resulting application of the simple interest rate generates a higher finance charge than the one disclosed?

A. The policy guide will apply if:

(1) The creditor's method of computing the payment schedule, as previously described, is used to compute the disclosed

finance charge (i.e., the total of payments less the amount financed).

(2) The final payment collected or scheduled under the contract (as generated by the application of the simple interest rate to the unpaid principal balance over the life of the loan) is greater than the one disclosed.

(3) The finance charge resulting from the first two conditions is understated.

9.   Q. Will reimbursement be required for demand loans with disclosures based on a one-year maturity when the demand loan contract calls for periodic payments that will amortize the loan over a definite time period?

A. Yes. A formal amortization schedule recorded in the demand loan contract is, under 12 CFR 226.17(c)(5), equivalent to an alternative maturity date, and disclosures based on the amortization schedule should be made, as opposed to the one-year disclosures.

10.   Q. Will reimbursement be required on demand loans when:

(1) An alternate maturity date is disclosed and reflected in the contract, but the finance charge disclosure is based on the year?

(2) There is no alternate maturity date disclosed or reflected in the contract, but the finance charge disclosure is based on a period of time less than one year?

A. In the first case, because there is an alternative maturity date in the contract, which is disclosed, the finance charge disclosure should have been based on that alternate maturity date, as required under 12 CFR 226.17(c)(5), not on the disclosure period to be used when the instrument has no alternate maturity date.

In the second case, the actual finance charge disclosure should have been based on a one-year period as required by 12 CFR 226.17(c)(5), not on some period less than that required when the instrument has no alternate maturity date.

After considering appropriate tolerances, reimbursement will be required in both cases if:

(1) The disclosed finance charge is less than the actual finance charge for the initial required disclosure period.

(2) The demand loan has been on the bank's books past the period for which finance charge disclosures were made.

Reimbursement will be calculated for the required disclosure period only. The amount reimbursed to the consumer is the difference between the finance charge actually paid and the finance charge disclosed (which may be increased by the applicable finance charge reimbursement tolerance).

If the demand loan has not been on the bank's books past the period for which finance charge disclosures were made (e.g., the finance charge was disclosed for a one-year period, but should have been disclosed for a five-year period, and only 10 months have elapsed), no reimbursement is required. However, if the bank takes no prospective corrective action (i.e., if it does not at least disclose in writing a refinancing of the original loan) and the loan remains on the bank's books past the period for which the original finance charge disclosures were made, reimbursement will be required as previously indicated.

Those concepts apply both to straight and variable rate demand loans whenever the disclosed finance charge is less than the actual finance charge after considering appropriate tolerances.

11. Q. How will the policy guide apply to violations of the early disclosure rules under Regulation Z?

A. As a general rule, the Policy Guide will not apply to violations involving early truth-in-lending disclosures, but will apply to violations of the pre-consummation disclosures required by section 226.17. However, if the creditor has provided erroneous early disclosures and has not made pre-consummation disclosures, the Policy Guide will apply to the erroneous early disclosures.

1. Q. Must reimbursements resulting from understated finance charges always be made as a single "lump sum" amount?

A. No. Reimbursements resulting from the creditor's failure to include prepaid finance charges in the total finance charge must always be refunded as a "lump sum" payment, but reimbursements resulting from failure to include finance charge components that accrue over time may be prorated on a straight-line basis (no time value) over the life of the loan and refunded under the lump sum/payment reduction method.

2. Q. Must a creditor use one reimbursement method consistently on all affected loans?

A. No. The creditor's right to choose between the two methods applies to each transaction.

3. Q. May a creditor apply a lump sum reimbursement to the consumer's loan balance on a loan requiring reimbursement instead of making a cash payment to the consumer?

A. If the loan is closed-end, the creditor must make a cash payment or a deposit into an existing unrestricted consumer asset account, such as an unrestricted savings, NOW account, or demand deposit account. However, if the loan is delinquent, in default, or has been charged off, the creditor may apply all or part of the reimbursement to the amount past due, if permissible under law.

If the reimbursement involves an open-end account, the creditor must make a cash payment or a deposit into an existing unrestricted consumer asset account such as an unrestricted savings, NOW, or demand deposit account. However, on a case-by-case basis, the agencies may permit the creditor to credit the consumer's open account by the amount of the reimbursement if the consumer consents. Creditors should be aware that crediting open-end accounts might create credit balances subject to the requirements of 12 CFR 226.11. In addition, if the open-end account is delinquent, in default, or has been charged off, the creditor may apply all or part of the reimbursement to the amount past due, if permissible under law.

4.   Q. If a transaction involves more than one consumer, to whom must reimbursement be made?

A. The reimbursement is the property of, and is to be made to, the primary obligor in the credit transaction. If there is more than one primary obligor, reimbursement must be made jointly. If the primary obligor(s) is deceased, the payment should be made pursuant to the estate and escheat laws of the state. If the creditor is unable to locate the primary obligor(s), after having at least mailed the reimbursement amount to the consumer's last known address, the amount of the reimbursement is subject to the escheat laws of the state.

5.   Q. How will the policy guide apply to residential mortgage transactions that have been assumed by a third party?

A. Reimbursement will be made only to the original borrower and only to the extent of overcharges that occurred before the assumption if:

(1) A reimbursable violation is found on the original borrower's disclosure statement; and

(2) The original borrower is not released from liability on the loan. The original transaction will be considered terminated with respect to the original borrower on the date of the assumption and the rules for application of the Policy Guide to terminated loans will apply.

Reimbursement will be made to the original borrower for the period before the assumption occurred if:

(1) A reimbursable violation is found on the original borrower's disclosure statement.

(2) The original borrower is not released from liability on the loan. However, in the event the subsequent borrower defaults and the original borrower must again assume payments on the loan, such payments will be based on the payment amount that would have been calculated under the lump sum payment

reduction method at the time of reimbursement, had no assumption occurred.

If a required disclosure to a subsequent borrower contains reimbursable violations, that borrower shall be reimbursed for the period after the assumption occurred, based on the new disclosure.

Non-Disclosure of the APR or Finance Charge

1. Q. How will the policy guide apply to loans for which no disclosure statements are on file?

A. If there is no evidence that the creditor furnished disclosures or if there is a preponderance of evidence that disclosures containing violations subject to reimbursement were destroyed before the record retention period expired, either violation is treated as a failure to disclose the APR. The creditor will be given the opportunity to substantiate the claim that an accurate disclosure was made before final action is taken. The absence of compliance documentation should be viewed relative to known practices of the creditor for record retention and Regulation Z compliance.

2. Q. How will the policy guide apply if a creditor did not provide required disclosures to the consumer before consummation, but did supply them after consummation?

A. If required disclosures were not provided before consummation of the transaction, the transaction will be viewed as having no APR disclosed, and enforcement action is in order. If the creditor's failure to provide disclosures included the credit life and accident and health insurance disclosures, the insurance premiums must be treated as finance charges.

3. Q. Will the policy guide apply when a creditor has disclosed the APR as "2% OP" to mean a fluctuating rate of 2 percent over the prime rate, or has disclosed similar prime rate terminology instead of the APR?

A. If the disclosure statement (not the note) clearly provides the numerical value of the prime rate as it pertains to the credit transaction, as of the time disclosures are given to the consumer, that rate (the prime rate or 2% OP) will be considered to be the disclosed APR under the Policy Guide. If the prime rate is not provided on the disclosure statement, the transaction will be viewed under the policy guide as if no APR had been disclosed.

4.   Q. Will reimbursement be required on demand loans when the variable rate feature has not been disclosed and the rate is increased?

A. Yes. If the consumer has not been notified in writing of the rate change on or before the date of the change, reimbursement will be required if the bank has not made the variable rate disclosures.

Each time the rate is changed and the customer is not given written notification of the new rate, the rate-change period(s) will be treated as if no APR had been disclosed, and the policy guide will apply. The rate on the most recent notification will serve as the contract rate.

Improper Disclosure of Credit Life, Accident, Health, or Loss of Income Insurance

1.   Q. Are the credit insurance provisions of the Policy Guide applicable to terminated loans?

A. Yes. The credit insurance provisions apply if such loans originated within the policy guide's corrective action period for terminated loans.

2.   Q. How will the policy guide apply if the cost of credit insurance premiums is disclosed as a rate (e.g., as a percentage or in dollars and cents per hundred per month) in a closed-end transaction?

A. Regulation Z permits creditors to disclose credit insurance premiums on a unit-cost basis in closed-end transactions by mail or telephone under 12 CFR 226.17(g), and in certain closed-end transactions involving an insurance plan that limits the total amount of indebtedness subject to coverage.

In all other closed-end credit transactions, however, the dollar amount of insurance premiums must be disclosed. If the premium cost in those cases is disclosed as dollars or cents per hundred or as a percentage, it will be treated as if no disclosure of the cost has been made and the policy guide will apply accordingly.

3.   Q. How will the policy guide apply if:

(1) The creditor does the not include premiums for credit life, accident, and health insurance in the APR or finance charge disclosures; and

(2) The creditor fails to disclose the optional nature of the insurance; but

(3) The creditor has afforded the borrower the option of taking or refusing the insurance by checking a block or initialing a line opposite statements similar to the following, both of which are disclosed in writing to the borrower: "I desire credit life, accident, and health insurance" and "I do not desire credit life, accident, and health insurance?

A. In those cases, the policy guide will apply because the creditor has not disclosed to the customer in writing, as required by section 226.4(d)(1)(i) of Regulation Z, that the credit life insurance or accident and health insurance are optional.

4.   Q. How will the policy guide apply if:

(1) The consumer is charged for credit life, accident, or health insurance premiums; and

(2) The creditor did not include the premiums in the APR or finance charge disclosures; and

(3) The creditor disclosed the optional nature and cost of credit life insurance to the consumer in writing and the customer signed or initialed close to those disclosures; and

(4) Either no affirmative statement indicating a desire to obtain the insurance was provided or the appropriate box or line was not checked or otherwise marked to indicate whether the customer did or did not desire the insurance?

A. If the disclosure provided a choice to the customer through statements, such as "I desire the insurance" and "I do not desire the insurance," and neither choice has been marked by the customer, enforcement action is in order because the creditor did not meet the requirements of 12 CFR 226.4(d)(1)(iii).

If no affirmative statement indicating a desire to purchase the insurance has been provided, and the customer has only signed or initialed near the optional nature statements or cost disclosures, the Policy Guide will apply because the creditor did not meet the requirements of 12 CFR 226.4(d)(1)(iii).

5.   Q. How will the policy guide apply if:

(1) The creditor does not include premiums for credit life, accident, and health insurance in the APR or finance charge disclosures; and

(2) The creditor provides disclosures stating that the insurance is not required; and

(3) The creditor provides the cost of each type of insurance, with a statement that the customer's signature will indicate a desire to purchase the insurance and the customer signs once, below the cost disclosures, but does not initial each type of insurance desired?

A. If the disclosures clearly indicate that the customer, by signing where indicated, elects to purchase each type of insurance for which the cost has been provided, the Policy Guide will not apply. However, prospectively the creditor shall clarify such disclosures by obtaining the customer's initials for each type of insurance selected, or by changing the manner in which the customer signs for credit insurance when more than one type is offered.

6.	Q. If vendor's single interest (VSI) insurance is written in connection with a credit transaction, the insurance premiums are not included in the finance charge, and the creditor does not obtain a waiver of the right of subrogation from the insurer, is the resulting finance charge understatement subject to reimbursement under the Policy Guide?

A. Yes. However, if the insurer has not exercised such rights of subrogation and agrees to prospectively waive that right for outstanding loans, the Policy Guide will not apply to those loans.

Obvious Errors

1.	Q. What are examples of obvious errors described in the Policy Guide?

A. Consider a situation where the APR is disclosed correctly and the correct finance charge is $600, no adjustment would be required if the amount of the disclosed finance charge is shown as $60 or less. Likewise, if the finance charge is correctly disclosed and the correct APR is 18.568 percent, no adjustment would be required if the disclosed APR is shown as 1.8568 percent or less.

Laws

15 USC 1601 et seq., Truth in Lending Act (TILA)
15 USC 1666, Fair Credit Billing Act
15 USC 7001 et seq., Electronic Signatures in Global and National Commerce Act
Credit Card Accountability, Responsibility, and Disclosure Act of 2009
Public Law 111-94, Credit Card Technical Correction Act of 2009

Regulations

12 CFR 226, Truth-in-Lending Regulation
12 CFR 34, Subpart B, Adjustable Rate Mortgage Regulation

OCC Comptroller's Handbook Booklets

Community Bank Supervision
Compliance Management System
Internal and External Audits
Large Bank Supervision

Software

APRWIN Program www.occ.treas.gov/aprwin.htm